WOMEN AS HEALERS

Women as Healers
Cross-Cultural
Perspectives

Edited by
CAROL SHEPHERD McCLAIN

RUTGERS UNIVERSITY PRESS
New Brunswick and London

Library of Congress Cataloging-in-Publication Data

Women as healers : cross-cultural perspectives / edited by Carol
  Shepherd McClain.
    p.   cm.
  Bibliography: p.
  Includes index.
  ISBN 0-8135-1369-3. ISBN 0-8135-1370-7 (pbk.)
    1. Women healers—Cross-cultural studies.   2. Medical
anthropology.   3. Folk medicine—Cross-cultural studies.
I. McClain, Carol Shepherd, 1939–
GN296.W65 1989
610′.88042—dc19   88-16896
                                                                              CIP

British Cataloging-in-Publication information available

Copyright © 1989 by Rutgers, The State University
All Rights Reserved
Manufactured in the United States of America

FOR MY MOTHER

CONTENTS

viii   Contents

ACKNOWLEDGMENTS

The idea for this book began to take shape in 1984, when I was invited to lecture to the first-year class of medical students at the University of California, San Francisco, on women in healing roles in other cultures. As I prepared my talk, my search for examples that would contribute to an understanding of the cultural significance of female healers led me deeply into both medical anthropology and feminist anthropology. It seemed timely for a collection of original essays that would under one cover reflect the richness of interpretations of women as healers as well as point to new interpretive directions.

My thanks go first to the contributors, whose interest and patience brought the project to fruition. I also wish to acknowledge the cogent advice of colleagues who read and commented on drafts of the introduction: Carole Browner, Brigitte Jordan, Linnea Klee, David Landy, Ellen Lewin, and Naomi Quinn. Marlie Wasserman of Rutgers University Press worked tirelessly on behalf of the project from its earliest stages and deserves special thanks for her guidance. Finally, I thank the curanderas, parteras, espiritistas, and mothers and grandmothers of Ajijic, Mexico, who shared with me at my asking their lived experiences as healers.

CONTRIBUTORS

CAROLE H. BROWNER is Associate Professor in the Departments of Psychiatry and Biobehavioral Sciences and Anthropology at the University of California, Los Angeles. Her research has concerned the effects of socioeconomic development on women's roles and women's health in both rural and urban Latin America. She is currently engaged in research on the health of women who work in electronic assembly plants on the U.S.–Mexico border.

RUTHBETH FINERMAN received her Ph.D. in anthropology at the University of California, Los Angeles. For the past twelve years she has conducted research on family health care systems of indigenous populations in the Andes and the Amazon lowlands of Ecuador. She is Assistant Professor of Anthropology in the Applied Medical Anthropology Program at Memphis State University.

MARGERY FOX received her Ph.D. is social anthropology fron New York University. She has been on the faculty at Fairleigh Dickinson University in Teaneck, New Jersey, since 1975, where she has taught medical subjects and gender roles. She has served as Director of the Women's Center, Coordinator of the Gerontology Program, and is a founder and coordinator of the Women's Studies Program. In addition to her work in Christian Science, she is the co-author of two published studies of women's friendships. Her current research is on women performers in the professional theater.

ROBERTO GARCIA is the Coordinator of Training at the Hispanic Health Council in Hartford, Connecticut. He has participated in several studies on health and illness in the Puerto Rican community and lectured widely on the topic of Espiritismo. Mr. Garcia is currently coordinating several projects designed to prevent substance abuse, premarital pregnancy, gang violence, and AIDS among Hispanic youth. He is especially concerned with the development of adolescent peer leaders and culturally appropriate prevention materials for Hispanics.

EDWARD C. GREEN is Coordinator of Behavioral Science at The Futures Group, a research and consulting firm in Washington, D.C., that holds several major contracts with the Agency for International

Development. After two years of dissertation fieldwork among the Maroons in Suriname, he spent five years teaching anthropology before beginning a career in development anthropology in 1980. He has since worked in the areas of environmental health, maternal and child health, family planning, and most recently AIDS. He worked as an applied medical anthropologist in Swaziland between 1981 and 1985, and has also directed research and health programs in Nigeria, Bangladesh, and the Dominican Republic. He edited *Practicing Development Anthropology* and has authored numerous articles and book chapters.

LAUREL KENDALL is Assistant Curator in Charge of Asian Ethnographic Collections at the American Museum of Natural History. Her current research on contemporary Korean marriage practices concerns such topics as matchmaking, romance, commercial wedding halls, reinvented traditions, and Confucian morals. She is the author of two books on Korean shamans and the editor of books on Korean women and religion. Her experience of Korea and Korean shamans dates from the early 1970s, when she served as a Peace Corps Volunteer. She later returned for anthropological fieldwork as a Fulbright and Social Science Research Council Foreign Area Fellow. She holds a Ph.D. in Anthropology from Columbia University.

BARBARA KEREWSKY-HALPERN is Adjunct Professor of Anthropology at the University of Massachusetts at Amherst. Long interested in processes of communication, she holds an M.A. in linguistics and a Ph.D. in anthropology and is certified as a teacher of the Feldenkrais Method of neuromuscular reeducation. Outside of academia she works in both group and private practice as a clinical medical anthropologist, often applying techniques learned from conjurers in Serbia and healers in Laos and Brazil. She is a National Science Foundation "Woman in Science" and author of many publications on ethnomedicine and communicative modes in patient/practitioner interactions.

CAROL SHEPHERD McCLAIN is currently affiliated with the Medical Anthropology Program, University of California, San Francisco. She has conducted field research on health behavior and women's reproductive health in Mexico and in the San Francisco Bay Area. Her most recent research interests include women's choices regarding childbirth care and new reproductive technologies, and delayed childbearing and maternal adaptation in American culture.

CAROLYN NORDSTROM received her Ph.D. from the University of California, Berkeley, in 1984, where she now teaches in the Peace and Conflict Studies Program. Her current research interests include women in war and the impact of war on women; riots, community conflict, and guerrilla warfare; and contemporary patterns of warfare and conflict resolution. She also continues to conduct research on complex plural health care systems in Sri Lanka.

MARGARET REID has been a faculty member in the Department of Social and Economic Research and the Department of Community Medicine, Glasgow University, since 1973. Her research interests include various aspects of the maternity services in Great Britain, home birth in Britain and the United States, prenatal screening, and the social dimensions of neonatal care. She is currently involved in a project establishing and evaluating a model well-woman clinic in Glasgow and a project studying the effect of parental visiting in neonatal intensive care units on the parents and the staff.

CAROLYN SARGENT is Associate Professor of Anthropology at Southern Methodist University, Dallas. She has recently completed a book on women's decisions concerning reproductive health in urban West Africa, and is currently conducting research in Kingston, Jamaica, on parental strategies for children's health care.

MERRILL SINGER is a medical anthropologist with primary interests in folk healing, illness behavior, sufferer experience, critical approaches to illness and treatment, and substance abuse. In addition to his work on Espiritismo, he has studied folk healing among Voodoo practitioners in Haiti, Black Hebrews in Israel, and Christian Scientists in Washington, D.C. Dr. Singer serves as Director of the Alcohol Research and Programs Unit of the Hispanic Health Council in Hartford, Connecticut, and as Assistant Clinical Professor in the Department of Community Medicine, University of Connecticut Health Center.

WILLIAM WEDENOJA studied psychological and psychiatric anthropology at the University of California, San Diego, and received his Ph.D. in 1978. Currently, he is Associate Professor and Coordinator of Anthropology at Southwest Missouri State University. Dr. Wedenoja has been conducting field research on socialization, personality, mental disorders, religious cultism, and folk healing in Jamaica since 1972, and has published several articles on those subjects. He has also published a book and two articles on a project involving the development of a multicultural curriculum for elementary schools in the Ozark highlands. His current research interests are Afro-Jamaican religious cultism and psychobiological and evolutionary approaches to human behavior.

CAROL SHEPHERD McCLAIN

Reinterpreting Women in Healing Roles

> And when the baby had arrived on earth, then the midwife shouted; she gave war cries, which meant that the little woman had fought a good battle, had become a brave warrior, had taken a captive, had captured a baby.—Sahagún; translated from the Aztec by Dibble and Anderson 1969

In less than two decades medical anthropology and the anthropology of women have emerged as new specialties within the parent discipline. Each has contemplated women in healing roles, but from different perspectives and with different objectives. Medical anthropologists interested in reproduction have largely focused on traditional midwives and childbirth in non-Western settings. Most have assigned themselves the task of describing other birthing practices and comparing these practices and their corresponding systems of meanings with biomedicine's treatment of pregnancy and childbirth. Gender seldom emerges as an issue in this body of literature. Other medical anthropologists have examined female ritual practitioners, and it is in their work that we are likely to encounter observations about gender, particularly the gender symbolic dimensions of societies' medico-religious systems. These studies, however, are still few. The larger body of literature on ritual curing, and on shamanism in particular, has not considered the sex of ritual practitioners as problematic; in most studies, commentary that can only be described as perfunctory may occasionally be found on whether women become ritual practitioners or have special qualities or purposes as ritual practitioners.

For their part, feminist anthropologists have not dwelt on healing roles, although some have noted that midwifery, curing, shamanism, and other medical occupations and pastimes can permit women to achieve status or prestige outside their domestic lives. In these studies, healing is interpreted as serving women's economic or political self-interest or as an avenue for women to participate in central cultural institutions of significance to both sexes. In other feminist anthropological (and social anthropological) writing, healing is seen to embody cultural images of femaleness as nurturing or as mediating between realms of existence (e.g., nature and culture, the living and the ancestors, purity and pollution).

Despite the uneven treatment of women healers that characterizes both medical anthropology and the anthropology of women, anthropologists are increasingly focusing more critically on broader social and cultural implications of women's healing. This volume is a collection of case studies that illustrate this growing concern; they are brought together to ask how recent conceptual schemes in feminist anthropology inform studies of the domain of healing and, reciprocally, how the ethnography of healing either supports or refutes those schemes.

All but one of the contributions are original. The overall thrust of the volume is eclectic, without particular methodological or theoretical arguments pressed to the exclusion of others. The chapters in Part One consider women in informal healing roles; those in Part Two describe female metaphors in healing. Chapters in Part Three detail the life histories of ritual specialists, and in Part Four the final chapters consider women's healing in the context of culture change. Each chapter presents a case study of a particular healing role performed predominantly or exclusively by women. Most of the world's major culture areas are represented in the cases, which consider women healers within African, South American, Asian, European, Caribbean, and North American cultural groups. The case studies are richly descriptive and interpretive, illustrating the ways in which women's healing articulates with particular features of gender relations, gender ideology, or gender symbolism in the societies in question.

The Emergence of Gender in the Anthropology of Healing

A number of conceptual schemes that stand out in the anthropological treatment of women have relevance to the healing domain. Three of these, the familiar domestic/public, nature/culture, and particularistic/ universalistic contrasts, provide a framework for viewing the sex of healers in the context of societies' wider gender formulations, although few anthropologists have as yet attempted such integrative analyses. A fourth construct, which can be abbreviated as the "women-as-muted" notion, is implicit in much of the discussion on women in informal healing roles. Although the assertion that women do not articulate either their interests or their perceptions of the world has provoked some feminist debate, the implications of mutedness, including whether it is one of a variety of social strategies women use to gain valued ends, have not been fully explored. Finally, a kind of informal functionalist argument in anthropology sees certain forms of healing—specifically, cults of affliction—as serving particular interests of low-status individuals, including women. The significance of each of these five conceptualizations for the study of women healers will be explored in the remainder of this essay. In the introductions to each of the book's four parts, the same conceptualizations will be examined in light of the new ethnographic material presented by the case studies.

Classification and Contrasts in Medical and Feminist Anthropology

Like all systems of human inquiry, folk and formal, anthropology uses classification as one means of making sense of the world. Without contemplating the tendency itself, which is perhaps genetically encoded in the primate (mammalian?) brain, it is useful for our purposes here to examine briefly the classificatory schemes that medical and feminist anthropologists employ to explain healing and gender. Classification, particularly the construction of presumed oppositions, enjoys a long and respected tradition in the anthropologies of medicine and religion. To cite a familiar example, anthropologists have for decades expended a great deal of intellectual energy demonstrating either the presence or the absence of European mind/body and natural/supernatural oppositions in native epistemologies (Evans-Pritchard 1937; Galdston 1959; Glick 1967; Radin 1957; Rivers 1927). The preoccupation has given way in recent years to hermeneutic approaches to illness and healing (Comaroff 1982; Good and Good 1981) and to political-historical accounts of European influence on traditional medical cultures (Janzen 1978; Worsley 1982). Yet oppositions thrive as labeling heuristics in other medical anthropological discourses, for example, the comparison of medical systems. The folk/professional, traditional/modern, ethnomedicine/biomedicine, and similar other oppositions infuse and color most comparative treatises on healing systems (Kleinman 1980; Leslie 1977). It is both interesting and significant that gender seldom emerges as an important principle in medical anthropological classifications, the majority of which ignore the significance of the sex of patients and practitioners (see, e.g., Foster's [1976] personalistic versus naturalistic medical systems, and A. Young's [1983] externalizing versus internalizing medical discourses). This inattention is understandable; medical anthropology is heir to the same androcentric biases that plague anthropology in general. Now, however, as the anthropologies of women and healing begin to converge at some points, feminist ethnography promises to expand and invigorate medical anthropologists' treatment of women in healing roles, and this may lead to a rethinking of how classification may conceal as well as reveal important cultural principles.

The same question may legitimately be asked of feminists' classifications, that is, do they assume more than they explain? Since gender is a central focus of this volume, feminist constructs merit close inspection. Those that bear most directly on the healing domain are a form of particularistic/universalistic opposition, illustrated most vividly in Strathern's (1981) treatment of Hagen gender symbolism, the domestic/public dichotomy (M. Z. Rosaldo 1974, 1980), and the nature/culture opposition (MacCormack and Strathern 1980; Ortner 1974).

Strathern writes that in Hageners' views, women are situated within individual households, consume rather than produce goods, and draw men's attention away from important public affairs. Women thus are seen as indulging in narrow self-interested behavior as opposed to promoting social welfare, which appears to be defined by Hageners as the economic and political pursuits of men. The argument parallels the more familiar universalist/particularist dualism that asserts that men's concerns are universalistic, women's particularistic. For Hageners, men are to women as social good is to self-interest, prestige to rubbish, and positive autonomy to negative autonomy. Each of these dichotomies illustrates dimensions of gender contrasts, although Strathern makes clear that women and men as persons may possess the attributes culturally ascribed to the opposing sex. Thus women who contribute to their husbands' investment schemes acquire a certain degree of prestige, and men who are weak and dependent are viewed as rubbish.

Strathern emphasizes the symbolic dimensions of the universalistic/ particularistic polarity, whereas Rosaldo focuses on its structural dimensions (M. Z. Rosaldo 1974). If women are particularistic, characterized by self-interest, and consume rather than produce social and economic goods, it is because of their primary location in households. That women contribute to a greater or lesser extent to economic and political life in particular societies is not seen as violating the domestic/public construct, because it is still they and not men who carry out the domestic (i.e., particularizing) activities that are overarched and integrated by public enterprises. A great deal of ethnographic evidence has been summoned to verify or reject the domestic/public dichotomy (see esp. Collier and Yanagisako 1987), and Rosaldo later modified her views about the extent to which the dichtomy accurately portrays women's lives (M. Z. Rosaldo 1980).

Recent writing on the domestic/public opposition rejects its more rigid assumptions. An example is Mathew's (1985) account of the Mesoamerican civil-religious hierarchy, an institution that has long been thought to be an exclusively extradomestic male preserve. Mathews found that in the Oaxacan village where she worked, the civil-religious hierarchy was in part dependent on contributions made by women from domestic bases: "Households, not individual men, compete for prestige through service involving the expenditure of surplus resources. The labor of both male and female household members is vital in accomplishing this goal, and the prestige earned through service is shared equally by the members of the household unit" (Mathews 1985, 296). She also found that limitations on women's participation in civil offices more generally are due not to their inability or reluctance to venture forth from households but to historical circumstance in which state-level forces have favored men in state-village interrelationships.

Men also occupy domestic spaces, in households or elsewhere (e.g., men's houses). In households of men, women, and children, the extent to which tasks, authority, prestige, and so forth are genderized—that is, differentially distributed between men and women—differs from one culture to the next. Maltz (1985) found that among Scottish pentecostals, husbands have authority over wives and that gender concepts stress male authority rather than the separation of men and women into different domains. Domestic relations also have public and political significance. For example, women exercise power and influence on men through their movements from natal to marital households in such diverse contexts as rural Taiwan (M. Wolf 1972) and highland New Guinea (Strathern 1972; see also March and Taqqu 1986). Domestic and public thus take on different meanings that themselves must be discovered through empirical research (Borker 1985; Harris 1981).

The domestic/public contrast is beginning to find its way into medical anthropological discourse through such empirical research. Ethnographers with special interests in informal healing have discovered that its practitioners are for the most part ordinary women whose domestic role obligations include the care of other household members, children in particular (Finerman, this volume; Graham 1985). Also, in an interesting symbolic reversal, women who become ritual or other specialized practitioners of medicine and who in the process are liberated from actual domestic obligations, infuse powerful female symbolism, including the metaphor of maternal nurturance, into their healing practices (Wedenoja, this volume).

The nature/culture contrast, unlike the domestic/public, claims a broader anthropological constituency, and in particular has shaped much anthropological work on female pollution. Symbolic studies of healing rituals frequently describe cultural images of women, particularly their reproductive substances, as representing uncontrolled and thus dangerous forces (La Fontaine 1972; Poole 1981) and as embodying the boundary between culture and order, on the one hand, and nature and disorder, on the other (Douglas 1966; Goodale 1980). Feminists and structuralists have devoted loving attention to the universality or cultural specificity of nature/culture contrasts (Lévi-Strauss 1969; MacCormack 1980; Ortner 1974; Strathern 1980); new ethnographic evidence offered in the course of this discussion shows not only that nature/culture contrasts differ from society to society, but that different societies juxtapose gender symbols with those of nature and culture in distinct ways (MacCormack 1980). As with the domestic/public dichotomy, Euro-American definitions of nature and culture may have little to do with contrasts that other cultures use to order the world. Strathern (1980) claims, for example, that Hageners do not categorize reality into nature and culture, but into "wild" and "domestic" and that these contrasts do not stand in the same relationship to each other as do Western notions of nature and culture.

Few medical anthropologists have borrowed the nature/culture paradigm to explain gender asymmetry in healing. But the idea that women are marginal, positioned not between culture and nature but between different social worlds (e.g., between this world and ancestral worlds) does appear in the medical anthropological literature. Women's symbolic marginality is the central explanatory theme in Ngubane's (1977) interpretation of women diviners among the Zulu. She identifies gender symbolism as the driving force shaping women's dominant position among Zulu diviners. As diviners communicate with ancestors, they are structurally similar to mothers and chief mourners (also women) at funerals. In both roles, women are marginal, positioned at the boundary between society and the world of the ancestors; it is through birth (through female bodies literally) and death (through females symbolically) that people move between the two worlds. In Ngubane's words:

> [that] the mother and the chief mourner [are] channels through whose bodies spiritual beings cross from the other world to this world and from this world to the other world . . . applies also to the diviner, who is a point of contact with the spirits who return to this world. Through a woman the transition of spiritual beings is made. This point is crucial in that it explains why diviners are women and why men must become transvestites to be diviners (Ngubane 1977, 88).

Marginality, then, can mean positioned between culture and nature or between this world and that of ancestral spirits. Ritual specialists who communicate with ancestral spirits on behalf of their living descendants are marginal in the second sense. Women occupy these roles in some societies, but not in others. Where they do, as among the Zulu, and where the spirits with whom they communicate are socially important, women ritual specialists are also socially important (see Bourguignon 1976 for a Haitian example).

As discussed earlier, the domestic/public dichotomy has more frequently entered medical anthropological writing, but not as a central conceptual focus. Ethnographers comment that the onset of menopause releases women from the symbolic associations and social obligations of still fertile women. Postmenopausal women enter the public domain, exercise authority, and acquire prestige in the same way men do (see Brown and Kerns 1985 for a more extended discussion). Women's reproductive status is sometimes noted by ethnographers, but with few exceptions (McClain 1975; Paul and Paul 1975), investigators rarely discuss the specific age at which recruitment to the healing role occurs and why this is so. Where women become healers before menopause, they are exempted from domestic restrictions despite their continued fertility. Attention has only recently been focused on the usefulness of the domestic/public contrast in the comparative analysis of informal healing. The ethnographic evidence thus far indicates that most informal healing is accomplished by women in domestic contexts. Its symbolic associations in these instances become intertwined with other female symbols, as is illustrated in several chapters in this volume.

Functionalist Interpretations
of Female Healing

Medical anthropologists have borrowed functionalist explanations from social anthropology to spell out how medical beliefs and behaviors satisfy individual, social, and cultural needs and contribute to social cohesiveness. Most employ the functionalist paradigm loosely to demonstrate that a given cultural complex—for example, the incest prohibition or spirit possession—contributes in particular ways to the integration or the adaptation of the society itself, or to the adaptation of a subgroup or subcategory of the society. As will be discussed further below, the dominant interpretation of spirit possession cults is a functionalist one that treats gender asymmetry as a principal theme (Lewis 1971, 1986).

Ethnographers studying medical systems, particularly when focusing on social relations, attribute particular adaptive, integrating, or maintaining functions to medical beliefs and behaviors. The treatment of illness has traditionally been seen by anthropologists to "reintegrate" patients into social groups (Madsen 1964), to increase social cohesiveness (V. Turner 1969), to confirm and sustain cultural belief systems (Comaroff 1981), to alleviate role stress (O'Nell and Selby 1968), and to allow the projection and safe discharge of hostility and aggression (Kluckhohn 1970; Spiro 1952). Generalizations about medical beliefs and behaviors at once reflect and reinforce functional explanations at the ethnographic level. Thus, Young writes:

> People maintain their medical traditions because they affect undesirable biological states in expected ways, and because they are effective ways for dealing with disruptive events that cannot be allowed to persist. A consequence of these meanings is that some kinds of sickness episodes also perform an ontological role— communicating and confirming important ideas about the real world (A. Young 1976, 5).

Comaroff extends the functions served by medical beliefs to the reinforcement of existing cultural epistemologies:

The onset of illness frequently occasions the perception of more deep-seated contradictions in the encompassing socio-cultural order. At the very least, the healing process mobilizes potent symbolic resources; for in the attempt to redress the breaches made by illness, healers everywhere manipulate symbolic media. . . . Healing affirms the hegemony of established images of the self and social context (Comaroff 1981, 369).

For symbolic anthropologists also, the interpretation of healing rests ultimately on identifying the functions that symbols and their manipulation in ritual perform in the service of maintaining the larger social system. Turner's description of the social benefits bequeathed by rites of status reversal, a form of "societal" healing in which normative age and gender hierarchies are purposefully, albeit temporarily, dismantled, is particularly explicit:

structural superiors, through their dissensions over particularistic or segmental interests, have brought disaster on the local community. It is for structural inferiors, then—(in the Zulu case, *young women* . . .), representing communitas, or global community transcending all internal divisions—to set things right again. They do this by symbolically usurping for a short while the weapons, dress, accoutrements, and behavioral style of structural superiors—i.e., men (V. Turner 1969, 184; emphasis in original).

As women normally represent weakness and men strength, rites of status reversal act to cleanse society of structurally induced stresses and "enable a sober return to a now purged and reanimated structure" (V. Turner 1969, 185).

Lévi-Strauss's (1967, 181–201) elaborate exegesis of a Cuna Indian shaman's cure is one of the most familiar symbolic/functionalist passages in the anthropological literature. It also vividly portrays gender asymmetry in action, although this effect was certainly not the author's conscious intention. Lévi-Strauss does not dwell on the sex of the healers who are the actors in the curing episode, but for our purposes, the distinction is quite important. A midwife, a woman, fails to enable a woman in labor to deliver her child. The shaman, a man, is called in when the problem becomes life-threatening. The shaman uses his greater power to direct the sick woman's conscious attention away from her pain to participate in the mythical battle between the shaman and his tutelary spirits and the malevolent spirit who has caused the illness (and who, incidentally, is female). Eventually the woman recovers and successfully delivers her infant. We may presume that during the protracted and intense symbolic battle waged by the shaman the ineffectual midwife is somewhere on the sidelines cheering him on. The sex asymmetry so patent in this account is not belied by the existence of a powerful female spirit in Cuna mythology. Vigorous female mythical representations need not equate with feminine prestige in real life, and among both indigenous and modern Cuna at least, women seem not to enjoy particular advantages (Swain 1982; for a psychobiological view of this same healing performance, see Laderman 1983, 1987).

Lévi-Strauss's objective in this essay is to demonstrate the effectiveness of symbols—how they function to ease distress and resolve very real illness. But his analysis further illustrates that functionalist interpretations can and do ignore important social realities that are manifest in healing performances; gender hierarchies are clearly among these. At least one survey of women's position in preindustrial societies concludes that shamans are predominantly male and that male shamans are more powerful than female shamans (Whyte 1978). To entertain the view that the most powerful healers are typically men means that male primacy in healing is as problematic as is their monopoly on social prestige, their hegemony in the public domain, the advantages secured by them through marriage, and so forth. It also means that the inevitable exceptions—female healers who acquire male attributes (see, e.g., Landes 1971) or female healers who are powerful in their own right—need explanation.

The most carefully constructed and ethnographically rich exposition of the significance of the sex of healers is I. M. Lewis's (1966, 1971, 1986) functionalist account of women participants in spirit possession cults, first as patients, then as spirit mediums. Lewis claims that through participation in "cults of affliction," women compensate for social and material losses suffered as a result of their structural subordination to men. The most dispossessed women are married, and cult members are largely wives seeking to gain strategic advantages over their husbands who in practical affairs enjoy privileges and rewards denied women.

> For all their concern with disease and its treatment, such women's possession cults are also, I argue, thinly disguised protest movements directed against the dominant sex. They thus play a significant part in the sex-war in traditional societies and cultures where women lack more obvious and direct means for forwarding their aims. To a considerable extent they protect women from the exac-

tions of men, and offer an effective vehicle for manipulating husbands and males relatives (Lewis 1971, 31).

Because the possessing spirits strike capriciously, their female victims
are held blameless and therefore not responsible for the burdens in-
curred by their male relatives in the course of treatment. Secondary
gains of a psychological nature result from the increased attention and
sympathy given to victims by others (see also Bourguignon 1976; Freed
and Freed 1967). Lewis posits that the spirits involved are "amoral" and
"peripheral" in the sense that "they play no direct part in upholding the
moral code of the socieites in which they receive so much attention" and
"originate outside the societies whose women they plague" (Lewis 1971,
31). The argument that women's rituals involve peripheral spirits is
required for the theory to make sense, for if women's rituals were socially central, would they not confer on women practitioners the same
prestige and status that male ritual specialists enjoy? Bourguignon
(1976, 34–36) questions Lewis's argument on this point and claims that
Haitian vodou violates Lewis's insistence that the possessing spirits of
subjugated individuals must be peripheral.

Other researchers also interpret spirit possession cults as a cultural
"safety valve" that allows women, and in some cases low-status men, to
gain temporary rewards from higher-status males and to achieve limited
prestige and authority that do not threaten the stability of the culture or
the dominant gender hierarchy (Hamer and Hamer 1966; Messing 1958).
Still others focus on role stress, hypothesizing that culture-bound illnesses
such as *susto* (O'Nell and Selby 1968) and participation in spirit possession cults (O'Connell 1982) alleviate individuals' anxieties over their failure to conform to social role expectations. Critical to this view is the
assumption that gender role stress falls more heavily on women than on
men because other avenues for relief are not as available to women as
they are to men. Morsy (1978) reasons that since not all women succumb
to illness designed to provide them with secondary gains, and since some
men also suffer the same illnesses, the locus of explanation must lie at the
intersection of gender systems with systems of power and authority, and
reference to gender hierarchy is not by itself a satisfactory explanation.

The idea that women's expressions of illness or their assumption of
healing roles derive from their low prestige and lack of access to valued
public roles has been criticized from at least two additional perspectives.
Some contend that Lewis and other "cult of affliction" writers overlook
the most obvious reason that women join together as victims and healers:
to cope with very real disease. Thus, women who participate in spirit

possession cults among the Luvale of Zambia have devastating personal experiences with infertility, pregnancy loss, and child mortality (Spring 1978). Spirit possession cults provide at once a practical and an expressive response. For example, new mothers with previous fertility problems may be secluded with their infants in specially built compounds for periods that may last for months. The goal is protection from aggrieved ancestors; the material result is effective quarantine. Spring reports that during an epidemic of measles, those children behind the "big fence" survived in greater numbers than those not ritually protected.

In a more recent study, Holmberg (1983) criticizes interpretations of spirit possession cults as "compensatory politics" and as psychotherapeutic. To understand the role of gender in the ritual structure of the Temang of highland Nepal, Holmberg instead focuses on the meanings that both shamanism (associated with femaleness) and Buddhism (associated with maleness) hold for the Temang. Although shamanic rites and their mythic referents reflect a feminine perspective—females as mediators between patrifocal households—these social divisions and their meanings are as important to Temang men as they are to women.

Harvey's (1979) study of female Korean shamans describes women as structurally peripheral, but in the two senses of social and psychological deviance. She addresses two trends in the interpretation of religious healing that have remained somewhat separate: the functionalist view of spirit possession cults that we have been exploring here, and the suggestion that culture ingeniously arranges useful roles for shamans of both sexes who suffer from certain personality disorders or psychopathologies. Harvey relates the life histories of six female shamans to affirm a series of rhetorical assertions she introduces at the beginning of her book:

> Could it be that Korean culture has developed patterns of systematically mobilizing the psychological insights and strengths of individuals, who, through traumatic personal experiences, have achieved psychological conditions suitable (through the role of shaman) for counseling others in the resolution of conflicts? Could it be also that Korean culture has assigned to shamans the additional function of serving their society as "deputy lunatics" by depriving them of the usual support system available to women through the family and kin group? And for those shaman families that remained together and shared the social ostracism of the shaman, could there have been hidden gains? Was the institutionalization of the shaman role specifically for women a way of allowing females

an indirect means of exerting influence and thus compensating them for their position of inferiority to males in authority and decision making (Harvey 1979, 6)?

Harvey's vivid accounts notwithstanding, deviance need not always be socially condemned. Like Korean shamans, highland Mayan midwives are also deviant in the sense that their domestic and conjugal roles are incompatible with their ritual roles (Paul and Paul 1975). Unlike the Korean shaman, however, the Mayan midwife's deviance is rewarded; as a ritual specialist, she commands deference and respect. Nor does her family suffer ostracism as a result of her departure from the household. Whether deviance in a ritual practitioner is rewarded or punished, then, depends upon cultural and social contexts.

Women's Symbolic Worlds and Healing

One line of discourse in the anthropology of gender asserts that women's lives are less well understood than men's because women occupy different symbolic worlds as a consequence of their structural subordination to men. To the extent that public discourse is dominated by men, women's codes of expression are less accessible within the society and to outside observers who would interpret the culture. Women thus project an image of themselves as muted. The ethnographer's task, according to this view, is to break into this world through other forms of feminine expression such as myth and ritual, and describe its contents. The twin ideas that women construct different models than men and that they do not expose their models to others originated with E. Ardener's analysis of Bakweri women's rituals, from which he constructs a general explanation:

> the models of society that women can provide are not of the kind acceptable at first sight to men or to ethnographers, and specifically . . . they do not so readily see society bounded from nature. They lack the metalanguage for its discussion. To put it more simply: they will not necessarily provide a model for society as a unit that will contain both men and themselves. They may indeed provide a model in which women and nature are outside men and society (E. Ardener 1972, 137).

Muted groups other than women exist (e.g., children), but it is women's hidden world views, signifying a separate order of social existence for themselves, that demand attention in the analysis of gender (E. Ardener 1972; S. Ardener 1978b).

Other ethnographic evidence fails to support Ardener's formulation, even where male ethnographic bias seems not to be a confounding factor. The Mundurucú provide one example. In describing indigenous Mundurucú gender relations, Yolanda and Robert Murphy (1974) discovered that changes brought about by development in the Amazon region affected men and women differently, including their reconstructions of the past:

> Mundurucú men reveled in the recall of the past, of times of valor and strength, of a more abundant life, of a period when the benevolent spirits were still vital and active in the affairs of man. The women, on the other hand, never had anything to say within our hearing about the "good old days"; in fact, they hardly ever talked about times past. It was men who mourned the end of the ceremonial cycle, the forgetting of myths and of lore, and the passage to a future dominated by outside forces. . . . The women, to the contrary, never expressed to us even a hint of grief for the death of the old (Murphy and Murphy 1974, 180–181).

This passage shows that Mundurucú women's lack of nostalgia about the past reflects not mutedness or a uniquely feminine perception of their former lives but rather their appraisal of their position vis-à-vis men in that life. That men and women have different values and causes for celebration, as illustrated so concretely in this description, does not mean that they occupy different symbolic worlds and by itself says little about women's idioms of expression, which probably differ according to social context in any case. Some ethnographic accounts tell us that women share men's conceptualizations through willing participation in men's worlds in whatever role is assigned to them, including sharing to a greater or lesser extent men's evaluations of them (Strathern 1981 devotes considerable attention to this issue in her analysis of Hagen gender imagery). Others describe societies in which women's models clearly depart from those of men (Collier 1974).

Women create and project images of themselves to gain economic, political, or social ends (Browner and Lewin 1982; Lewin 1979). One of these images, not surprisingly, is that of mutedness. If ethnographers notice women's separateness or silence, they may nevertheless overlook the purposeful elements these impressions hide (see, e.g., Keesing 1985). A case in point is Okley's (1975) analysis of Gypsy women's structural and symbolic relationships with Gypsy men and with the surrounding, dominant European society of non-Gypsy men and women ("Gorgios"). Within Gypsy society, women are polluting to men, a belief articulated strongly by both sexes and supported in daily ritual avoidances. However, Gypsy women construct a separate image of themselves in relationship to Gorgios, particularly Gorgio men, an image not revealed to Gypsy men. While accepting their subordinate status within Gypsy society, when "calling" (conducting economic enterprises among the Gorgios), Gypsy women enjoy an entrepreneurial independence denied them within Gypsy society. "Calling" allows intermittent escape from some of the more unpleasant aspects of gender hierarchy, but it does not threaten the social order.

In sum, what women can and will say about themselves depends upon historical circumstance and micropolitical context, including not only gender relationships but also encounters with ethnographers (both male and female). As Keesing points out, "lack of success in eliciting rich accounts of self and society from women cannot be taken as evidence that they are ultimately unable, because of life experience and societal role, to give such accounts" (Keesing 1985, 27).

How does the medical anthropological literature either challenge or support the argument that women are muted? Do women healers, for example, construct and share healing discourses that define gender differently than do men's discourses? Are these discourses accessible, either to men or to ethnographers? Medical anthropologists' treatment of women healers, principally indigenous midwives and spirit mediums, provides only limited and inconclusive case material. In some societies, the management of pregnancy and childbirth are exclusively the business of women (Sargent 1982), both in knowledge and in practice, whereas in others, men also participate, either symbolically, as in the couvade and other ritual practices (Paige and Paige 1981), or practically, as in supporting their wives during labor (Jordan 1983) or presiding over particularly difficult or ominous labors (Laderman 1983). Certain African spirit possession cults attract mostly women with fertility-related illnesses (Spring 1978). Cult adepts call on their female ancestors, through trance and possession, to reverse their reproductive misfortunes. In the process, ties among women are promoted and strengthened, both laterally among cult members and vertically between female ancestors and living female descendants. Men neither participate in these cults nor directly benefit from them. Elsewhere women manipulate men directly through healing, as in cults of affliction, or they withdraw permanently from ordinary female role obligations, as do highland Mayan midwives (Paul 1978b).

Women healers do not just act on their own behalf or collectively advance the interests of women against those of men. As ritual specialists (Finkler 1981, 1985) and secular curers (Lieban 1981), women alleviate the illnesses and the suffering of both sexes, just as do men healers. Why gender is significant to some healing discourses but not to others is a question that awaits further study. The question is central to several of the essays in this volume.

New Contributions to the Study of Women Healers

This collection is organized into four parts according to the predominant themes of the essays. Two chapters in Part One describe women as unnamed and informal healers, and the third comments on why women are reluctant to assume public healing roles. Together they illustrate the increasing attention paid by ethnographers to women's everyday lives. As case studies in the anthropology of women and in medical anthropology, each places women as domestic and local healers in the larger context of gender relations. The chapter by Finerman considers domestic healing by Saraguro Indian women in a rural Ecuadorean Andean community. Of particular interest is the author's discussion of mothers' responsibility for illness prevention, particularly on behalf of children. Nordstrom's essay describes local-level women healers in Sri Lanka and compares them with healing specialists. She suggests that it is in the context of ordinary healing of mundane illnesses—not the acute illnesses occasioning the intervention of traditional or biomedical specialists— that cultural conceptions of health and "dis-ease" are negotiated and given meaning. Browner describes the strict egalitarian ethos in a Chinantec-speaking Indian community in rural highland Oaxaca that inhibits men and women alike from differentiating themselves from their fellow villagers. In the case of women, one consequence is that only a few midwives exist, and these women do not achieve particular recognition or reward for their occasional work. Further, reproductive and medical knowledge is widely and evenly dispersed throughout the community, among men as well as among women, and the most frequent attendant at a woman's birth is her own husband. Among Chinantecs, conformity to sex role norms reflects a larger ideological conservatism that acts collectively to defend the indigenous way of life against government and other forms of outside intrusion and forces of divisiveness. Few women in this social context are willing to risk social censure to achieve a status that offers few personal rewards.

The chapters in Part Two illustrate the ways in which female and mother symbols characterize women healers' curing practices. Both patients (male and female) and the healers who treat them enact their respective roles metaphorically as children (patients) and mothers (healers). But to become healers, women must take on responsibilities beyond the confines of the household and the workplace and outside the boundaries of kinship roles. In so doing, they gain degrees of freedom, prestige, and influence denied to them by the more routine dimensions of their lives. Fox provides an exegesis of Christian Science theology and the role of women healers in Christian Science practice. She presents two views of these practitioners, the secular view of the surrounding dominant society that women's healing is less prestigious than men's public activities, and the Christian Science view in which women healers have normative power and prestige just as do men teachers and administrators. Kerewsky-Halpern describes the Serbian *bajalica,* the postmenopausal woman who cures fellow villagers with oral charms and conjurings. Although past reproductive age themselves and thus free of female pollution, mothering and other feminine metaphors pervade the ritual incantations of the *bajalice.* Like Ngubane's (1977) Zulu diviners, bajalice, as women, are closer to society's boundaries and thus are imbued with mysterious power that they summon in healing rituals. Wedenoja's account of the religious healing cult in Jamaica known as Balm draws on psychoanalytic interpretation. Wedenoja describes the female balmist healer as a source of maternal nurturance, protection, warmth, and comfort, whose ritual cures satisfy patients' dependency needs in addition to reversing their misfortunes. Balmists are women because healing is associated with mothering, a culturally pervasive symbolism that Wedenoja documents for Jamaica and suggests may be universal.

The three chapters of Part Three are life histories of women who are ritual specialists. Singer and Garcia trace the events in the life of a Puerto Rican woman that eventuate in her recruitment to Espiritismo and her assumption of the leadership of a spiritist center. Kendall's description of the life of a Korean *mansin* is similar, emphasizing less the characteristics of her healing work and more the biographical experiences that led her to take on the shaman role. Green describes the troubled personal circumstances of a young Xhosa woman of South Africa and their resolution through her apprenticeship with an older female diviner-medium. In each chapter, the women in question had suffered difficulties in their domestic relationships, a form of sex-role stress that appeared to have precipitated their search for new sources of personal satisfaction. Further, all had experienced visions, an ability that suited them for the ritual role they eventually attained. The women in these chapters conform in some respects to Lewis's (1971) belief that spirit possession is a vehicle for oppressed individuals, particularly women, to escape, if temporarily, the confines of role stress. As ritual specialists, each indeed overcame personal misfortune and gained status enhancement. However, other requirements of Lewis's thesis fail to explain ethnographic details found in these case studies. For example, the mansin in Kendall's account is possessed by centrally significant, not peripheral, spiritual beings, and her "clients" include both men and women who are not themselves destined to become healers. The same may be said about the spiritist healer described by Singer and Garcia. Although spiritism may be considered in one sense peripheral to the dominant Catholicism of the Puerto Rican community, it is vital to segments of that community, and patients of both sexes and different ages seek out spiritists to ease affliction and illness. Men as well as women achieve leadership roles within the temples. That Lewis's ideas about sex asymmetry and certain kinds of spirit possession cults fail to explain existing cultural diversity in gender and healing is a cause for neither alarm nor celebration. Indeed, it would be surprising if new scholarship in medical and feminist anthropology did not lead us to reexamine familiar explanations.

In Part Four, the final two chapters deal with women in traditional healing roles in the context of culture change. Sargent compares midwifery, childbirth care practices, and ideas about proper maternal comportment in rural and urban settings in the People's Republic of Benin, West Africa. The inevitability of the decline of traditional midwifery in urban areas contrasts with new occupational opportunities for urban Bariba women. The gains are not commensurate, however, with the losses. Urban women have their babies in clinics attended by biomedically trained practitioners. The possible margin of safety provided by biomedicine is achieved only through the loss of the autonomy still held by rural Bariba mothers, who for the most part still deliver at home and decide who their attendants will be. At the same time, the prestige and influence previously attached to the most accomplished midwives is disappearing, as evidenced by the fact that urban women and, increasingly, rural women as well do not seek to become midwives and instead prefer to pursue other avenues of self-determination. Reid's chapter traces the lay midwifery movement in the United States from the late 1960s to the present. She highlights the tensions between the ideologies of sisterhood and professionalism, both of which claim midwives' loyalties and structure their personal goals. As lay midwives find they cannot subscribe to both philosophies at the same time, they make compromises that separate them from their previous loyalties to sisterhood and bring them closer to the more restricted definitions of care giving required by mainstream biomedicine.

Taken together, the essays illustrate the ways in which medical anthropology both contributes to and benefits from cross-cultural studies of gender. Ethnographers have more intensely scrutinized how gender informs the study of other cultural domains—for example, kinship and marriage, religion and ritual, power and politics, production and reproduction. This volume, in documenting the significance of gender in healing roles and statuses, begins to bring similar balance to the domain of medicine.

PART ONE
Women as Informal Healers

Medical anthropologists interested in healing practitioners tend to concentrate their attention on specialists: shamans, spirit-mediums, diviners, priests, midwives, and even secular healers who treat mundane illnesses or perform simple medical services, such as bone setters, herbalists, injectionists, and the like. The study of self-treatment is relatively new, and the idea that individuals who carry out such informal healing make up a category of "healers" worthy of investigation is even more recent. Thus, the existence of a "popular" sector in plural medical systems that contrasts with "folk" and "professional" sectors has gained currency in the medical anthropological literature (Kleinman 1980; Leslie 1977). But the study of women as informal healers within this sector has lagged, and the interest that has been demonstrated reflects not so much a medical anthropological question about healing roles as a feminist concern with documenting women's lives and their contributions to culture. Because most illnesses are managed in the popular sector (Kleinman 1980; Parker et al. 1979), however, attention by some medical anthropologists has necessarily and appropriately shifted to domestic healing and to women as informal or domestic healers. In this domain, the curing strategies of first resort are those that women employ in households; mothers and grandmothers treat children, wives treat husbands, daughters and daughters-in-law treat parents and parents-in-law, and so forth. Grave illnesses and serious injuries are usually recognizable as such and in these cases, family members immediately seek the care of specialists, either indigenous or biomedical (J. C. Young 1981). But most illnesses are not life-threatening and their entire course plays out in domestic contexts. These contexts can extend to include local neighborhoods where informal networks (usually of women) act to bind together separate domestic units (March and Taqqu 1986).

In this section the chapters by Finerman on Andean Saraguro mothers and by Nordstrom on Sri Lankan local-level female healers present rich ethnographic detail on the context and content of informal healing. Both authors contrast informal healers with the range of specialist practitioners in the communities in question and show how gender hierarchies and their supporting ideologies determine the distribution of medical roles between the sexes. Both authors interpret informal healing as a social maintainance device that in the case of the Saraguro mothers perpetuates the integrity of the family and in the case of the Sri Lankan local-level healers mediates between formal and local interpretations of cultural beliefs and precepts.

The chapter by Browner describes the position of midwives in a Chinantec community in which medical knowledge is widely distributed, egalitarianism is a prevailing and guiding ideology, and standards of comportment for women are enforced by public opinion and reaction. The consequence is that few women choose the occupation, and midwifery takes on none of the characteristics typical of formalized healing roles in other cultural contexts: specialized or arcane knowledge, specialized skills, exceptional community regard (usually positive, but in some cases negative, as some healing specialists are feared as witches), and the attribution of sacred qualities.

In these chapters, women's healing is defined as informal, that is, as occurring in domestic spaces without jural-political accoutrements, and as promoting models of reality that do not depart, either secretly or in confrontation, from dominant cultural models articulated by men in public arenas. Nordstrom contends that central Sri Lankan religious and moral principles are held equally by men and by women, and that it is the business of local-level healers to translate these principles to the domain of mundane but ubiquitous misfortune and disorder, including illness. Far from being muted, women as healers not only do not subscribe to separate, feminine models but readily articulate the dominant models of Sri Lankan culture, just as do male Buddhist priests and shamans in more dramatic fashion in public contexts.

Neither do Saraguro mothers as domestic healers challenge male cultural constructions. The cultural models, including disease concepts, that underlie domestic healing in this peasant Andean community do not distinguish women's worlds from men's, nor are they women's secrets. Saraguro mothers, as do their male kin, view the home as a fortress against an unpredictable, dangerous, and uncontrollable environment. The models of the world that are discrepant are those of villagers and outsiders. Saraguros consult biomedical specialists for the treatment of disease only with reluctance. It is interesting that this reluctance extends to indigenous specialists as well, which suggests that other forces in addition to cultural conservatism must be at work to perpetuate the domesticity of healing and the primacy of women as nonspecialist healers. These forces may parallel those exigencies and constraints described by Browner as inhibiting women in the Chinantec community of San Francisco, Mexico, from becoming midwives: strong social expectations regarding women's proper place and behavior and a code of egalitarianism that extends from economic and social domains to include medical knowledge and practices.

Yet another dimension of informal healing is its symbolic relationship to nurturance. Finerman makes explicit the cultural equation between maternal nurturance and domestic healing among Saraguro Indian peasants. In the Chinantec community Browner discusses, diagnostic and therapeutic knowledge is uniformly held by adults of both sexes, but gender role relationships assign to women the task of applying nonesoteric medical knowledge to the care of household members. The mother metaphor that imbues informal healing with meaning in these chapters derives from women's primary domestic responsibilities. As will be seen in Part Two, certain specialist healers also nurture patients, an association that suggests that the re-creating of domestic relationships in public contexts is therapeutic.

The Forgotten Healers: Women as Family Healers in an Andean Indian Community

Few societies today are limited to a single source of health care. A number of traditional and introduced therapeutic alternatives, providing different treatment costs and benefits for residents, may be available in a community. Although cross-cultural studies of therapeutic systems have often pointed out the pluralistic nature of community health care, few have detailed the full range of treatment alternatives available.

In many cases, descriptions of community health resources identify categories of traditional and biomedical health practitioners such as doctors, nurses, pharmacists, midwives, bone setters, masseurs, herbalists, and shamans. Individuals who do not bear a formal title are more commonly described as clients of health agents, and not as active health care providers. As a result, investigations that focus on specialized healers can provide only a parital understanding of the individual's role in treatment.

Investigations of women's roles in family health care illustrate the need to broaden our inquiry beyond the study of specialized healers. Some studies detail women's participation in selecting therapeutic agents (Litman 1979, 78, 85; J. C. Young 1981) and in childbearing (Jordan 1983; Kay 1982; Newman 1985; Romalis 1981). However, most research has perpetuated the image of female heads of household in their role as clients of practitioners (Romalis 1981). Those few studies that have explored women's roles as family curers characterize treatment as though it were Bandaid therapy: simplistic practices directed at the relief of minor complaints. Chrisman, for example, states that mothers and grandmothers caring for family members tend to "diagnose common illnesses and treat them with the materials at hand" (quoted in Helman 1984, 44). Such descriptions underestimate the complexity and breadth of women's contribution to family health.

The failure to identify mothers as family healers is understandable, since the term "mother" does not immediately evoke the connotation of health practitioner. Still, healing activities can be interpreted as an extension of child-care duties, and we can view the nurturant, protective image associated with mothers as a reflection of their responsibility for family health.

Saraguro Indians in the southern highlands of Ecuador provide an exemplary case of women's contribution to family health. Despite the availability of numerous professional care resources, female heads of household in this population treat most family health complaints themselves, employing a complex system of therapeutic beliefs and practices in the treatment of a broad range of illnesses. A twelve-month survey of illness episodes in 140 families indicates that Saraguro mothers are the first and most frequently used source of therapeutic care. They treat 86 percent of all family illness complaints and act as the first source of care for 75 percent of all ailments recorded. In contrast, physicians were consulted for fewer than 20 percent of all complaints surveyed over the one-year period (see Finerman 1985 for details). Saraguro women, then, make a quantitatively overwhelming contribution to health care.

Saraguros are not an ethnographically extreme or unrepresentative case of women's participation in curing. Cross-cultural studies show that women and, in particular, female heads of household represent a major source of therapeutic assistance in many societies.

A number of reports discussing self-treatment, lay healing, or the popular health care sector identify women (mainly mothers) as primary health care providers. Young states that "the first, and by far the most frequent response to illness in Pichátaro is to attempt home or self-treatment. In doing so people have at their disposal a wide variety of remedies" (J. C. Young 1981, 104). He notes that "women, especially, have detailed knowledge in this area (1981, 104). Other investigations of lay healing and self-care directly identify mothers as primary health care providers. Helman states that in the popular or lay sector of therapy, "the main arena of health care is the *family*; here most ill-health is recognized and then treated. It is the real site of primary care in any society" (Helman 1984, 43–44, emphasis in original). He continues by noting that "the main providers of health care are *women*, usually mothers or grandmothers" (1984, 44, emphasis in original). Spector similarly indicates that information on traditional health care can be best understood through interviews with mothers or grandmothers, since "nurturance has been the domain of women in most cultures and societies" (Spector 1979, 32). Cheney and Adams (1978, 82); Manzanedo, Walters, and Lorig (1980, 195); and Clark (1970, 163) find that middle-aged or elderly Mexican-American women direct lay healing for family members as well as neighbors and friends, and Martinez and Martin (1979, 184) estimate that more than 85 percent of Mexican-American mothers surveyed about folk illnesses can list home remedies used in their treatment. Kleinman, too, details the participation of Taiwanese family members in health care and in the selection of treatments, where decisions "often came down to the choice made by a key family member, usually the mother or grandmother if a child was ill" (Kleinman 1980, 197). Litman notes that for families in Minnesota, "the mother was found to serve as a prominent influence in matters of health and nutrition. As a matter of fact, perhaps the most persistent theme running through our three generation study was the rather pervasive role played by the wife-mother in the health and health care of the family" (Litman 1979, 85).

Home treatment systems are portrayed in many of these reports as rudimentary and relatively ineffective. Young states that in Pichátaro, self-treatment "generally offers the lowest likelihood of cure, relative to the other alternatives" (J. C. Young 1981, 168). Similarly, Herrick finds that, for the Iroquois, "self-treatment or lay health-actor treatment would be undertaken in cases of mild illness or misfortune," but "experts would be sought especially if symptoms were of a more serious nature" (Herrick 1983, 150). Detailed accounts of ailments treated and remedies administered at home indicate, however, that in many societies family therapy is highly complex. Young observes that in self-treatment "people have at their disposal a wide variety of remedies, including both traditional herbal remedies and commercially produced types, as well as a considerable store of knowledge concerning their use," and that informants (especially women) "often in just a few minutes could list twenty or thirty different remedies and the illnesses for which they are used" (J. C. Young 1981, 104). Herrick, too, notes that Iroquois families had individuals with knowledge of herbs that "reduce fever; induce sweating, vomiting, urination or defecation; stop diarrhea; soothe sore throats; expel phlegm; tranquilize; stimulate; cleanse the blood; stop toothache, and so on" (Herrick 1983, 150). Similarly, Woods and Graves find that self-treatment in Guatemala "includes the use of inexpensive patent medicines purchased at the pharmacies, home remedies such as herbs, poultices, juices, and alcoholic beverages, or quite commonly, a combination of the two" (Woods and Graves 1976, 345). Home remedies outlined in these studies reflect a high degree of complexity, sharply contradicting the depiction of lay treatment as ineffective.

Investigations reporting frequencies of therapeutic recourse identify lay, home, or "self-treatment" as the single most common response to sickness. Young states that "the first, and by far the most frequent response to illness in Pichátaro is to attempt home or self-treatment" (J. C. Young 1981, 104). He determines that home or self-care was the initial response in 72 percent of disease episodes recorded and was used in 49 percent of all cases. In only 2–6 percent were forms of specialized care employed as a first resort, and specialized care represented only 4–18 percent of all health care (1981, 131). Woods and Graves report that in Guatemala, no treatment and self-treatment "are high-frequency responses for the majority of Lucenos, both Indian and Ladino" (Woods and Graves 1976, 345). Here, no treatment and self-treatment were employed for 73 percent of Indian, and 70 percent of Ladino illnesses; medical resources treated only 27 percent of the Indian and 30 percent of the Ladino cases documented. In his discussion of lay health care, Kleinman states that "in the United States and Taiwan, roughly 70 to 90 percent of all illness episodes are managed within the popular sector" (Kleinman 1980, 50). His survey of sicknesses recorded in a one-month study of 115 Taiwanese families indicates that "93 percent of these episodes were first treated at home, and 73 percent receive their only treatment there" (1980, 68). Furthermore, "in 98 percent of all episodes of adult sickness and 100 percent of all episodes in the elderly, recourse was made initially to self-treatment" (1980, 187). Similar findings are reported for Hong Kong (Lee 1976) and the United States (Levin, Katz, and Holst 1979; Litman 1974, 1979).

Why do individuals rely on mothers for health care? My own research conducted in Saraguro from 1978 to 1988 suggests that dependence on mothers as curers is not a result of cultural conservatism (unwillingness to exploit new health care services) or lack of access to other (indigenous or biomedical) therapeutic resources. Instead, medical choice was found to be related to the environmental, social, and cultural costs and benefits of consulting specialists and mother-healers. Women's responsibility for their family's health can be understood only in relation to the overall therapeutic system of a population. This chapter examines Saraguro women's curing activities within the context of gender role allocation and health care decision making in the indigenous population.

Methods

I began my research on Saraguro health practices in the summer of 1978. I expanded the initial investigation with a fourteen-month field project conducted between July 1980 and August 1981, and with follow-up studies undertaken in the summers of 1982, 1984, 1986, and 1988. I recruited Saraguro women who had given birth to one or more children as primary informants, because they are recognized by the indigenous community as the principal health care providers for the family. Members of Saraguro women's health and community development groups in four barrios were invited to participate in the research. One hundred forty women volunteered to complete interviews conducted each month between September 1980 and August 1981, at which they related details of family illness and treatments used over two-week periods. Approximately two-thirds of the participants completed surveys in any specific month, and most women completed a majority of the surveys. Birth histories, contraceptive knowledge, and economic conditions were also recorded with a subsample of 76 volunteers from the 140 health-survey participants (see Finerman 1985 for additional details on health surveys, and Finerman 1984, 330, for information on pregnancy and contraception histories). During this period I undertook in-depth interviews and participant-observation with fifty volunteers to record family health care activities. Health professionals in the community were also interviewed and observed to compare specialized medical services available to Saraguros.

Health Conditions in Saraguro

Saraguro Indians are a bilingual Quichua- and Spanish-speaking population numbering between fifteen and twenty thousand people. Approximately six thousand live within the *cabecera cantonal,* or county seat, of Saraguro in the southern Andes of Ecuador. Others reside in smaller parishes throughout the highland province of Loja, and in the past century some Saraguros have begun exploitation of the lowland tropical forest. The Saraguros are subsistence-based agropastoralists who supplement maize and potato cultivation with sheep and cattle herding and limited marketing of dairy products and crafts (for details see Belote 1984; Stewart, Belote, and Belote 1976).

Indians living in the canton of Saraguro have settled in dispersed barrios around the town center. Since the turn of the century the town itself has been populated almost exclusively by artisans and merchants of Spanish descent, locally referred to as *blancos*. Currently some two thousand blancos reside in Saraguro. Indigenous residents are readily distinguished from non-Indians through dress and hair style. Blanco hair and attire are styled in accordance with Western fashion. In contrast, all Saraguro Indians wear hand-spun and woven clothing of a distinctive local style derived from indigenous and colonial influences, and both men and women plait their hair in a single long braid (for additional information, see Meisch 1980–81). Saraguro dress and hair reflect the Indian population's strong ethnic identity, and cutting off one's braids or changing one's clothing indicates rejection of Saraguro culture.

The Indian population of Saraguro suffers high infant and adult morbidity relative to U.S. and Ecuadorian national averages (Finerman 1983, 1292). Infants and children are exposed to recurrent parasitic infection (with resulting complications from diarrhea and dehydration) and epidemic outbreaks of measles and whooping cough. Although Saraguro children currently display few signs of malnutrition, it is expected that the increasing availability of high-calorie but nutritionally inadequate processed foods (e.g., sugar and noodles) will adversely impact Saraguro health in the future. Adults exhibit high rates of symptomatic and asymptomatic tuberculosis (estimated to affect up to 50 percent of the residents of some barrios in Saraguro), and a significant percentage of the adult population suffers from the complications of alcohol abuse (a problem common to many post-Conquest indigenous societies; see, e.g., Finkler 1983, 85; Flores-Ochoa 1966, 43–44). Saraguros identify a number of culture-specific illnesses that also threaten individuals, including witchcraft (*brujería*), evil eye (*mal ojo*), envy (*envidia*), evil airs (*mal aire*), nerves (*nervios*), magical fright (*susto*), soul loss (*espanto*), and water-fright illness (*bao de agua*).[1]

Health Care Resources in Saraguro

Health is a prominent concern in the indigenous community, particularly because of high illness and death rates. A number of therapeutic services are available to Saraguros. Resources include traditional curing specialists such as *curanderos* (shamanic ritual curers), herbalists, and midwives, as well as biomedical professionals such as pharmacists, nurse practitioners, and physicians. Each therapist offers specialized forms of treatment, aimed at satisfying different health needs. People select practitioners by evaluating curing needs in relation to the relative costs and benefits of exploiting a given agent. An examination of treatment alternatives in Saraguro provides indications for continued indigenous reliance on mothers as healers.

Curanderos

At present two curanderos practice in Saraguro. They treat supernatural illnesses, including witchcraft, envy sickness, and soul loss, and more rarely chronic complaints and emotional disorders associated with alcoholism, sterility, and unrequited love (see Furst 1972; Kiev 1968; and Sharon 1978 on curanderismo). Curanderos are distrusted, because they accept payment both to cast spells at the request of a client and to remove spells on the behalf of a victim. Many residents also express dissatisfaction with the expense or efficacy of care.

Herbalists

Six herbalists in Saraguro treat natural and supernatural illnesses. Therapy involves administration of a series of herbal teas and advice on diet (for details see Bastien 1980, 1981). Since most Saraguros are already proficient in the use of medicinal plants, herbalists are usually consulted only after homemade herbal remedies prove unsuccessful.

Midwives

Several indigenous midwives practice in Saraguro, assisting in labor and delivery and advising on fertility, contraception, and prenatal and postpartum care. They employ massage, baths, and herbal remedies and make recommendations on diet, hygiene, and child care (Cosminsky 1978, 1982). Saraguro midwives are not biomedically trained or licensed, although the Ecuadorian government has sponsored midwife training programs in other rural communities (Baquero et al. 1981; Schreiber and Philpott 1978, 181). Saraguro women are unwilling to relinquish control over childbirth (Finerman 1982). As a result, most midwives are employed only after self-care proves ineffective (e.g., for problem deliveries).

Pharmacists

Two pharmacies and several small druggist shops operate in Saraguro. Pharmacists sell medications and herbal preparations and make suggestions on diet and therapy. Prescriptions are not required for purchases, so many Saraguros consult pharmacists rather than physicians. Some pharmacists sell expensive or unnecessary medications to customers, and reliance on druggist recommendations has made overmedication and misuse of drugs a common problem (Finerman 1983, 1295). Still, pharmacies remain a heavily exploited source for remedies.

Nurses

Eight Saraguro Indian nurse practitioners (*enfermeras*) are available for free consultations. They operate health posts in most barrios, where they administer vaccinations, treat minor complaints, and lecture indigenous mothers on nutrition and hygiene. Health posts are poorly stocked, however, often lacking basic supplies and medications. In addition, nurses are not trained to handle major medical emergencies. Despite favorable community sentiment, lack of institutional support is currently limiting the efficacy of nurses as health promotors.

Physicians

Physicians practicing at Saraguro's community hospital are first-year interns assigned to the rural post to fulfill one year of compulsory service. Patients undergo physical examinations and laboratory tests before receiving prescriptions for medications, which individuals must then purchase from pharmacists and administer at home. As already noted, patients often circumvent this process by consulting directly with pharmacists. Saraguros disapprove of the public and impersonal nature of hospital care, and many describe physicians as inexperienced and unsympathetic to Indian patients (Finerman 1985).

Traditional curers in Saraguro are no longer actively engaged in health care. Curanderos continue to practice witchcraft but rarely treat other forms of illness. Herbalists have been largely replaced by druggists, who supply pharmaceuticals as well as plant preparations. Few indigenous healers have apprentices, and traditional curing knowledge is not being passed on. Biomedical resources, because they are imposed from the outside, continued to operate regardless of community approval or disapproval.

Dissatisfaction with specialized resources available in Saraguro has reinforced reliance on family therapy. The preeminence of Saraguro women's positions as curers, and their beliefs and practices, will be compared with those of other treatment specialists to explain the popularity of family healers.

Family Curing Roles

Economic factors like the division of labor have helped to shape the allocation of curing duties. Saraguro women are allotted curing responsibilities as part of the differentiation between home and subsistence labor. Within the indigenous community, the division of labor by sex is more highly restricted for domestic activities than it is for agricultural and pastoral work. This distinction has affected the delegation of curing duties, primarily by assigning family curing activities exclusively to women.

Saraguro men and women often participate together in many phases of subsistence and cash crop production (although the most strenuous cultivation activities, like plowing, are performed almost exclusively by men). Together husbands and wives perform complementary roles, which makes the family the primary economic unit within the community. Males spend a majority of their time managing herding and husbandry, while females spend more time directing household activities. Nevertheless, Saraguro women regularly take charge of agricultural and pastoral production when spouses and other male relatives are not available to assist. In the twentieth century, as Saraguros have begun exploitation of land in the tropical forest, women have been forced to assume greater responsibility for cultivation and herding. Many men now leave Saraguro for several months each year to graze cattle in the Amazon lowlands, and during this period their wives are in charge of homes, families, agricultural fields, and livestock.

Labor is less flexibly defined within the domestic sphere in Saraguro.

Men's household duties are confined to collecting and splitting firewood and weaving fabric for clothing. Women manage all family care and household tasks (cooking, cleaning, and child care) and also spin wool, weave belts, and sew and dye garments. Since women spend more time supervising household activities than men do, mothers in Saraguro (as in most societies) are more accessible to their children.[2] Mothers therefore come into contact with children's health complaints on a regular basis, and fathers confront family illness less frequently. Women learn to recognize the early symptoms of illness in family members. In this manner, the Saraguro sexual division of labor and the prolonged absence of males shape the allocation of healing roles within the family.

Socialization practices also guide females to informal healing roles. By age twelve most Saraguro girls demonstrate considerable proficiency in health care. In contrast, Indian boys of comparable age display little or no knowledge about curing. All children learn to present health complaints to mothers, because they are the consistently accessible parent. As children grow, the role of mother as healer is continually reinforced. Children learn about the symptoms and treatment of disease and about patient and healer roles through personal experience with sickness and observation of ill siblings. Role differentiation in healing begins as older girls learn more about treatment by assisting mothers in the preparation and administration of remedies and by caring for younger siblings who are sick. By the time a girl reaches puberty she becomes her mother's assistant in supervising and curing siblings. She learns remedies through observation, imitation, and questioning. Adolescent boys do not undergo training in health care, because they are removed from the home environment by age six to assist their fathers with farming and herding. As a result, curing skills and knowledge are passed on exclusively to daughters.

During adolescence, when they assume a more substantial role in sibling care, Saraguro girls become immersed in health care training. Their therapeutic skills are refined as they gain the ability to prepare remedies without maternal supervision. The instruction and experience girls receive at this point give them greater confidence in their curing abilities and instill a sense of responsibility for the family they themselves will eventually establish.

Saraguro women assume the role of family curer after their first successful pregnancy. Mothers gain experience by treating their family, and their knowledge is broadened by experimentation and through discussions with female friends and relatives.

Informal yet strong social sanctions reinforce women's self-image and perpetuate their commitment to family curing. Saraguro mothers regularly compliment each other on the health of their offspring. Ruddy skin color and fatness are considered signs of health, and women comment on these features as an expression of approval for proper child care. Overt social censure for poor family care is less visible. Although mothers rarely face direct criticism for family illness, women with chronically sick children become the targets of gossip. For Saraguros, gossip and censure act as a more powerful tool than praise in encouraging role conformity.

Saraguro women fix the blame for illness on sources beyond their control. They trace most childhood illnesses to agents outside the home and recognize only falls and burns from hearth fires as being of home origin. Contagions, poisonings, and virtually all natural and supernatural disorders are attributed to outside sources. Viruses, colds, and fevers, for example, are traced to contact with schoolmates or neighbors, and poisoning is believed to result when children eat toxic plants while playing outside. Body aches, malevolent airs, magical fright, envy, and evil eye are also associated with contamination from forces outside the house. Saraguros view the home as a sanctuary from illness and the outside world as dangerous and filled with disease (Finerman 1987).

I interpret this tendency to view the home as a refuge from illness and the environment as a source of disease as a coping mechanism for dealing with sickness and death. By attributing illness to forces external to the home (rather than to carelessness within the home), people minimize personal guilt and social censure; women cannot be held accountable for unpredictable environmental agents. In this way Saraguro women protect their self-image and their reputations as family therapists.

Saraguro mothers also assume domestic healing roles to enhance their social status. Women in Saraguro predominate in the low-status domestic sphere, "those minimal institutions and modes of activity that are organized immediately around one or more mothers and their children" (M. Z. Rosaldo 1974, 23). Indian males dominate the higher-status public domain of "activities, institutions, and forms of association that link, rank, organize, or subsume particular mother-child groups" (M. Z. Rosaldo 1974, 23). Indian males achieve status through economic pursuits and participation in religious and community groups. Females manipulate status by taking part in women's groups but also by securing authority over domestic decisions (Graham 1985; Lamphere 1974, 99, 105; Mella 1987; Romalis 1985; Schlegel 1975, 174; Stern 1986). Exclusive control over health decisions and family curing gives

Saraguro women power within the household. Mothers refuse to surrender responsibility for care even in cases of life-threatening illness. When specialists are consulted, women continue to claim responsibility for the outcome of treatment.

Preventive Care in Saraguro

Because Saraguros view the home as safe and protective and the outside environment as dangerous and filled with disease, mothers take pains to protect children leaving the home. Infants wear little clothing at home, but mothers wrap infants taken outside in blankets and tie a red cord around wrists or ankles to ward off envy and witchcraft. Mothers swaddle infants to restrict movement and carry them on their backs, covered by shawls to minimize attention and avoid social censure. Older children also wear red cords, and when they leave the house they dress in several layers of clothing and wear hats for protection from the elements. Bundling children prevents excessive exposure to the sun and cold winds, which are believed to induce illness from hot and cold humoral imbalance (Colson 1976; Currier 1966; Foster 1953; Logan 1977).

Saraguro women associate family hygiene with the prevention of illness. Mothers consider bathing to be dangerous on very cold or very warm days, since temperature extremes disrupt humoral balance. They may add herbs to bath water to compensate for hot or cold humoral extremes. Hygiene concerns extend to hair care and waste disposal. Loose hair strands are collected from combs and burned to prevent harm by witches, who use hair in the performance of contagious magic. Excrement, like hair, can be used to cast spells, and individuals take care to defecate in sheltered areas and bury waste.

Saraguro mothers supervise diet as a preventive health measure. Foods categorized as cold (e.g., rice, potatoes, eggs, milk) are served in conjunction with foods classified as hot (e.g., beans, corn, beef, plantains), or the hot and cold balance is adjusted by incorporating medicinal plants in food preparation (e.g., adding them to soups or drinks) and by altering cooking time (raw foods are cold; dishes boiled for several hours are considered extremely hot). Individuals avoid eating food prepared by strangers; dishes made at home are thought to be healthy and nutritious. Food consumption and body weight are directly associated with health: a heavy physical build and large appetite are signs of well-being; weight loss and diminished appetite are perceived as symptoms of physical or emotional illness.

Diagnosis and Treatment

Extensive exposure to family ailments helps Saraguro mothers recognize illness symptoms before family members actually complain of sickness. Many women stressed the importance of early recognition and diagnosis to check the progression of illness.

Early symptoms of illness identified by Saraguro mothers include appetite or sleep loss, fatigue, or restlessness. Family members may also complain of physical pain, nausea, or bleeding. Mothers then examine them for symptoms such as fever or chills, unusual (pallid, flushed, or yellow) skin tone, rashes, blemishes, swelling, inflammation, unusual color or smell of urine or spittle, external or internal pain or bleeding, and menstrual, bowel, or bladder dysfunctions. Individual symptoms are classified as hot or cold, and the combination of complaints affecting the sufferer guides diagnosis.

Mothers also question family members to determine the cause of sickness. They ask the sick person about diet, dress, hygiene and daily habits, emotional disturbances, exposure to climatic extremes (which are believed to produce humoral imbalances), and unusual incidents or dreams that would indicate a disorder had supernatural origins.

Diagnoses are derived from extensive experience with family illness. Young Saraguro mothers are considered less competent diagnosticians than older women because they are less practiced in examining patients and interpreting disease syndromes. Younger women frequently listed individual symptoms (fever, coughs, sore throats, headaches) as family problems, while older women commonly identified complex disease syndromes (colds, whooping cough, and measles). Women who had never married or borne children demonstrated little knowledge about illness and curing despite what they may have learned from their mothers.

Once a preliminary diagnosis is established, Saraguro mothers initiate treatment. Saraguro mothers treat hot and cold humoral imbalances with allopathic measures (Finerman 1985). Humoral treatment includes physical therapy (massage, baths, and rest), diet control, and herbal remedies administered in a number of forms, often in conjunction with pharmaceuticals. Medicinal plants are cultivated in house gardens (*huertas*), collected in diverse ecological zones (paramo, intermontane basin, tropical forest), and purchased at markets in other cities. Saraguro mothers have a great deal of botanical expertise and make use of more than 350 medicinal plant species. They can detail the effectiveness of individual herbs for specific disorders and the methods for preparing each plant for use in curing.

Saraguro women believe that therapy is accelerated by lending emotional support to those who are ill. Although Saraguros do not identify psychological satisfaction as a specific goal in treatment, they frequently attribute recovery from illness to the quality of support provided and are unwilling to employ services that fail to provide emotional support. Three informants stated, for example, that "they treat you like an animal in the hospital" and that "it would be better to die at home than to go to the hospital." In a tragic case in 1982, a forty-three-year-old Saraguro mother miscarried in the seventh month of pregnancy. Friends, relatives, and nurses were unable to convince her to seek professional care for her hemorrhaging. She refused, stating that it would be better to die at home than to consult strangers. After four days, she and her child died. This case, though unusual, underscores the value Saraguros place on therapy that is familiar, private, and personalized.

Saraguro women promote their image as nurturant guardians. Home therapy is characterized by familiar, private, and personalized care. Mothers guarantee familiarity by caring for sick family members in commonplace surroundings and by using vernacular terminology and recognizable treatments (Aamodt 1977, 1978). Privacy is valued as a means for concealing personal achievement or misfortune from public attention and thus for avoiding gossip (Foster 1967, 89, 165; Redfield 1970, 32–33). Treatment at home shields mothers and sick family members from public view and social censure. Saraguros believe that personalized care helps individuals cope with stress, physical pain, and frustration over incapacitation, which are thought to hinder convalescence. The compassion and interest Saraguro mothers convey toward sick family members are thought to encourage recovery. Patients can be successfully treated without psychological support (Press 1971), but satisfaction with care can influence people's willingness to make long-term use of health services. Individuals who undergo a successful but stressful therapeutic experience may refuse similar treatment in the future.

Discussion

Cultural conservatism (Baquero et al. 1981, 10; Foster and Anderson 1978, 84, 106; Goodenough 1966, 91) has been suggested as an explanation for failure to employ specialized health care resources. In many ways Saraguro typifies the conservative South American peasant community: Indian residents maintain a strong ethnic identity, reflected in dress, language, and values, and make little use of biomedical specialists. However, several aspects of Western therapy, such as disease terms, pharmaceuticals, and some notions of disease causation, have been successfully integrated into health care in Saraguro (and in other populations; see Erasmus 1952; Leslie 1977; Logan 1973). Here, it appears that nonuse of biomedical practitioners is due not to any innate conservatism but to a rational analysis of the costs and benefits of employing biomedical or traditional specialists. Conservatism does not, in itself, present a powerful explanation for medical practices in Saraguro.

Others have argued that lack of geographic and financial access may explain the nonuse of health specialists. Young, for example, states that the Pichátaros of Mexico are "a people with an awareness of, and often as not a genuine enthusiasm for, modern medical treatment, but who are at the same time frequently denied full access to such services" (J. C. Young 1981, 176). In this case the tenacity of traditional health beliefs and continued reliance on native practitioners "may be seen as aspects of the community's ongoing adaptation to its position of economic and social marginality in relation to Mexican society" (J. C. Young 1981, 176). In contrast, alternative treatment resources are readily available to Saraguros. All services are physically accessible: traditional specialists and nurse practitioners live and work in Indian barrios, and pharmacists and physicians practice in the town center, within walking distance of most patients. Treatment is also economically affordable for most Saraguros. Consultations with traditional specialists cost little, and since a majority of Indians earn cash incomes through land and livestock holdings, most can afford to pay practitioner's fees. Most significantly, however, biomedical care is provided free of charge in Saraguro. Under these circumstances, individuals might actually reduce health care expenses by consulting physicians before purchasing medications, because without such advice mothers regularly purchase expensive and frequently inappropriate pharmaceuticals for use in home remedies. Nevertheless, Saraguros lack confidence in cost-free biomedical services (Finerman 1983, 1296). Lack of geographic and economic access to health services is clearly an inadequate explanation for failure to employ alternative health services in Saraguro.

Foster and Anderson point out that time can pose further limitations on the use of specialists. They note that "when patronizing a government health service for prenatal or postnatal care, or any of the other services that in themselves may seem desirable, means loss of a major chunk of valuable working time, we can speak of the economic costs to the potential user" (Foster and Anderson 1978, 247). In Saraguro, however, family care requires a greater investment of time than does the use of alternative services. Home treatments necessitate the cultivation, collection, and preservation of medicinal plants (often harvested in distant ecological zones or purchased at markets in faraway cities), trips to town to purchase pharmaceutical ingredients, processing and administering herbal remedies, and continuous attention to sick family members. Under these conditions, recourse to specialists would actually reduce the amount of time Saraguro women expend in family health care. The use of alternative therapeutic services in Saraguro is thus also not determined by time constraints.

Reliance on mothers for family care appears to be shaped by the social and psychological costs of consulting treatment specialists. The cost and benefits of home and specialized care are apparent in their distinct approaches to training and therapy. Mothers, like traditional specialists, acquire curing knowledge and training through experience. However, traditional specialists treat specific health problems in a large patient population; women treat a large range of health complaints suffered by the same individuals. Mothers gain an intimate understanding of the idiosyncratic symptoms family members manifest when ill. Women further broaden their treatment knowledge by participating in community health meetings and discussions with female friends and relatives. Traditional specialists do not discuss practices with other healers, because remedies and curing knowledge are considered trade secrets. Consequently, Saraguro women often have more extensive knowledge about medicinal plants than herbalists do, and mothers have a more eclectic understanding of health care. Saraguro mothers also see their own experience in curing as comparable (if not superior) to that of biomedical specialists, whom they view as inexperienced or inadequately trained or supplied. Specialists treat patients in a public, impersonal setting and often delegate responsibility for treatment to staff members, the patient's family, or the patients themselves. In contrast, mothers personally prepare and administer home remedies and provide private, personal care and emotional support to sick family members. The social and psychological costs of consulting therapeutic specialists in Saraguro have therefore encouraged reliance on mothers for healing.

Studies of medical care in Saraguro and in other societies suggest new directions for research and applied health programs. Few studies have detailed women's contribution to family treatment or the association between parental healing roles and the social role of the curer. Reports tend to ignore modal health care behavior and focus instead on descriptions of traditional and biomedical specialists who, in reality, make a colorful but quantitatively less significant contribution to health care. Kleinman (1980) states that although the popular sector of health care is the most frequently employed source of treatment, this system has been ignored in research on traditional curing systems. He notes that "self-treatment by the individual and family is the first therapeutic intervention resorted to by most people across a wide range of cultures. This is only one of the essential activities taking place in the popular sector (and especially within the family)" (Kleinman 1980, 51). He further suggests that the "relative inattention given to this sector is responsible in part for the fact that so much past work in medical anthropology and cross-cultural medicine and psychiatry has been irrelevant to practical issues in health care" (1980, 51).

The cultural embeddedness of domestic curing has implications for the introduction of new treatment services in Western and traditional societies. In Saraguro, for example, efforts to initiate change at the community level by enlisting specialized curers may prove ineffective, because specialists are rarely consulted. Therapeutic change in the indigenous population cannot be effected at the individual level until researchers address the special role and status of mothers as healers. Kleinman notes that medical anthropologists have failed to recognize the therapeutic, preventive, and health maintenance functions of lay healing (Kleinman 1980, 53). It is not yet clear whether, as he optimistically states, "increasing concern among social scientists and public health experts with self-care should remedy this oversight" (1980, 53).

Notes

Research funding was provided in part by the UCLA Committee for Health Services Research and by the UCLA Department of Anthropology. I am grateful to Thomas Collins, Linda Bennett, Susan Scrimshaw, Allen Johnson, Douglass Price-Williams, Carole Browner, George Foster, Sheila Cosminsky, and Ross Sackett for sharing many thoughts with me on drafts of this paper; I assume full responsibility, however, for any errors in material presented here. The assistance of the Department of Anthropology of Memphis State University, the Museo de Antropología of the Banco Central of Ecuador, the Instituto Nacional de Patrimonio Cultural of Ecuador and the staff of the community hospital of Saraguro is gratefully acknowledged. Deepest appreciation is extended to the people of Saraguro, without whose generous cooperation and support this research would not have been possible.

1. See Finerman 1985 for details on these syndromes, and see also Foster 1953; Martinez 1978; and J. C. Young 1981. Bao de agua appears to be an illness category exclusive to Saraguros. It is described as a form of soul loss in young children and is attributed to magical fright and exposure to water. Symptoms include some or all of the following: fever, diarrhea, skin rashes, facial swelling, loss of appetite and/or sleep, and persistent crying. Treatment includes vapor baths, herbal teas, and a *sopla* in which the patient's body is sprayed with herbal preparations.
2. For additional information on time allocation studies on male and female participation in child care see Erasmus 1955; Johnson 1978; and Nag, White, and Peet 1978.

It's All in a Name: Local-Level Female Healers in Sri Lanka

Sri Lanka has a highly complex and sophisticated system of medicine. A number of medical and religious healing traditions are available to the general public to provide concepts of disease prevention and treatment regimes for most of the illnesses and other misfortunes that afflict people. The average Sinhalese sees these different traditions not as separate epistemological domains but as different options within a coherent and integrated universe of knowledge and practice.

Within the extensive array of health practitioners is a group of people who provide primary health care, here defined as treatment options of first choice beyond home remedies, and who circulate important medical knowledge. They are mainly women who reside in virtually every community and who both receive recognition for their medical knowledge and are avidly sought as medical practitioners. Yet unlike *dostoras* (allopathic doctors), *vedas* (Ayurvedic physicians), *aduras* (exorcists), "FHWs" (family health workers), Buddhist and lay priests, astrologers, and fortunetellers, all of whom provide health care, these women are not recognized collectively as healers or referred to by a generic term like *veda hamine* (female Ayurvedic physician). Thus, they do not appear as health care providers in surveys or in other research on medical practices and health care utilization patterns in Sri Lanka.

This chapter examines these female healers and explores their role in medical care and the distribution of medical knowledge. To provide a context for this discussion, I will first present an overview of gender roles and medical pluralism in Sri Lanka. The relationship of these informal[1] healers to the larger medical system will then be traced. I will argue that they are central loci of sociomedical knowledge and are key to understanding how illness behavior and ideology are negotiated in everyday situations in Sri Lanka. The analysis is built upon the view that illness is a disruption in social and personal meaning for patients and their families and networks and that illness behavior is essential to give meaning to the disruptive state of sickness (Comaroff 1981; Nordstrom 1984, 1986; Taussig 1980). Medical care, in this model, entails the construction and negotiation of meaning out of the unique circumstances, personal characteristics and relationships, and illness symptoms of individual patients.

Fieldwork for this research project was carried out in a southern province of Sri Lanka for two years in 1982–1983 and during the summers of 1985 and 1986. The study, conducted in both urban and rural locations, focused on the dynamics of the health care system as manifested in the daily lives of ordinary people. Data collection methods included the review of government and other official descriptions of the medical system, participant-observation of patient/practitioner relations in practitioners' offices, the recording of patients' health care–seeking activities, and the administration of a household survey to follow the illness episodes and outcomes of family members. Special attention was given to the Ayurveda/Sinhala medical tradition.[2]

Gender Roles

A shorthand statement of gender roles in Sri Lanka is that women manage household and domestic affairs and men are responsible for agricultural and other extradomestic work. Certainly this was largely the case in the past, although there exists considerable overlap in the sexual division of labor, a trend that has recently intensified. Strong family ties continue to be important, and men as well as women take an active interest in raising children and in maintaining the household. Women increasingly supplement household resources and finances by small-scale agriculture and cottage industry and by employment outside the home (Gombrich 1971; Goody and Tambiah 1973; Kapferer 1983; Obeyesekere 1981; Yalman 1971). Further, adults of both sexes are expected to be involved in politics, understand the complexities of Buddhist thought, and stay abreast of current events. That certain areas of cultural knowledge remain associated more strongly with one sex is not incompatible with a prevailing ideology of gender symmetry. The distribution by gender of skills, occupations, knowledge domains, and the like says less about gender ideology than do the values attached to them. In particular, men's roles are not consistently valued above women's. Women's conceptualizations of gender symmetry are especially explicit, as exemplified in one informant's statement in response to my question about whether women wished they could perform certain exclusively male roles:

> Oh, I suppose sometimes I wish I could do a *kapua*'s [lay priest's] work. But there are many things I do that men cannot. We [the Sri Lankans] are a poor people, and without my work my husband, the men in my family, could not survive. My work is essential, as is my husband's. Sometimes the men must wish they could do what I can, in the same way that sometimes I wish I could do men's work. We are all needed—everyone's work is needed to survive. I cooked the special *kande* [conghee] to eat during the procession, and cleaned the house and area as the ritual prescribes. There could be no ritual without these things too.[3]

Gender symmetry is also reflected in broad socioeconomic trends. For example, though one of the poorest countries in the world, Sri Lanka has a literacy rate of 80 percent for both sexes (Sri Lanka Dept. of Information 1981). Men dominate in the professions, but women are increasingly represented, especially in medicine, law, and education. Women's political participation is also growing; Sri Lanka was the first country in the world to elect a female prime minister, S. Bandaranayaka.

Health Care in Sri Lanka

The Sinhalese call upon several distinct medical, religious, and cosmological traditions to control illness and ensure well-being. The various options are well understood by the general populace, and health care knowledge is taken seriously. Medical knowledge is continually circulated and updated in communities through daily conversations and frequent public media presentations concerning illness and health. Sri Lanka enjoys one of the highest set of health indices among Third World countries, despite its low economic standing (Pollack 1983; Simeonov 1975; Sri Lanka Ministry of Health 1982, 1983). The complex of medical traditions and intense popular interest in health partially explain this apparent paradox.

When a Sri Lankan becomes ill, a wide range of healing treatments is available. Ayurvedic or allopathic (biomedical)[4] treatment can be sought, either by going to a practitioner trained in these formal traditions or by home remedy. Aduras (ritual specialists for problems caused by demonic or malign influences) relieve illnesses caused or compounded by some evil external to the patient. Buddhist priests and kapuas (lay priests specializing in godly intervention) help correct disease through ritual and spiritual intervention. Astrologers (*gurunnanse*) and fortunetellers (*shastra-karaya*) use what the Sinhalese consider to be empirical means to identify and advise on difficult health problems. *Pena-karaya* ("see-ers" utilizing trance states) and *anjanam-karaya* (lamp readers; "see-ers" who do not utilize trance) use metaphysical ritual for the same end.[5] More extensive descriptions of health care in Sri Lanka are found in Obeyesekere (1969, 1975, 1976) on Ayurveda; Wirz (1954) and Kapferer (1983) on exorcism; Kemper (1980) on astrology; Amarasingham (1980) and Waxler (1976, 1979) on mental illness; Wijeratne (1979), Simeonov (1975), and the Sri Lankan Annual Health bulletins on medical pluralism; and Silva (1983) and UNICEF-WHO (1977) on community health care.

What I will term local-level healing receives little mention in these accounts. Nor do health officials and clinical allopathic practitioners acknowledge this informal system as a distinct and important health care resource. Local-level healers form a loosely articulated and informal network. I first discovered its existence in interviews with patients and in research on their health care activities. Although I use the term "local level," I wish to emphasize that it is not a translation from Sinhala; even in the colloquial language no single name can be found that refers collectively to informal healers. To refer to them collectively in Sinhala, one says something like: "those women who aren't dostoras or veda hamines who provide curing services in their community." "Local level" is further meant to emphasize the particular forms of knowledge and styles of interaction that characterize these practitioners and their patients.

S. Ardener (1978b, 22) observes that "the right to be addressed, and the way you are addressed, are important determinants of a person's place in the structure of any society." All of the practitioners mentioned above, with the exception of local-level healers, are referred to and addressed by a generic name. People use the generic name when describing illnesses and their treatment. For example, one frequently hears "I went to the dostora mahattaya/nona" (doctor sir/lady) or "I took treat-ment from the Veda mahattaya/hamine" (Ayurvedic sir/lady). One need not identify the individual occupying the role.

Ardener also notes that "the actual choice of name or title in a system of address also has great significance. . . . A name may not only ac-knowledge personal existence but also has continuity of personal and social definition" (S. Ardener 1978b, 22). In both referring to and ad-dressing local-level healers, people use personal terms (since occupa-tional terms are absent). Thus, one hears "I went to D.'s house [or location] for this problem," *D* being the house or property name, or the location or hamlet, of the healer. One also hears individual healers referred to by personal titles like *kanda amma* (conghee mother), *Veda amma* (Ayurvedic mother), *Karunawathie akka* (elder sister named Karunawathie), and so forth.

Two kinds of local-level healers can be identified. One provides what I call "grandmothers' medicine"; they are women whose home remedies have gained them respect and fame in a community. The second kind of healer, in addition to treating patients, transmits to them and their families systematic medical knowledge, learned either from other heal-ers in the family (*paramparawa*) or through her own experience. In both cases the women do not heal on a full-time basis, but as a supplement to domestic obligations or to employment outside the home. Most do not charge set fees, but accept goods in exchange for their services.

Part-time healing and reciprocal exchange set local-level healers apart from the other categories of health practitioners in Sri Lanka. Most formal healers practice medicine or perform healing rituals full-time. All charge set fees. Further, particularly in allopathy and Ayur-veda, practitioner/patient interaction is typically "clinical" in the sense that diagnosis and treatment occur in institutional settings (whether pub-lic or private, hospital-based or in shops) and conform to theoretical principles set in formal written doctrines.

Gender Ratios among Healing Practitioners

The sex ratios found within the various healing systems show several marked patterns, though these are currently in flux. Allopathic institu-tions have traditionally been dominated by men. In the last several decades, however, increasing numbers of women have sought medical degrees. At present, there are roughly twice as many male as female graduates.

In the case of Ayurveda, a distinction must be made between two different educational systems when considering sex ratios. A smaller percentage of Ayurvedic physicians are graduates of the College of Indigenous Medicine, which combines Ayurvedic theory with the infrastructural principles of allopathic care. At this time the admittance ratios are equally divided between men and women.[6] The largest number of indigenous physicians have learned their skills through apprenticeship (*paramparawa*), usually to an older family member. They are referred to as Vedas, and are considered Sinhalese, rather than Ayurvedic, medical practitioners (the term Ayurvedic is reserved for college graduates). Vedas have traditionally been male, but female Vedas (Veda hamini) are now in evidence in most communities.

Buddhist and lay priests and exorcists are predominantly male, although a few women practice as lay priests or exorcists. Astrologers, fortunetellers, and see-ers can be of either sex. Although most local-level healers are female, male local-level healers also exist and tend to specialize in the treatment of mens' occupational problems and sexual disorders.

Women are increasingly entering formal healing roles, a pattern that can likely be linked to an expanded need on their part for economic resources to help support themselves and their families. This trend is in turn traceable to a growing class system based on economic transactions and market principles that is supplanting former caste-based service relations. Also contributing to the trend are population increases, which reduce per capita agricultural holdings, and an escalation of unemployment, which strains family finances.

In sum, formalized institutionalized healing—medical and religious— tend to be male-dominated. This asymmetry holds more strongly for religious and exorcistic traditions than it does for medical traditions. Noninstitutional healing, available at the local level or within households and not requiring formal education, has more frequently been the domain of women. Women's increasing entrance into professional medicine, both Ayurvedic and allopathic, is beginning to change these established patterns, however.

Health Ideologies

At the onset of an illness severe enough to cause discomfort or interrupt daily routine, Sinhalese begin a course of treatment and follow a set of "correct actions": diet, bathing, and activity patterns deemed correct for a sick person (*leda*) and for the particular problem at hand. Ayurveda/ Sinhala medicine and allopathy are the major empirical medical traditions in Sri Lanka. Decisions about which is the most appropriate are made on the basis of the type of disease and the specifics of the illness episode. In addition, if a patient suspects that a malign influence is compounding the illness, or if he or she wishes to remain protected against such an attack, the services of an adura may be sought.

Religious ceremonies are often conducted to ease patients' minds and speed recovery by spiritual means. Horoscopes may be checked for answers about precipitating etiological agents and for advice concerning the correct actions required to cure the condition. Fortunetellers or see-ers may be approached for the same reasons (Amarasingham 1980). These ritual specialists may recommend further medicinal therapy, religious actions, or *aduru-kama* (exorcism). This cycle of advice and treatment will be continued and expanded until the patient recovers, is deemed incurable, or dies.

Ayurvedic theory provides the central conceptual framework that defines the body in illness and health for most Sri Lankans. Thus, whether allopathic, Ayurvedic, or ritual treatment is preferred for a particular illness, popular Ayurvedic explanatory principles are applied to give meaning to both the social and the physical dimensions of the problem (popular is used here to mean socially shared, community-level knowledge [Bakhtin 1968; Ginzberg 1982; Obeyesekere 1966]). Popular Ayurvedic theory coexists with allopathic doctrines without contradiction in the minds of the Sinhalese. Within a general explanatory Ayurvedic model, germ theory and contagion are commonly recognized and the isolation of victims of infectious disease is widely practiced. Vectors for the more common diseases in the area (malaria, filariasis, rabies, waterborne diseases, etc.) are known.

The concepts of balance and of Tridosa—the doctrine of the three humors—are fundamental to Ayurveda. The humors are wind (*watha*), bile or heat (*pitha*), and phlegm or water (*sema*). Sinhalese view the humors as engaged in a constant dynamic process. The dynamic is not relegated solely to the physical realm, but is in constant interplay with social and universal forces. The state of the individual is dependent on the state of the humors, which in turn are affected by both internal and external variables. Treatment is directed toward correcting imbalance and returning the humors to their correct proportional relationships. For treatment to be effective, all the etiological factors affecting the body

must be addressed, whether of psychological, physical, social, environmental, or cosmological origin.

The textual traditions used by specialist practitioners are distinct from
the social knowledge people use to orient themselves toward illness and
its treatment. Clinical and religious practitioners generally uphold the
integrity of the doctrines in which they are schooled when they interact
with patients, which thus perpetuates separate and formalized sets of
healing traditions. In popular practice, on the other hand, individuals
approach the different traditions as alternative options in a single health
care universe. They choose specific treatments based upon shared popular knowledge encompassing the separate healing traditions.

These separate traditions must thus be accessible and comprehensible
to everyone. Local-level healers translate, mediate, and perpetuate traditional medical knowledge, linking it with respected social traditions in
interaction with patients and patients' families. They contextualize allopathy, Ayurveda, Buddhism, and exorcism in a single framework that
also includes daily prescriptions for cleanliness, good nutrition, proper
social relations, environmental sanitation, and the like, all viewed as
crucial to the maintenance of health. They articulate the information
they select in discourses familiar to their patients.

Local-Level Healing

An illness episode in a Sinhalese family typically progresses as follows.
When a family member shows symptoms of an illness, an adult woman,
usually the mother or female household head, makes a diagnosis. On the
basis of the symptoms and the history of the sick person, she decides
which home remedies will work best and whether further care is needed.
If the illness is simple and the patient is expected to recover quickly with
these ministrations, no outside medical advice is sought. However, if the
family is uncertain about their diagnosis, if the illness is disrupting the
daily activities of the patient and causing discomfort, or if the mother
isn't sure that the home remedies are sufficient to treat the problem, a
local-level healer will be consulted. If the illness is serious or life-
threatening, professional clinical care will be sought at once.

The family will choose a local-level healer whose area of specialization or renown for certain treatments matches the illness at hand.

Examples of the more common medical specializations of local-level healers include stomachaches, mild diarrhea (i.e., not associated with cholera or dysentery), uncomplicated fevers, headaches, toothaches, minor sprains, and simple fractures of fingers and toes. They also treat pregnant and lactating women who have minor ailments and children who are restless, suffering minor upsets, or prone to cry during the day or in their sleep. Malaise caused by a minor fright, resulting from a malign supernatural encounter or the actions of an evil person, can also be corrected by local-level healers, although serious cases are taken to an adura. Some local-level healers specialize in treatments for particular illnesses or conditions, for example, hepatitis, snakebites, or bone, joint, and muscle problems. Others are generalists.

Local-level healers do not usually stock medicinal supplies; either they prescribe remedies for the mother to purchase, or the patient's family brings medicinal ingredients for the healer to prepare on her premises. Herbal decoctions are generally given for internal and humoral disorders, and oils are applied for external and structural ailments, although in some instances, a healer will suggest allopathic drugs that she has found through experience to be successful in treating particular conditions.

In addition to providing curative services, some local-level healers perform minor religious or exorcistic rituals, act as see-ers, or read horoscopes to ascertain whether complications are accompanying a particular illness or to improve treatment efficacy. For example, they may chant over medicine before giving it (*maturanawa*). Chanting can include mantras (verses protecting against malign presence) or Buddhist verses. For stomach ailments, frights, headaches and the like, conghee, coconut water, or even plain water may be chanted over before being administered. Chanting counteracts evil and soothes patients, making them more receptive to treatment and thereby allowing the medicine to "answer" or work more effectively (cf. Kerewsky-Halpern, this volume).

Treatment is taken three times; in the morning, the evening, and the following morning. The patient's family and the healer reassess the case after the third visit, and if the patient's condition is improving as expected, the healer will prescribe a course of action for convalescence. If the patient is not responding as hoped, the family consults a clinician and discontinues the services of the local-level healer, although they may continue to ask her advice about the case.

During the consultation healers discuss with the patient and the family the intervening factors that may be compounding the case. They may address the patient's diet, daily routines, and other habits and point out healthful alternatives. They will inquire frankly into personal difficulties or problems at work, and consider supernatural and environmental causes that may be contributing to the illness. Each etiological agent thus identified will be targeted by specific ritual and empirical treatment procedures.

Recruitment bears directly on the type of therapy a local-level healer performs. Some have learned traditional Sinhalese medicine from a family member who was a practitioner of that indigenous medical system. An increasing number today add personal experiences and informal study to a general knowledge of home remedy, in which case recruitment is situational. For example, a woman may become sick and go to a specialist (either allopathic or Ayurvedic) for treatment. If she has a particular interest in healing, she may make notes of the symptoms and the diagnosis and treatment regimens, including the ingredients of the medicines she takes. Then, when someone she knows suffers from the same problem, she recommends the same course of treatment. If the response is positive, the sick person relates the success to others, and the novice healer begins to build a reputation and a clientele. The ritual elements of informal healing are also learned informally, from a family member, from books, or from personal experience as a former patient.

Local-level healers are also thought to have a special propensity for healing. People agree that not just anyone can go to a practitioner, write down treatment formulas, and become a healer. Aside from the commitment and discipline required to learn techniques, formulas, verses, and so forth, a healer's remedies must "answer," or work. Building a clientele depends upon word-of-mouth recommendations; if treatments do not cure, patients do not return.

When people are asked why the majority of local-level healers are women, their answers fall into two categories. The first emphasizes practicality. Local-level healers tend to work from their homes. A man's work, however, may take him quite a distance away for a major portion of the day. People want to be able to come to a local-level healer for help at any hour of the day or night, and therefore they feel that their chances of finding the healer and getting care are greatly increased if she is a woman. Others note that one is never sure what state a man will be in around the house. One may arrive to find him drunk or socializing with friends. (Drinking is popular and widely accepted among men but negatively sanctioned for women.)

The second reason given to explain why these healers are often women is grounded in the belief that certain practitioners—of any healing tradition—are graced with *athquniya* (or *athwachchi*), the "gift" or "touch." This means that a practitioner not only is disposed toward healing, but due to his or her kindness, compassion, and gift for healing, is better able to help patients. The Sinhalese say that if the same medication is given to a patient by two different practitioners, one with athquniya and one without, the medicine will "answer" more successfully for the former. A person who has meanness or evil in them, or who is jealous and unkind, by definition cannot have the touch. Athquniya is not considered to be a mystical or supernatural gift by the Sinhalese, but one based on the personal attributes of a person.

Female local-level healers are believed to have a greater propensity for athquniya because they do not provide medicine as an occupation but rather are motivated by a desire to help people. In the minds of the Sinhalese, that these healers work out of their homes and that they more commonly work according to a service, not a market (fee-for-service), principle attest to this altruism.

Making Illness Meaningful

It is the disruption of social roles and the inability to interact normally that signal the advent of true illness and prompt the search for a cure. Sickness challenges people's most fundamental conceptualizations, both in terms of their relationship with their bodies—the physical state—and in terms of their relationship with their universe—the existential state. In essence, it challenges the everyday meaning that culture provides its members (see Berger and Luckmann 1966; Langer 1942; and Schutz 1962 for more detailed discussions of culture and meaning).

During an illness, people seek help not only for the physical disability but for the social "dis-ease" it generates in their lives. The Sinhalese expect a healer to address both the physical condition and the personal and social circumstances surrounding the illness. Advice on life style as well as the provision of medicine is thought to be crucial to the treatment process. Thus health care is an attempt both to correct the physical disability of the patient and to undertake a reconstruction of meaning by which the patient and all those involved with the illness episode can make sense of the new set of circumstances encountered. As sickness is a periodic experience for virtually everyone in a community, this reconstruction of meaning is both ongoing and extensive.

Nichter (pers. comm.) suggests that nonacute or everyday health problems, not life-threatening ones, provide the context in which health beliefs and behaviors are developed and expressed. Certainly major illness (both chronic and acute) profoundly challenges conventional meaning and disrupts social relationships, but people's lives are far more frequently affected by simple illness. In the case of acute illness or injury, trauma and the need to find immediate and life-saving treatment prevent the patient and the patient's family from exploring and evaluating accepted explanations of cause and therapeutic action. People are more concerned with surviving these acute states than becoming educated about them. It is the everyday and nonacute health problems, however, that provide the occasion, and also the opportunity, to build meaningful explanations of the nature of illness and health and of therapeutic action.

In Sri Lanka, local-level healers play an important role in the formulation and dissemination of knowledge about health and illness. Such knowledge is not confined to the physical domain. It also encompasses the social, environmental, and supernatural forces that influence human health. Popular Ayurveda, with its theoretical emphasis on balance and the interrelationships of dynamic forces, is the framework within which local-level healers weave knowledge from all the medical traditions—allopathic, religious, cosmological—so that all possible contributing causal factors are properly dealt with in the course of therapy.

Because of variations in the incidence of illness and the changing circumstances of individuals and families, people reassess the medical knowledge available to them when confronted with illness. In Sri Lanka, local-level healers are the social nexus where this process occurs at its most fundamental level. In the course of their own healing activities, local-level healers consult practitioners of other medical traditions, make detailed notes on diagnosis and treatment, read about and discuss current problems that people face and the therapies used to correct them, and consult with their own patients about the patients' ailments and complaints. They integrate these diverse strands of experience and information into a knowledge framework that closely fits the needs and demands of people in their communities.

In the course of these activities, local-level healers uphold respected social and healing traditions. They mediate new medical information with the old by translating it into terms compatible both with general Ayurvedic theory and with existing cultural understandings widely shared throughout the community. Continuity of meaning is thus ensured, but the specific content of medical knowledge is able to change. The knowledge constructed from this renewal process not only meets

patients' immediate needs but gradually reconstitutes popular definitions of illness and health without requiring a wholesale recasting of
health beliefs and ideologies.

In very concrete ways, local-level healers are rooted in the social affairs
of the community in which they practice. They are familiar with the
histories of their patients or, if not, at least with the particular social
background from which they come. They know the life styles of their
patients and the traditions they hold to be important. They sit down and
talk to the patients and their families. Thus, unless the condition is of such
severity that it requires immediate clinical attention, people prefer to go
to a healer who will take the time to make the illness comprehensible.

Gender Representations and Local-Level Healing

The social location of local-level healers provides a commentary on the
dialogue in the feminist literature on the nature/culture and domestic/
public constructs and their relationships with issues of gender and power
(see especially Ortner 1974; M. Z. Rosaldo 1974, 1980; Strathern 1980).
In particular, the argument that females are more closely associated with
nature (by virtue of their physical and social roles in reproduction) is
challenged by gender alignments in the Sri Lankan medical system.
Professional medical physicians, on the one hand, are predominantly
male. They concern themselves mainly with physiological distress and
confine their therapeutic endeavors also to the natural realm of the
physical body and its biological processes. In this context, males are
more closely linked to the natural realm. Local-level healers, on the
other hand, who are mostly female, place physical distress in a larger
social context. Their concern is with issues of culture and society and the
links between these domains and the physical body.[7] Both in dealing
with disease as a sociomedical process and in generating a commu-
nitywide body of knowledge with which people can meaningfully confront disease, local-level healers occupy a position more closely aligned
with culture. Local-level healers further participate in activities that
mediate between public and private domains, which demonstrates in yet
another cultural context that women as well as men move between
public and domestic arenas (Maltz 1985). They stand outside clinical

institutions but transmit the knowledge and practices associated with clinical medicine into domestic frameworks and popular discourses. They connect public and domestic medicine, and insofar as medicine is embedded in other social traditions, they constitute a bridge between public and domestic spheres of social interaction.

Although local-level healers are important links between official medical traditions and the ordinary citizenry, they do not receive formal recognition by the government, health agencies, or other organizations concerned with health. Some healers have commented that lack of official recognition prevents them from competing with professional allopathic and Ayurvedic practitioners for funding and other forms of aid. Others have noted that this invisibility frees them from the bureaucratic restrictions imposed on licensed practitioners. It is precisely the freedom from governmental attention and regulation that permits them to practice the integrated healing that they do.

Why official descriptions and scholarly studies of health care systems should so consistently ignore informal healing by women is unclear. E. Ardener (1972) and S. Ardener (1978b) assert that women are "muted," and that part of the reason for this is that researchers' theoretical paradigms fit more cohesively with those used by men in a society. Also in this view, men's models of both men's and women's worlds are more accessible, both ideologically and in the field context, to researchers or other outside observers (Keesing 1985). This presupposes that men and women do indeed have separate perceptions of their respective worlds and that men are more articulate in defining theirs, which thus gives men's world views the force of encompassing social realities.

My data on the Sri Lankan medical system fail to support this argument in its entirety. Part of E. Ardener's exegesis is based on the nature/culture dichotomy that places women closer to nature in a hierarchical representation of nature and culture. In Sri Lanka, local-level healers, as we have seen, are neither socially mute nor symbolically closer to nature (as opposed to culture) than are other healing practitioners. Indeed, the relationship is arguably quite the reverse, for the significance of local-level healers lies in their "vocalness," their ability to synthesize and communicate sociomedical knowledge. Further, the definitions of illness and health that they articulate form part of the community's general store of knowledge. This knowledge generates the available repertoire of means for coping with illness for both men and women. Unlike the erudite doctrines of the major medical traditions, sociomedical knowledge remains comprehensible to the public in general.

The attribution of "muteness" to women, then, fails to explain the lack of recognition accorded to informal female healers in Sri Lanka. Nor are women viewed differently from men as they increasingly enter the formerly exclusively male preserves of professional and ritual medicine. Women are fully accepted as allopathic and Ayurvedic physicians. In these systems, except for intimate or gender-specific disorders, people care little about the sex of a practitioner. They are more concerned with the reputation for successful curing and the interpersonal manner of individual practitioners.

Local-level healers remain unrecognized in official accounts of health care in Sri Lanka because they represent a different order of healing than that associated with the major medical traditions and because they lie outside the control of official medicine and its definitions of health and illness. The location of local-level healing in domestic contexts both perpetuates its invisibility and explains why its practitioners are predominantly women. Yet despite their anonymity in the larger health care system, local-level healers provide the official medical traditions the indispensable service of making their ideologies accessible to the rest of society.

Notes

1. *Informal* is used here to mean in contrast with professional medical traditions. Informal healing lacks codified documentation and its practitioners are unlicensed and unregulated.
2. Ayurveda is the indigenous empirical medical system in South Asia. However, in popular usage the Sinhalese apply the term Ayurveda to medicine practiced by graduates of the College of Indigenous Medicine. The Sinhalese refer to home remedy and the medicine practiced by those who have gained their education through apprenticeship—the largest forms of indigenous care in Sri Lanka—as Sinhala medicine.
3. Both Obeyesekere (1963a, 1963b) and Kapferer (1983) argue that women are subordinate to men within Sinhalese society, and that widespread wife beating is a primary mechanism to control and subjugate young wives. Both also note that women are not passive recipients of such abuse, but are equally—though mostly verbally—abusive toward their husbands. My data corroborate the existence of domestic violence but do not find it as universal as described by Obeyesekere and Kapferer. Although tension between the sexes is patent, the fact of its existence by itself does not signify female subordination. A fuller understanding of the relations between the sexes requires a much broader discussion.

4. Allopathy is equivalent to biomedicine. I choose it here to follow usage by Sri Lankans, who prefer allopathy to any of the other terms also equivalent to biomedicine (scientific medicine, cosmopolitan medicine, modern medicine, Western medicine).

5. I call these two groups "see-ers" because they are consulted to "see" the circumstances surrounding a problem and advise on it.

6. There are several smaller schools of Ayurveda in the country, many of which accept only men. The number of practitioners they introduce into society is small, however, compared to the college graduates and paramparawa-trained practitioners described here.

7. Kapferer (1983), in addressing the question of why women seek exorcistic healing more frequently than do men, invokes the earlier version of the nature/culture dichotomy (Ortner 1974). He asserts that women's subordination to men is the product of an ideology that sees women as "weak." Women are primarily connected to biological (reproductive) and domestic (cultural) activities; "they are the linch pins of culture" (Kapferer 1983, 108). Although women's close association with childbearing and domestic responsibilities is indisputable, the notion that these activities are always subordinate to other spheres of activities is arbitrary and reflects observer bias. I do agree with Kapferer's point that "women, as conceived by culture are, more frequently than men, a major point of articulation between nature and culture" (Kapferer 1983, 105). However, rather than seeing women as weak because of their association with nature—in both reproductive and health care responsibilities—my data lead me to a different conclusion. As women control and define reproduction and informal health care, they occupy a social position of "strength," invested with the responsibility, in both arenas, to span domestic and public domains.

CAROLE H. BROWNER

The Management of
Reproduction
in an Egalitarian Society

In early 1958, the Mexican federal government approved a petition by local authorities to establish a midwife training program in the rural *municipio* (township) of San Francisco.[1] The wife of the man who was president at the time had recently died in labor. Although the local lay midwives who attended the birth were not formally charged in the woman's death, local authorities vowed to reduce further maternal mortality by seeking training for local women in modern childbirth techniques. A government physician was dispatched to San Francisco, where it was planned that he would live for two weeks at a time during the proposed several-month training program. About twelve women, the majority young and married, in the prime of their childbearing years, volunteered. The first two training sessions were well attended, but by the third, all but two of the class members had permanently abandoned the course. Those who dropped out said they quit because they had too much other work, because their children needed their attention, or because their husbands had rescinded permission for them to attend. Only one of the two who completed the course had shown genuine interest in the profession. (She died soon after completing the course.) The second, Fernanda, had been ordered to attend by her husband, the president's right-hand man (*síndico*). And like the others, Fernanda also wanted to quit. Her husband, however, forbade it because he felt personally bound by the commitment he had made as a public official. Fernanda worked as a midwife for the next twenty-five years. But although her knowledge of biomedical midwifery was recognized throughout the community, she was not asked to attend most deliveries, nor was her social status in any way enhanced by virtue of her work.

Why did Fernanda's technical knowledge not equip her to become a specialist whose services were widely sought? Why could she not transform this knowledge into prestige and wealth? This account seeks to answer these questions.

Introduction

This chapter considers the social position of midwives practicing today in San Francisco, a community of Chinantec-speaking Indians located in highland Oaxaca, Mexico. It considers why the role of midwife is not highly developed and why few choose it. I will show that ubiquitous social pressures toward conformity and egalitarianism lead women to resist differentiating themselves from their peers. These same pressures make it uncomfortable for midwives to accumulate much specialized knowledge. One correlate of these social processes is a high level of self-sufficiency in the treatment of women's reproductive health problems and a large number of women who give birth without outside assistance. Another is that the status of women who become midwives depends more on their personal characteristics than it does on their experience or specialized skills within the reproductive domain.

Methods and Background

The data offered here were collected during a 1980–1981 field study designed to examine how knowledge of medicinal plants for reproduction and reproductive health was distributed throughout a homogeneous, unstratified peasant community and to understand the implications of this distribution of knowledge for fertility outcomes and for relations between the sexes. A total of 306 individuals (over half the community's adult women and men) were interviewed, and additional in-depth interviews were carried out with the community's five midwives and two most prominent healers. Others who practiced healing occasionally or only for specific conditions were interviewed in less depth about their healing activities.[2]

The municipio of San Francisco consists of about 1,800 individuals, the vast majority of whom are subsistence cultivators who live in a combination of concentrated and dispersed settlements. About a third live permanently in the dry mountainous *cabecera* (head town); the rest either divide their time between the cabecera and tropical lowland *ranchos* (hamlets) or live permanently in the lowlands. Only 5 percent of the households rely solely on wage labor, but another 80 percent report cash income from at least occasional wage work or petty commodity production.

Despite the availability of government-subsidized, low-cost health care services in the cabecera and within a bus trip of the lowland ranchos, health care practices in San Francisco are still largely traditional. For example, 91 percent of the women interviewed had had their last child at home without a nurse or physician in attendance, and 82 percent used only herbal or other traditional remedies for postpartum recovery.

Gender roles and responsibilities in San Francisco are generally similar to those described elsewhere in indigenous highland Mesoamerica (e.g., Bossen 1983; Harris 1978; Maynard 1974). The public and domestic domains are physically separate and sexually distinct. Adult, married men are obliged to conduct all the municipio's public political and religious activities. Women are formally excluded but play important supportive roles (Browner 1986a, 91; see also Slade 1975). Women's other tasks revolve around meeting their families' domestic and economic needs. Women have primary responsibility for child care and housework, but they are also expected to cooperate fully with their husbands in subsistence cultivation and in earning cash. The vast majority of Franciscanas regularly engage in agricultural labor, and households where women work for wages or engage in petty commodity production are in no way stigmatized.

Due to the municipio's dispersed settlement pattern, the actual division of domestic labor is somewhat flexible. The competing demands of the agricultural cycle and the mandatory educational system separate many families for months on end. Increasing numbers of men have become semipermanent labor migrants as well. As a result, many adults find themselves performing tasks that would ordinarily be assigned to the opposite sex. Men may cook and do their own laundry when, because they are cultivating their fields, they are separated from their wives; women may haul, clear lands, and perform other heavy tasks if their husbands are absent. Moreover, because families who do not have children of primary school age may reside for long periods in isolated hamlets that consist of only one or two households, couples tend to become interdependent and help one another with daily tasks. Thus the overt ideology of male superiority and male dominance is moderated by economic interdependency along with a genuine respect for the value of women's work (Browner 1987). This relatively flexible division of labor is, however, confined to the economic domain. Women are prohibited from publicly performing religious or political activities even when their husbands have been absent from the municipio for years.

San Francisco still embodies many characteristics of a traditional closed corporate peasant community, including the intensive practice of subsistence cultivation, communal land tenure in the vast bulk of the municipio's extensive landholdings, and local government by consensus (E. R. Wolf 1955, 1957). Both parents of more than 98 percent of the population are native to the community. The only outsiders who live for any extended time in San Francisco are a handful of government school teachers and health workers. Although San Francisco is not truly autonomous or self-sufficient, for most inhabitants daily life revolves around the subsistence cycle, and few have regular contact with outsiders.

Maintaining independence from state control and domination was a fundamental goal of the traditional closed corporate peasant community. Because it also served state interests to allow such communities a measure of self-determination, there was no inherent contradiction between the community's goals and those of the state (Dennis 1979; K. Young 1976, 1978). One way that closed corporate peasant communities preserved independence and limited external intervention was by requiring manifestations of unity in all public affairs. In such communities unity was regarded as more than an abstract ideology. Members recognized that divided communities were much more vulnerable to land loss, incorporation by the state, or complete destruction. Yet unified communities are increasingly rare in contemporary Mesoamerica, as enduring factions have caused many bitter and seemingly permanent splits (Chinas 1973; de la Fuente 1949; Stebbens 1984; Ugalde 1973). San Francisco's success at avoiding factionalism has been attributed to the local authorities' ability to marshal public support. When an issue with potential for splitting the community has emerged, the ideology of unity has been uncompromisingly evoked. Villagers are required—at least publicly—to accept the local authorities' position, regardless of their personal opinions.

A powerful means of maintaining unity in communities like San Francisco is by negatively sanctioning any behavior that separates individuals from the rest (Leslie 1960; Nash 1967; Whitecotton 1977, 250). Although in many other Mesoamerican communities, the consequences of migration have eroded the effectiveness of this type of social control (e.g., Dinerman 1982), in San Francisco this has not yet been the case. For example, when in the late 1970s a native-born schoolteacher built an electric corn mill in the cabecera for public use, the project was an immediate success, and demand for the service was initially great. But soon after the mill began operation, local authorities, using the municipio's communal resources, built another. Business at the schoolteacher's mill soon fell to near zero. All who were asked said they preferred the communal mill because they did not want any one individual to profit at the expense of others. The relentless criticism directed at the community's shop owners undoubtedly had a similar source, as did the repeated public censure of a small number of local women who worked on programs they believed would promote positive change. Although the women saw their acts as beneficial to San Francisco as a whole, they were sanctioned for dividing the community and manifesting egotistical behavior (Brown 1986a).

The Social Position of San Francisco's Midwives

Powerful social pressures discourage Franciscanos from economically or socially differentiating themselves from their peers. These same pressures help to explain why midwives in the community do not enjoy a higher social status than ordinary women and why individuals are reluctant to assume the midwife role. Few benefits of any sort accrue to midwives. They are not rewarded with prestige or respect and may instead be criticized for having assumed the role. Nor can they feel that they are performing a vital or even a valued social function, since most births occur without them. Furthermore, there is little financial incentive to become a midwife since villagers are unwilling to pay much for the service.[3]

These social dynamics are more clearly seen when we consider the backgrounds and experiences of the women practicing midwifery today in San Francisco. At the time of the research, there were five midwives.

Four of them were older, married women who worked in the cabecera. With the exception of Fernanda, whose training by the government physician has already been described, none of these older midwives had had any formal instruction. In contrast to these four was the fifth, who was a young married woman who had studied nursing and midwifery in a government training program. She lived and worked in one of the permanently occupied ranchos. Because most of my data collection took place in the cabecera, and because social and political dynamics differ somewhat in the two locales, I will limit my remarks to the midwives practicing in the cabecera.

The four midwives ranged in age from forty-five to past sixty. All were married and lived with their husbands. Their formal schooling varied from none to two and a half years. Each reported more than twenty years of midwifery practice. One spoke excellent Spanish, two were minimally conversant, and one spoke no Spanish whatsoever. With regard to their educational backgrounds and linguistic competencies, the midwives did not differ significantly from other Franciscanas.

Recruitment and training varied among the four. As previously noted, Fernanda had no personal wish to become a midwife but had been pressured into accepting the role by her husband. The others were all self-selected, generally in response to significant personal experiences with childbirth. For example, Carmela's first labor was protracted and painful; she was convinced that she would die. To distract and help calm her, the attending midwife told Carmela to pay attention to what she was doing so that Carmela herself could become a midwife one day too. When she recovered, Carmela asked the older woman to train her, and eventually she developed her own practice. Adela's work as a midwife began when she discovered she would have to help deliver her first grandchild, because no other plans for a birth attendant had been made. The prospect frightened her, and she prayed to God that the birth would turn out well. When it did, in thanks she promised to help other women, should they ask. Although Adela identified God as the source of her knowledge and skills as a midwife, she did not believe she had been "chosen" by God, contrary to other midwives elsewhere in Mesoamerica (Cosminsky 1976, 1983; Paul and Paul 1975). None of these three midwives is very active; each delivers fewer than six children a year. The fourth, Imelda, is San Francisco's most popular midwife. She delivers about a dozen children a year. She learned midwifery primarily from her mother, also a midwife, often accompanying her on her rounds when still a child. Imelda's popularity as a midwife is credited to the fact that she is also a curer who specializes in witchcraft-caused diseases. She is most frequently consulted when there is the suspicion that a pregnant woman may be bewitched, for this could lengthen or in other ways complicate the delivery.

San Francisco's midwives do not elicit much trust from the community. Most residents do not consider them particularly knowledgeable or competent. This may in part be due to their lack of an extended apprenticeship and to the absence of divine intervention in their selection (cf. Sargent 1982). It may also be due to a general lack of trust that Franciscanos express in *any* healer practicing today in their community. When those interviewed were asked, "Who knows how to heal in this community?" 39 percent replied, "No one"; an additional 6 percent named modern health care practitioners only. And although twenty individuals were named in response to this question, only Imelda was mentioned more than 15 percent of the time. Three others were mentioned by about 10 percent of the people.

Nor was greater confidence expressed in the deceased healers of an actual or mythical past; there was little agreement on who had been the best or most powerful healers in earlier times. Yet at the same time it was not unusual for Franciscanos to answer the question "Who knows how to heal?" with, "Many people know, in fact almost everyone" or "Here there is no one; we help one another among ourselves." Others simply named themselves or other household members in response to the question.

There appears to be no tradition in San Francisco of powerful, high-status shamans (of either sex) as has been reported for some other indigenous Mesoamerican communities (Holland 1963; Vogt 1969), where such healers are considered to be the guardians of their community's spiritual well-being. Typically healers are divinely inspired male elders whose power and status derive from the fact that they link the community's spiritual and political domains. In sharp contrast, in San Francisco those recognized for their healing abilities are often physically handicapped and consequently unable to participate fully in the community's political, economic, or social affairs. At least two of the most renowned male healers, one currently practicing and one deceased, were blind,[4] and another has severe, handicapping birth defects (Rubel and Gettelfinger-Krejci 1976). These men do not experience elevated social status because they cure. They are not recognized as spiritual guardians, nor is their political position in the community enhanced by virtue of their healing activities.

These data provide a context for understanding the lack of confidence Franciscanos express in their local midwives. They indicate that, in general, healing and obstetrical knowledge are thought to be widely dispersed throughout the community rather than controlled by a select group of individuals. Concrete evidence for these attitudes is seen when the herbal and other technical knowledge of San Francisco's midwives and of ordinary women and men are compared (cf. Finerman 1982). All 306 individuals who were interviewed, as well as all the midwives, were asked whether they knew any herbal or other remedies for the treatment of each of the eight reproductive health conditions Franciscanas most commonly suffer. All were also asked to describe any remedies they knew to speed labor or diminish labor pains and to promote postpartum recovery.[5] Surprisingly, all the herbs and other techniques reported by the midwives were also mentioned by others in the community. Moreover, the remedies and techniques that the midwives described were those most widely known by the general public. For instance, the overwhelming majority of the herbal remedies reported for the management of reproduction and the treatment of women's reproductive health problems had multiple uses. But although there were thirty-seven remedies for which a specific use was mentioned by just one informant, in no case was a midwife the source of this information. It may have been that the midwives mentioned only the most widely known remedies, either because they wished to preserve secrecy (cf. Ngubane 1981) or because they wished to avoid singling themselves out by admitting that they possessed specialized knowledge. When laywomen described their parturitions, however, they reported that the midwives had administered the same remedies that the midwives themselves had named. Rarely did a woman say she did not know what herbs the midwife had used, which led me to conclude that the midwives did not withhold herbal information during the interviews.

What has been reported as distinguishing healers from the rest of the population in some other Mesoamerican communities is not their herbal knowledge, which may be widely shared, but their control of ritual knowledge (Metzger and Williams 1963). In this regard it is significant that Imelda, San Francisco's most popular midwife, is also the community's most renowned healer. As previously indicated, she attributes most illnesses to witchcraft, which she is skilled at healing. Like the other midwives, the prenatal routine Imelda follows involves monthly physical examinations and massage. Additionally, she will diagnose and, if necessary, treat the pregnant woman if she discovers witchcraft. Yet despite the special services Imelda offers, even she assists at relatively few deliveries.

Many families, even nuclear ones, feel competent to deliver children without any outside assistance. During the 304 home deliveries about which I have data, a midwife attended in only 49 percent of the cases, and was significantly more likely to be present at a woman's first than at subsequent deliveries ($x^2 = 11.20$, $p < .001$). (An additional twenty-eight births [9 percent] occurred in a health center or were attended at home only by a doctor or a nurse.) Although a few (6 percent) reported that no one at all had been present for the birth, most births were attended by relatives. The woman's husband was the most common birth attendant (45 percent), followed by his mother (30 percent) and her mother (29 percent) with about equal frequency. So widespread was the practice of fathers attending the births of their children that only 11 percent of the men interviewed indicated that they had never helped during any of their wife's deliveries, while 53 percent participated in major ways such as preparing herbal beverages or giving massages to speed the labor. The following account describes one man's recollections of his wife's most recent delivery. It was her fourth pregnancy and the third child they had had together.

Several days before the baby was due, we decided not to use the health center or any of the midwives because they all charge a lot. My wife and I decided that we would struggle together, whatever the outcome, but that it would be a home cure just like the curers do it because, as you know, there are women that injections don't agree with because the injections are very hot and there's always the risk that they will cut off the flow of the milk. So together we decided it would be better if we didn't seek any help from anywhere.

It was 1:00 in the morning when my wife was seized by a pain in her womb that we knew meant that it was time for the birth. I felt very tired as I got up and went to the kitchen to light the fire and then I went to look for Saint Mary's herb. I put some up to boil in a pot of water on the fire and when it had boiled, I poured my wife a cup to drink. As soon as she finished drinking the tea, the pains began to come more quickly. So I boiled some chocolate and gave her a cup of that and she drank it. And right after that I massaged her womb with almond oil that I had warmed up just a little, and while I was massaging her, the baby was born.

I picked the baby up and wrapped him in a clean, warm cloth and after two or three minutes I cut the umbilical cord, that is, the cord that comes from the placenta. The baby was born at 2:20 A.M., last October 4. Twenty minutes after the baby was born, the placenta was delivered. While we were waiting, I gave my wife two cups of *aguardiente* with salt. (That is, you put a little bit of salt in a clean cup and then add about two cups at the most of aguardiente to dissolve it quickly and you give it to the patient to drink. The placenta will fall right after that.) My mother also helped me care for the newborn while I took care of the mother of the baby. I also gave the mother a little *mescal* to warm her body.

By 3:00 A.M. we were saved [everything was all right] although there wasn't any mother's milk until the following day when I went to look for an herb that in Chinantec we call *ma'3 li4 too2 dsea2*[6] that I put around her waist. But first I had to buy a quarter of a liter of mescal and a quarter of aguardiente, five pesos of alcohol and five of *catalán*. I mixed the herb with the four types of liquor and spread this mixture over a cloth. Then I smeared some tallow over the herbs and I took a little liquor into my mouth and I blew it over the herbs until they were well soaked. Then I burned some pitch pine and mixed some of the smoke in with the herb. I covered the mother's entire waist with this mixture using a cloth that measured about 30 centimeters in width. You can leave the herbs in place for approximately one day and one night but then you must remove them and rub alcohol on the waist. The next day you have to do the same thing until the remedy has been applied three times. After the first cure the mother will have a little bit of milk for the baby, after the second, she will have a little more and after the third she has plenty. But while there isn't any milk, you have to give the newborn *yerba buena* [*Mentha citrata*] tea every so often and you can also give him a little bit of coffee to relieve his hunger.

Later, the mother should be given other herbs like *chamiso* [*Baccharis glutinosa*] or, if not, then the bitter herb that grows in the hot country, but this [bitter] herb needs to be cooked in a little pitcher and mixed with a little bit of mescal and given in the mornings and in the evenings for fifteen days. Not caring for the mother in this way can cause other illnesses such as a swollen face or swollen feet.

The newborn also needs care. His umbilical cord must be warmed using a little ball of tallow wrapped in a warm, clean little cloth so that it will dry out quickly. This must be done twice a day until the stump falls off. In the case of my [last-born] son Mauricio it wasn't possible to save the umbilical cord because it fell off among the bedclothes and I couldn't find it so that it wasn't possible to hang it up in a tree as I had done with my son Elias's umbilical cord.

I found this work interesting. I was like a midwife and I thank God I came out of it without more difficult problems. Three days after the birth of my son I went to register him at town hall where they took the information they needed. I did this because if you delay with the registration, the child's parents are fined by the authorities.

The author of this account neither considers himself nor is considered by others to be especially knowledgeable about midwifery or healing. Nor is he an especially self-confident individual; in fact he is regarded by most as one of the community's less successful and less competent men. Yet he recounts his role in the recent birth of his son with complete self-assurance. And although his account is unusual in its completeness, the activities he describes are not. Nearly half the men interviewed could name specific herbal remedies that could be used during the pre- and postpartum periods, and most who named remedies had personally pre-pared them.

One corollate of the relative absence of midwife specialization in San Francisco is that the social status of the women who are midwives de-pends less on how they perform the midwife role than on how closely they conform to the standards of behavior set for women in general (cf. McClain, this volume; Whyte 1978). When informants were asked whether a particular midwife was respected or esteemed and why, the replies invariably referred not to her activities or abilities as a midwife but to other characteristics. Imelda and Fernanda were described by most in quite negative terms: that is, although Imelda was the commu-nity's most sought-after midwife and most renowned healer, she was not respected because she had been highly promiscuous sexually when she was young. Similarly, although Fernanda was the only person in the community to have studied biomedical midwifery, she was not seen as worthy of respect because she was considered a selfish woman whose only concern was her own family's economic advancement. In contrast, public opinion of Carmela and Adela was uniformly positive: Adela was respected because she and her husband had completed their community service; Carmela was respected because she was serious, hard-working, and responsive to her family's needs. In no case did these women's activities as midwives—and in Imelda's case as a healer—contribute positively or negatively to their social standing in the community.

Implications

There have been few analyses of the social position of midwives, either in Mesoamerica or elsewhere, which could provide a broad framework for interpreting these data. Cosminsky's comprehensive reviews of the cross-cultural literature on midwifery cite just a handful of articles, most of which are simply descriptions of the midwife's practices and activities (Cosminsky 1976, 1983). In part this may be because many cultures fail to recognize a specialized midwife role (Ford 1945). But even where a well-defined midwife role does exist, accounts reveal great variation in her social position (Lombard 1965, cited in Sargent 1982).

A number of theories have suggested that the social position of midwives varies according to the status of women in a society (Whyte 1978); the status of healers who are not midwives (McClain, this volume); the amount of technical or other skill that midwives possess (J. Kelly 1967; Sargent 1982), including whether they are responsible for complicated deliveries or whether in such cases they are expected to call upon other specialists (Lévi-Strauss 1967); and whether midwives are chosen by divine selection, self-selection, inheritance, or in other ways (Mac-Cormack 1982a; L. Paul 1978a). Yet no overarching theory that seeks to explain cross-cultural variation in the social position of midwives has been able to account for all the data. This material from San Francisco, Oaxaca, provides an additional set of factors that should be considered in future analyses of the phenomenon. It demonstrates that theories that seek to account for the social position of midwives cross-culturally need also to take into account local historical, socioeconomic, and political conditions.

Conclusions

Although any Franciscana may become a midwife, few choose to do so. This is partly a function of how the midwife role is structured in the community and partly a function of broader social processes. Information related to the management of childbirth is widely dispersed throughout

San Francisco, and most midwives do not control much esoteric knowledge. As a result, most families feel they can manage uncomplicated deliveries, particularly if the woman has already borne other children, without a midwife's assistance.

Yet the inability of Franciscana midwives to marshal status, prestige, or respect does not only stem from the unspecialized nature of the role. It also derives from the fact that in a community like San Francisco egalitarianism is seen not as an abstract social good but as a concrete means by which individuals, families, and even the very community have ensured survival. At its core, this egalitarianism consists of an economic system based on the collective control of communally held resources and a political process that requires manifestations of public unity on all local issues and on those that affect the community's relationships with the world outside. For such a social system to be effective, the bonds of cooperation must be dependable and consistent. In communities like San Francisco, pressures to conform are a basic means for ensuring egalitarianism, because divisions based on differential access to any social resource diminish the power of conformity as an organizing principle.

The pressures to conform that San Francisco's midwives face are therefore no different from those endured by the rest of the community. But these pressures lead to a lack of demand for the services of midwives and a lack of appreciation for their expertise and experience. Another outcome is that few individuals are attracted to the midwife role, and those who are, do not become highly specialized. The exception to this is Imelda, the curer-midwife. She is one of the very few in the community who can treat diseases and difficult labors caused by witchcraft. Yet even she is not respected for her control of esoteric knowledge, and her status, like that of the other midwives, depends on attributes unrelated to her performance in the midwife role.

In this account I have sought to show that in a community that jealously guards economic and social equality, little prestige, privilege, or social status will accrue to individuals by virtue of their activities as midwives. Rather, the means by which prestige and status are earned are universalistic. Nor in such an insistently egalitarian community is the midwife role likely to become highly specialized. And because many who do not consider themselves midwives control equivalent knowledge, those who sell midwifery services will not be in much demand. It is therefore not surprising that in an egalitarian society like San Francisco, although anyone may become a midwife, few do so. The role offers them little advantage.

Notes

The research for this essay was supported in part by grants from the National Science Foundation, NICHD, the Wenner-Gren Foundation for Anthropological Research, and the Committee on Research of the UCLA Academic Senate. Margarita Garcia Hernandez assisted with the data collection and Linda M. Hunt with the data analysis. Helpful comments on an earlier version of the manuscript were made by Alan Harwood, Carol McClain, Arthur J. Rubel, and Carolyn Sargent. An abbreviated version of this paper was presented at the 1986 joint annual meetings of the American Ethnological Society and the Southern Anthropology Society held in Wrightsville Beach, N.C.

1. All proper names are pseudonyms.
2. Copies of all interview schedules are available from the author.
3. The charge for delivering a child at the time of the research ranged from 50 to 100 pesos. Daily wage for a female laborer was 25 pesos plus two meals.
4. Onchocerciasis is endemic in San Francisco's lowland territories. No reliable statistics on visual impairment for the community exist, but estimates place it at about 15 percent.
5. Further information on the conditions named and the remedies themselves can be found in Browner 1985a, 1985b, 1986b, and Ortiz de Montellano and Browner 1985.
6. San Francisco Chinantec has three levels of tone: 4 is high, 3 mid, and 2 low. In addition, there are four tone glides (23, 24, 34, 42) that are a combination of the levels.

PART TWO

Healing with Female Metaphors

Female images that appear most often in the anthropology of curing, when they appear at all, are those of women as nurturers and mediators (Hoch-Smith and Spring 1978). As nurturers, healers protect, comfort, and guide patients to restored health in the same way that mothers care for their children. And like dependent children, patients look to healers to meet their physical and emotional needs. Nevertheless, the healer-as-nurturer metaphor is not found in all cultures, nor do all female healers nurture their patients (although Wedenoja in this section suggests that nurturance is a universal symbolic substrate of curing). Biomedical physicians in general and many types of folk healers, although they are in great demand and appear to satisfy at least partially patients' expectations (Lieban 1981; Press 1971), practice a perfunctory type of therapy that can hardly be described as nurturing. As mediators, healers cross symbolic boundaries, particularly those separating the human world from that of spirits or ancestors, and intervene with the latter on behalf of their patients or clients. In yet another sense, healers mediate between forces that cause illness when the body experiences imbalance: hot or cold, excess emotion like fright or anger, harmful natural qualities like the wind or the magnetism associated with eclipses, and so forth.

How nurturance, mediation, and other metaphoric associations of healing intersect with those of gender is an empirical question that has only intermittently attracted anthropologists' interest (Holmberg 1983; Lewis 1986; Ngubane 1977). But these intersections are key to understanding why men or women occupy particular healing roles. The chapters in this section explore these symbolic connections in three cultural contexts. In the essays by Wedenoja and Kerewsky-Halpern, women healers are metaphoric mothers, meeting the physical and affective needs of their patients in the same way that real mothers provide for their children. Kerewsky-Halpern describes how *bajalice* (elderly female healers) elaborate culturally specific and pervasive mother metaphors into vivid oral charms. Past reproductive age themselves, bajalice no longer threaten male well-being, and thus they move freely in and out of domestic households to conjure away illness and other distresses. The requirement that women must be postmenopausal to become curers or must achieve ritual cleanliness to do so if they are still young appears frequently in cultures that combine beliefs about female pollution with their enforced placement in domestic spaces (Brown 1985; L. Paul 1978a). Women who heal in these symbolic and empirical contexts—bajalice are one example—traverse public spaces at any time and interact intimately with men other than kin, behaviors prohibited for ordinary women.

Wedenoja finds mother metaphors to be the dominant symbolic imperative behind balm healing in Jamaica. Balm healers embody Jamaicans' idealized mother. The effectiveness of the metaphor derives from the power and resilience of the mother-child bond in Jamaican culture. Just as the balmist's patients view her as the archetypal mother, so the balmist herself finds her own projected need for nurturance filled by caring for others. Wedenoja's psychodynamic exploration of the balmist's personality further reveals traits far removed from maternal nurturance—hostility and authoritarianism, for example. It would not be surprising to find, too, that patients' views of the healer/mother are ambivalent and also include representations of the female healer as evil. Female symbols are rarely unidimensional, although they may be depicted as such in the literature (Hoch-Smith and Spring 1978 elaborate this point).

Fox's discussion of Christian Science healing practitioners compares the sect's gender images with those of the surrounding society. In Christian Science, God is androgynous, and the deity's masculine and feminine principles are distributed equally to men as administrators and lecturers and to women as healing practitioners and nurses. Women's formal roles are just as valued as those of men, despite the outward appearance that the sex typing characterizing these roles duplicates the familiar hierarchical ranking of men's and women's occupations found in the secular United States. According to Fox, it is the spirituality residing in healing that is most meaningful to Christian Scientists, and the more healing practitioners nurture ther own spirituality, the more prestige they accrue. That women gain palpable material reward and status enhancement from their healing accomplishments exposes the practical side of Christian Science gender symbolism and provides yet further evidence that women in healing roles take advantage of positive cultural images of themselves to pursue culturally valued goals.

The representations of women presented in this section are uniformly positive. Even the negative traits of Wedenoja's balmist healer are over-shadowed by her more desirable characteristics. But female images are of course not universally positive ones. Women are equated with rub-bish (Strathern 1981), with nature in the sense of being outside and below culture (Ortner 1974), with evil (Hoch-Smith and Spring 1978), and with mystical beings that threaten men (Harvey 1979; Nadelson 1981). Similarly, women's qualities, substances, or essences are widely perceived as harmful to men (Douglas 1966; R. C. Kelly 1976).

Men or their substances can also pollute, however. For example, both the Kafe and Hageners of the Papua New Guinea highlands view semen as well as menstrual blood as dangerous when out of place (Faithorn 1975; Strathern 1972). It is not, then, that women pollute men, but that all reproductive secretions are potentially polluting. In the domain of healing negative qualities can also be attributed to one sex or the other or both, and witches and sorcerers may be male or female. Further, both male and female witches are able to heal as well as to curse, but these individuals may build up a form of negative charisma that eventuates in their destruction or in their being cast out by ordinary members of society (Epstein 1967; R. P. Turner 1970). Thus, although unflattering and threatening images of women are associated with illness and misfor-tune, so also are those of men, and both sexes in these representations cause illness instead of curing it. Because cultural symbols change with social and historical context (Douglas 1970), the witch or sorcerer can heal on one occasion and curse on another.

WILLIAM WEDENOJA

Mothering and the Practice of "Balm" in Jamaica

This chapter deals with Balm, an Afro-American folk healing tradition in Jamaica that has not received much study.[1] Like many other studies of traditional medicine, what follows focuses on psychotherapeutic aspects of the healing relationship, although I do not mean to dismiss the biological aspects.

According to Jerome Frank (1974, 285–289), all forms of psychotherapy, including religious and folk healing, have four generic components: (1) a special place or setting for healing, (2) a rationale or myth that provides a plausible explanation for suffering, (3) rituals or procedures to overcome suffering, relieve distress, and regain well-being, and (4) a relationship based on a patient's trust and confidence in the healer. The first part of this essay provides a general description of illness and healing in Jamaica, and it briefly covers the first three components of healing. The rest of the essay focuses on the last component, which is probably the most important and complex of the four, the relationship between Balm healers and their patients.

The main concern of this chapter, like the others in this volume, is an almost totally unexplored aspect of healing, the gender of the healer. Many if not most Jamaican healers are women, and the relationship they establish with their patients is very similar to that between mother and child. Balm healing involves maternal transference, which encourages regression and dependency in patients, and it seems to be a ritualized extension of mothering. The main need that it satisfies is an emotional rather than a physical one, a desire for attachment under conditions of stress. The mothering element of healing and the need for attachment are probably not unique to Jamaican Balm; on the contrary, these are components of most, if not all, healing relationships.

Illness and Healing in Jamaica

Jamaican peasants show great concern for illness. It is a very common topic of discussion and a source of constant anxiety. There is, however, little understanding of the scientific theory of disease. Illnesses are blamed on drafts and exposure to cold temperature or imbalances of blood or bile in the body (M. F. Mitchell 1980, 28). They are also, perhaps more often, attributed to spiritual causes.

According to one Balm healer, the majority of illnesses are "chastisements" from God for "disobedience" to His ways. However, another said that "most sickness coming from nigromancy," which refers to Obeah (sorcery), and this is the most common belief. In the behavioral or perceived environment of Jamaican peasants, there are four types of malevolent spirits that can cause suffering: *duppies* (ghosts), fallen angels, demons, and the devil. In addition, ancestor spirits may punish their descendants. Jamaican peasants also worry that neighbors and relatives will turn, in envy or spite, to an *obeahman* (sorcerer), who has the supernatural power to manipulate spirits and use them to do harm.

The first resort in cases of illness is, of course, self-medication. Though Jamaica has a lengthy and extensive tradition of folk cures, it is dying out and rapidly being replaced by over-the-counter drugs. If an illness persists for several days, help may be sought from a private doctor or a government medical clinic, but there is widespread dissatisfaction with them. A sophisticated comparison of ninety-seven patients of healers and doctors in Jamaica by Long (1973, 217–232) showed that Balm healers are better liked, spend significantly more time with patients, and give more satisfying diagnoses than doctors.

The expense of a doctor's examination and prescription drugs is a serious drain on the financial resources of the average Jamaican, and seeing a doctor often involves significant travel and a long wait at the office. The greatest problem with the doctor-patient relationship, however, is communication, which is inhibited by cultural and class differences.

Doctors and patients normally come from separate subcultures of Jamaican society; they use different terms to describe symptoms and label diseases and they hold different beliefs about etiology and treatment.

Consequently, a doctor may find it difficult to elicit diagnostically meaningful symptoms from a patient, and a patient may not understand a doctor's diagnosis or the purpose of prescribed medication. In addition, a patient may regard diagnostic inquiry as a sign of incompetence, because it is the custom of Balm healers to divine an illness before speaking with a patient. These factors undermine a patient's faith in a doctor and his expectation of successful treatment.

Doctors and patients also normally come from very different social classes, which is a barrier to establishing a satisfactory relationship. According to social convention, an upper-class doctor should be authoritarian and impersonal or patronizing in his relationship with a lower-class patient, who should, in turn, be submissive and obedient to the doctor. Consequently, a patient may be reluctant to ask questions about a diagnosis or treatment that he does not understand because the doctor might regard this as a challenge to his position and authority. There is also a lack of warmth and rapport in the doctor-patient relationship. Peasants often complain that doctors are "rough" with them and, based on my observations, I would have to agree. (For an in-depth treatment of the problem of social class in medical treatment in Jamaica, see M. F. Mitchell 1980.)

In general, rural Jamaicans are dissatisfied with the treatment they receive from doctors and have little faith in their effectiveness. Moreover, they believe doctors are incapable of dealing with illnesses of a "spiritual" nature. Therefore, many turn to religion and folk healers for relief.

A patient may consult an obeahman or a "scientist," but these magical practitioners are not generally viewed as healers. Obeahmen are widely feared for their power to curse others and control ghosts. People turn to scientists principally for good-luck charms like rings and bracelets, which are used to avoid accidents or to bring success.

Balm, which has been practiced for over one hundred years in Jamaica, is closely associated with an indigenous religious cult called Revival. Although Jamaicans regard Revivalism as a Christian faith, it is actually a syncretic, Afro-Christian religion that relies heavily on the intervention of spirits, often through dreams and "trance" states. Revival cults are descended from Myalist healing cults, which emerged in the late eighteenth century to counter Obeah (Wedenoja 1988). Many Revivalist ceremonies and practices are concerned with the prevention or alleviation of illness and misfortune, and about half of all Revival cults offer treatment for outsiders as well as members. Some Revivalists operate *balmyards* devoted entirely to the practice of healing. These healing centers employ Revivalist beliefs and practices but are not Revival cult centers.

American Pentecostal sects have become phenomenally popular in the past two decades (Wedenoja 1980), and faith healing by laying on of hands and group prayer is a major feature of their services. Whereas Revivalism is widely regarded as old-fashioned and low class, Pentecostalism is often viewed as a more modern and respectable faith. A significant reason for its spread may be that it combines the respectability of the modern doctor with the spirituality of Revivalism.

Healing in Balmyards and Revival Cults

Jamaican peasant culture makes a distinction between the sacred and the profane, referred to indigenously as the "spiritual" and the "temporal." Revivalism is commonly called "the spiritual work" and Balm is often called "spiritual science," because they deal with spirits, treat spiritual afflictions, and rely on trance states. Although God is held to be the source of their healing power, the power is delivered to them through angels by means of the Holy Spirit. In contrast, Obeah is called "temporal science" because it can be learned and is not a gift. Moreover, Revivalists and balmists routinely rely on visions, dreams, precognition, glossolalia, and ceremonial possession trance, whereas the obeahman depends on magic and does not use altered states of consciousness.

The Balm healer is essentially a shaman, a person who has received—generally during a severe illness—a spiritual "calling to heal the nation" and the "spiritual gifts" of divination and healing. The balmist's power to heal is based on spirit mediumship; she works with angel familiars who advise her in diagnosis and treatment.

Balmyards can be identified by "banners" (flags) flying from poles, often next to a small wattle-and-daub structure. Generally, they are enclosed by fences and have an arched gateway guarded by a follower. In addition, there will be one or more "seals" on the grounds. These are poles, about five feet high, with a glass of water and fruit set on top to attract and feed angels.

Typically, one day each week is set aside for a healing ceremony. Although the majority of patients come on this day, balmyards receive patients for private consultations throughout the week. A Balm healer is usually supported by many devoted followers, often former patients, who assist her in her work. On a healing day, these "workers" offer a service for patients "to cheer up their spirit," and they frequently perform a counterclockwise group dance called "shouting" to remove "destruction" or evil from the patients.

Patients are called out of a healing service, one at a time, to a shed where they are bathed in water that herbs have been boiled in. This bath is normally accompanied by the recitation of psalms. After being bathed, the patient is led to a private room for a consultation with the healer.

In order to diagnose an affliction, a Balm healer will perform a spiritual divination or "reading," which psychologically is an institutionalized form of empathy. There are several ways to read a patient, but in all cases symptoms are never elicited from the patient prior to a reading. The balmist must demonstrate her gift of healing by telling the patient what his or her problems are. One of the more common methods of divination is called "concentration": typically, the healer will gaze intently at a silver coin or a plant leaf in a glass of water until a "message" from an angel is received in her mind. Other forms of reading include interpreting the movement of the flame of a candle, reading a patient's tongue, card cutting, passing hands over the body of a patient, interpretation of dreams, and palm reading. Very powerful healers may be able to read patients simply by looking at them.

Balm healers deal with every conceivable form of human suffering except serious wounds and broken bones, but the most common complaint is pain in any part of the body. Another frequent problem is a vague syndrome called "bad feeling," which is generally characterized by sudden onset, "feeling out of self," losing self-control, feeling weak and fearful, profuse sweating, and fainting. Other popular problems include weakness, indigestion, headaches, and a feeling of "heaviness" or "beating" in the head. Every healer sees some cases of paralysis, blindness, crippled limbs, deafness, and dumbness. Mental disorders are almost always blamed on spirits, and they are frequently treated by healers. Patients also complain of problems in living such as excessive worry or "fretting," difficulties in raising children, and conflicts with family members, boyfriends, girlfriends, or spouses. Many patients believe that neighbors or relatives are trying to "kill" them—that is, using sorcery on them. Some are filled with hate and want to harm others supernaturally.

A majority of Balm patients seem to suffer from chronic and stress-related afflictions like somatized depression, and they are demoralized; they feel "isolated, hopeless, and helpless" (J. D. Frank 1974, 314). Balm patients often eagerly related a litany of problems to me: they have too many children to support and care for, they can't find a job, the "baby father" won't support his children, they can't find enough to feed their family, their work is too hard, they can't get a visa to go abroad to work, and so on. Many of them are young adults who have come to realize the dismal fact that their grandiose adolescent expectations for life are totally unattainable.

Although different balmists employ different treatments for the same conditions, there is a limited range of common therapeutic techniques. All patients attending a healing service will typically be given a glass of water with a leaf in it, known as "consecrated water" or "the medicine." The great majority of healers give their patients "bush" or herbal concoctions, frequently in the form of "teas": purgatives to clean the stomach, tonics to build the body, cooling medicines to reduce pressure, and bitter medicines to clean the blood (M. F. Mitchell 1980, 30).

Jamaicans have great faith and pride in their bush medicines, and at least in past decades, the average person knew enough of them to treat himself. The use of herbs is now, however, being supplanted by vitamins and minerals, crude drugs, and over-the-counter medicines, which may be supplied by the healer but are more commonly prescribed by her and filled at a pharmacy. Patients may also go directly to a pharmacy, rather than seeing a healer, and ask the pharmacist to recommend a drug. They turn to healers when they fail to get quick results from other sources or when they think their problem is spiritual and therefore not in the realm of medical expertise.

Balm healers specialize in spiritual afflictions. Although they usually provide or prescribe herbal remedies and common drugs, they also use rituals and magical items to counteract spiritual forces. Balmists routinely tell their patients to burn candles or frankincense and myrrh, recite prayers, and read psalms. They often anoint patients with lavender oil and perfumes or tell them to fast to "build up the spirit." Sometimes they will open and close a pair of scissors over the head of a patient to "cut"—that is, to exorcise—a spirit or use a padlock to "lock" a spirit.

A belief that conversion to Christianity and the living of a Christian life will protect one from Obeah and ghosts has been prevalent in Jamaica since the eighteenth century. Revivalism had its origin in antisorcery movements, and many of its ceremonies involve ritual combat with ghosts. Revivalists sing and dance to overcome spirits and call on God's angels to protect and advise them. In ritual trance states, they joust with demons using wooden swords, wave banners to sweep demons from the church, and smash bottles of carbonated soda on the floor to "cut destruction" (evil forces). Regular attendance at Revival ceremonies provides ritual cleansing. In cases of serious affliction, a special ceremony may be performed for a patient. Those who recover from a serious illness are expected to devote themselves to the cult; otherwise, it is said that God will make them fatally ill.

Portrait of a Balm Healer

Ethnographic fieldwork is a fortuitous enterprise. By chance rather than by design, the hamlet I chose to live in had a very successful Revival cult led by a popular healer, who made me her "godson" on my first visit with her. During the following year and a half we spent a great deal of time together, and I came to know her as well as I have ever known anyone.

The Reverend Martha Jones, generally called "Mother" Jones (these are pseudonyms), is a stocky sixty-four-year-old black woman who stands about five feet five inches tall and weights about 140 pounds. She lives with about thirty followers and children in a large house next to her church, which she founded in 1950.

Mother Jones was born in the community where she now lives, and spent her first twelve years there. Her father, who died in 1953, made his living as a painter and was also a leader in the local Missionary Alliance church, where she was baptized. She describes him as a quiet, strict, stern, sober, and hard-working man, who was close to her. Her mother, who died in 1937, was a housewife who gave birth to ten children, four of whom are still living. She too was quiet, strict, and home-loving.

Mother Jones was sickly throughout childhood and worried constantly about getting ill or hurt. She contracted malaria and typhoid fever, and lost her hair. Because she was their youngest child and so sickly, her parents were very protective, even keeping her from school, and gave her a great deal of attention.

At the age of twelve Mother Jones went to Kingston to live with an older sister, and she worked there as a maid for eighteen years. She married a black American sailor when she was twenty-two but never had any children. In her late twenties she had a number of "spiritual experiences"—epileptiform states and visions—and went to a Balm woman who told her she had a "spiritual gift."

Mother Jones moved to Washington, D.C., when she was thirty to work as a parlormaid for the British ambassador, but she became "crippled" during her first year there and received a vision telling her to return to Jamaica and start a healing ministry. After another year in Kingston, she and her husband moved to her home town and started a "work." Her husband, however, left in the following year, and she has not seen or heard from him since.

Mother Jones was ordained in the National Baptist church in 1960 and appointed "overseer" for four or five churches in the area. They eventually broke away, and she changed her membership to another American sect.[2] Over the past twenty-five years, every moment of her life has been devoted to her church and healing. She once remarked to me, "my task is not an easy one, my time is not my own. I couldn't tell the day when I am able to rest my head on the pillow." Every Monday she holds a healing service and sees from ten to thirty patients. Throughout the week other patients come individually to her. And her church holds a variety of services and classes almost every day or night of the week.

The people in her community have great respect for Mother Jones, and she has many devoted followers throughout the island and among Jamaican communities in England, Canada, and the United States. No one doubts her integrity and devotion. Everyone refers to her as "Mother" and relates to her as a mother. She shows concern not only for her patients and followers but for the entire community and society as well. She likes children and they are attracted to her. About twenty children live with her: some are ill or handicapped and others have been left with her for discipline or because their mothers are unable to care adequately for them.

Mother Jones says that people come to her for healing when a doctor fails to find anything wrong with them and they think it must be a spiritual, not a physical, problem. She sends her patients to a doctor if she thinks they need one and, for her protection, usually insists that they see a doctor before coming under her care; otherwise she could be liable for prosecution. She does not normally treat someone who is on medication, because "you can't mix the spiritual and the temporal."

Mother Jones tells her patients that "the Lord will help them and they will be healed just through faith, if they believe." But, she laments, "Some people want more. . . . They want something to take way with them. . . . They seem to think it is someone's bad intents.. . . . They don't believe prayer and God will be able to keep them. . . . They feel they have to pay a lot of money . . . and get some superstitious something, or they are unsatisfied." Unlike some Jamaican healers, who blame many problems on Obeah and duppies and provide "guards" (protective amulets), Mother Jones often rebukes these patients by telling them "their thoughts are not right."

Mother Jones told me she wanted to be a preacher rather than a healer, but healing was the gift she received through the Holy Spirit. Although she says that spiritual healing is not a gift one can learn or teach, she does have pamphlets on gospel healing and an ancient book on anatomy, and she listens to radio talk shows on health problems.

One of Mother Jones's "spiritual gifts" is an ability to feel a patient's pain while she is "in the spirit." She also uses "concentration" to "read" a patient by staring at a glass of water with a leaf in it and asking the patient to drop a silver coin in "as a love offering" to an angel. Like most Balm healers, she does not ask patients to describe their symptoms, because she is supposed to be able to "read" them.[3] But after giving a rather general diagnosis, she will question the patient and discuss the problem in detail before prescribing treatment.

All of the patients at a Monday healing service receive a glass of consecrated water and an herbal bath before seeing Mother Jones. In her private consultations with patients she often assigns them specific chapters of Scripture to read and gives them a "healing prayer" to wear next to the place of their illness. The latter is a sheet of "spirit writing," a propitiation to God written in cabalistic script while in a state of trance. She gives her patients "bush medicine" or herbs, prescriptions for vitamins and over-the-counter drugs, and offers advice on living. But she attributes her healing ability largely to her gift for spiritually absorbing a patient's suffering into her own body: "If you take their condition, you draw it off, the people goes free." She constantly complains about the suffering she bears for others, and says her gift might kill her if she entered a hospital.

A Healer's Personality

Mother Jones is a dedicated and renowned healer who has served in that demanding capacity for thirty-eight years. Evidently the roles of healing meet at least some of her needs as well as those of her patients. This section examines relationships between the personality of Mother Jones and her healing roles. The analysis is based on innumerable observations and interviews with her, a life history, and two projective techniques (the Rorschach and the Thematic Apperception Test, or TAT).[4]

In terms of her persona or social self, Mother Jones is forceful, dynamic, charismatic, self-assured, caring, intelligent, perceptive, serious, responsible, and domineering. The projective techniques, however, reveal a somewhat different personality: very extratensive or sensitive and often anxious and fearful; emotionally labile and histrionic but repressed or constricted; fearful of losing control of her feelings and responding to threat with flight or dissociation; moralistic; and sometimes depressed. She shows trust in herself but mistrust for others, has a generally optimistic attitude, is keenly attuned to the affective needs of others but displaces her own affective needs, and has a lot of repressed hostility—particularly toward men. Her responses also show a need for nurturance, a need to nurture others, and a need for public attention and approval. The TAT responses suggest that she had to struggle for autonomy from her mother's overprotection in adolescence and, feeling guilty about this, identified strongly with her mother in adulthood becoming nurturing, protective, domineering, and moralistic.

Mother Jones's roles as religious leader and healer appear to meet most of her personality needs well. They give her autonomy and dominance over others and gain her love, affection, and admiration. As a surrogate mother for many people, she can identify with her own mother, which gives her a strong sense of identity and relieves her of guilt. Healing provides her with a defense mechanism, undoing, which disguises her hostility toward others. It offers opportunities to criticize others and impose her strong sense of morality on those she dislikes. It is also, by means of projection, a way to satisfy her own need for nurturance. Mother Jones's ritual roles provide frequent and sanctioned outlets for her dissociative tendencies in the form of visions, trance, and ceremonial possession states. And her entire life is governed by such a narrow range of role expectations that she is seldom threatened and finds predictability and security in them. This restrictiveness is, however, something of a problem too: Mother Jones is always, in a sense, "on stage" and performing roles, which limits her personality and makes her lonely.

In order to have a successful balmyard or Revival cult, healing or leadership roles must be gratifying to patients and followers as well as to the healer or leader. I found several individuals who had a strong desire to become healers or leaders and had tried many times to establish a Balm practice or Revival cult, but had always failed to attract a clientele or devotees. They were not lacking in spiritual knowledge, but they did not meet the psychological needs of others. Given the renown and large following of Mother Jones, it is apparent that she not only meets her own needs but satisfies those of her patients and followers as well.

Mother Jones's characteristic optimism is encouraging to patients and raises their expectations for relief. Her sensitivity to the affective needs of others—that is, her warmth and concern—evokes feelings of love and security in her patients and allows her to establish rapport with a patient quickly. The psychological tests also show her to be a very creative and intuitive person, someone who thinks in a holistic manner and can easily make convincing interpretations of a case on the basis of a few clues.

Scheff (1975, 1979) has emphasized both the need for emotional arousal in therapy and the importance of group support if therapeutic change is to persist, and these elements are amply present in Mother Jones's practice. Her healing services employ drums and tambourines, singing and dancing, histrionic preaching, and ecstatic behavior, all of which is emotionally rousing. She holds periodic "Patient Tables," which are lengthy and ecstatic ceremonies, to honor former patients. And her patients often become involved in the regular cycle of ceremonies of her church, at which members are expected to "testify" often to their salvation or personal rebirth; normally, this involves declarations of the important influence of Mother Jones on their lives. The changes she instigates in her patients are then reinforced by her presence and by the support of other followers.

Women and Balm

Jamaicans say that Balm and Revivalism have greater "spiritual power," including the power to heal, than other religions. Pentecostalism is also regarded as a significant spiritual power and healing resort, but less powerful than Balm and Revivalism. The "nominal churches" (denominations) are commonly said to be spiritless and lacking in healing power.

Spirituality and healing are largely associated with women in Jamaica. Denominational churches always have male ministers, and their officers are usually male as well. However, 16 percent of the Pentecostal churches in my research area were led by women,[5] and most of them had women in other positions of leadership too. Both of the balmyards in my area were operated by women, and ethnographers working in other areas of Jamaica have also noted that Balm healers are usually women. There are many women in positions of leadership in Revival cults and, in my area, 54 percent were headed by women. In addition, while only 46 percent of the male leaders of Revival cults practiced Balm, 64 percent of those headed by women did so. In Revival cults I have studied, men were never directly involved in healing.

This association of women with healing is not restricted to Balm and Revivalism. The medical system relies heavily on nurses and midwives, too. In rural areas, babies are delivered by government midwives, traditional *nanas,* or resident nurses at community clinics. The day-to-day operation of a rural hospital is managed almost entirely by the Matron and her nurses, with doctors serving mainly as surgeons and consultants. Obeahmen and scientists are, however, to my knowledge always men.

This sexual division of labor may be due, in part, to considerations of wealth and prestige. The practice of Obeah or Science is reputedly very remunerative and a source of great influence. But the practice of Balm, though it may bring one honor and respect, usually offers little in the way of income or formal prestige and power. As in most societies, men monopolize public positions of wealth and power and leave the less lucrative positions to women.

The association of men with sorcery and women with healing may also be based on cultural stereotypes about the sexes. In interviews and TAT responses, men are generally depicted as violent, troublesome, unreliable, untrustworthy, sexually aggressive, deceitful, and exploitative. Obeahmen are feared because they work in secret, with malicious ghosts (duppies), and cause harm or misfortune. Women, in contrast, are portrayed as peaceful, benevolent, nurturing, caring, responsible, and trustworthy. Correspondingly, Balm and Revivalism are benign institutions; their purpose is to counteract Obeah and malicious ghosts or provide protection from them. Thus we have a simple semiotic equation of Obeah with men, aggression, harm, and evil, on the one hand, and Balm and Revivalism with women, protection, helping, and good, on the other.

Mothering and Balm

Modern biomedicine can be effective even when the rapport between doctor and patient is poor, but success in psychotherapy or traditional healing depends on the personal qualities of a healer and her relationship with a patient. The most striking facets of Mother Jones's healing relationships are the childlike behavior of her patients and their strong attachment to her. They not only call her "Mother" but also relate to her as children do to their mother. She, in turn, acts like a mother toward them.

Mother Jones is idealized by her patients and followers, who believe she has a special spiritual gift to understand their problems and draw suffering from them. They believe she genuinely cares about them, and they readily put their trust in her. This is remarkable because Jamaican peasants are generally mistrustful and unwilling to confide in others; in particular, they worry about gossip and sorcery. But Mother Jones has a reputation for confidentiality, and she and other healers are perhaps the only people Jamaicans feel free to confide in.

Mother Jones is very firm and directive, even domineering or authoritarian, with her patients. Although she is supportive and shows a great deal of sympathy for them, she is also quick to criticize their life styles and is quite insistent, in a caring way, about their need to change. On numerous occasions I heard her berate a patient for sinful ways and prescribe, in some detail, the life he or she should be leading.

Patients and followers readily submit to Mother Jones's authority and direction. They often develop a strong attachment to her, and even act regressively in her presence. Most of her patients rely on her only temporarily, in times of crisis, but some become dependent on her. She is served by about fifteen workers, many of them former patients, who have devoted their lives to the service of her church and her healing practice.

Mother Jones's patients and followers cherish their personal relationship with her, but they know that to maintain it they must be obedient and follow her directives. People in her community were quite adamant in stating that she made her followers live up to very high standards. Because there is a great deal of gossip and Mother Jones has many ears who will report lapses to her, she has a kind of omniscience. This, coupled with the shame-oriented personality of Jamaicans, gives her considerable power or influence over followers and patients from the area.

Dependence on Mother Jones often leads to identification with her, which gives some patients and followers greater identity, autonomy, and self-assurance. Several have, in fact, gone on to start their own Revival cults or balmyards. On the whole, it was my impression that her devoted followers and former patients were more successful and better adjusted than the average person in the area. Long (1973, 233, 237) similarly concluded, in his comparison of patients of healers and doctors, that Balm patients were better integrated into their culture and had substantially better extrafamilial relationships.

The response of Jamaican peasants to Mother Jones may be due, in part, to their submissiveness, lack of self-confidence, and low self-esteem, since individuals with these traits are highly susceptible to therapeutic influence (J. D. Frank 1974, 115). But Jamaicans are not normally very receptive to direction from others; the heritage of slavery has made them very sensitive to this. They respond to Mother Jones in part because she is a woman, and women are more trusted and respected than men. They also respond to her because she is a motherly woman: someone who is kind, warm, and caring.

The relationship between Balm healers and patients is a ritualized version of the mother-child relationship, and this is openly recognized in Jamaican culture. Healers are referred to as "mothers" and they are expected to play a maternal role. They are idealized as supermothers and adopted as surrogate mothers. Moreover, healers often refer to patients as their "children."

Familial idioms are used extensively in Revivalism, and they are not merely metaphors. Cultists behave according to the familial roles associated with their positions. The social organization of Revival cults strongly reflects the mother-centered pattern of the family in Jamaica, and one of the attractions of Revival cults is that they are fictive family groups.

The "Mother" is usually the central figure in a cult, and everything revolves around her. The "Armor Bearer," Mother Jones's "right hand," is in charge of the day-to-day activities of the cult, a role resembling that of the eldest daughter in a large family. Other women are referred to as "sisters." Some of the younger sisters, who are known as the "workers," serve the Armor Bearer much as younger daughters work under the eldest daughter in a family.

In general, women have instrumental roles that involve a great deal of work but little recognition, whereas men are given expressive roles that have prestige but little responsibility. The "Father" or "Daddy" is sometimes the dominant but more often a removed but respected figure. Many of the men are deacons, and they seem to play the role of uncles. The pastor of Mother Jones's church, who was raised by Mother Jones, is a handsome and charming young public health inspector. His official duties are to preach sermons and perform weddings and funerals, but he also fills the familial role, common in Jamaican families, of a favorite son who is admired by all. Other men are referred to as "brothers." Mother Jones always called me "my son," and her followers referred to me as "Brother Bill."[6]

Mother Jones is a mother not just to her patients and followers but to the entire community. She is its moral standard and conscience and, more generally, a symbol of the love, affection, and devotion of mothers. There is a great respect for mothers in Jamaica, and the mother-child tie is the strongest bond in the society. Children are often reluctant to leave home and mother when they reach adulthood, and the most traumatic event in the life cycle is the death of one's mother. Mothers have almost total responsibility for their children; the role of fathers is largely limited to punishment for severe offenses. In addition, mothers delegate many domestic tasks and child-care responsibilities to their daughters, while sons are free to roam and play. The needs of rural children are therefore met largely by women.

The cultural patterning of the healer-patient relationship on the mother-child bond encourages maternal transference, regression, and the development of a dependency relationship. This can give the Balm healer a great deal of influence over her patients, because it makes them more receptive and suggestible. Moreover, the mother-child bond probably has some effect on all other relationships, because it is usually the first and most influenctial relationship in life. Maternal transference can thus provide the healer with an opportunity to make some rather fundamental changes in the personality and behavior of her patients.

Maternal dependency can be very supportive for patients. The healer, as a surrogate mother, consoles them, looks after them, and takes control when things go wrong. She gives them attention, affection, nurturance, encouragement, and offers them direction and purpose. Through attachment to her, they can regain a childlike sense of protection and security.

Western therapists would regard the dependency aspect of the healer-patient relationship in Balm as a problem, but it is not seen as one in Jamaica. Jamaicans are very sociable and they do not place much value on independence and self-reliance. Dependency is not condemned or discouraged.

Attachment and Healing

Human beings are a social species. We live in groups, forms bonds of affection, and depend on each other. The first and probably foremost bond in human life is the attachment of an infant to a caretaker, usually its mother. According to the attachment theory of Bowlby (1971), infants have a strong and innate predisposition to form a relatively long-term relationship with at least one (and perhaps more) individual. This bond is established and maintained by "attachment behaviors" like crying, smiling, vocalizations, excited bounding, reaching, approach behavior, clambering up, and clinging (Ainsworth 1977).

Bowlby (1971, 257) has remarked that "no form of behaviour is accompanied by stronger feeling than is attachment behaviour." It is especially likely to be activated when an infant is hungry, in pain, tired, sick, alarmed, or separated from its attachment figure (Ainsworth 1977), and it is terminated only by bodily contact (Bowlby 1971, 313).

Need for attachment or, to use an older term, dependency continues throughout life. As individuals mature, they develop additional bonds with, for example, siblings and other relatives, peers, and mates. Disruption of these bonds, particularly the loss of significant others, increases the probability of illness or emotional problems. Moreover, individuals continue to exhibit what Henderson (1974) has referred to as "care-eliciting behavior": a pattern of activity that evokes comforting responses such as close body contact or expressions of concern, esteem, or affection from another. Henderson regards dependency as the most fundamental determinant of social behavior and, in contrast to many therapists, he sees it as a normal behavior to the extent that it falls within the limits of tolerance of an individual or his or her society.

Need for attachment is heightened by anxiety, and under stressful, anxiety-provoking conditions like illness it is natural to seek the comforting security of a nurturing figure like Mother Jones. By meeting a patient's need for comfort and security, the healer can eliminate or reduce the emotional distress associated with sickness. This may be all that is called for with a self-limiting disease, but it can also have a physiological benefit by altering the secretion of hormones.

Illness and Emotional Needs

It is my clinical impression, based on numerous observations of Balm healing and interviews with healers and patients, that the primary function of Balm is to provide psychological and particularly emotional support. This impression is supported by the research of Long (1973, 220, 233), who found that Balm patients had more psychologically related disorders and "interpersonal diseases" than patients of medical doctors in Jamaica.

Emotional needs are probably an element of most illnesses. Western medical practitioners, having a physical bias, tend to ignore them, either dismissing them as illegitimate demands or regarding them as beyond their expertise. These emotional needs are important to patients, however. Balm healers approach illness from a spiritual perspective and work with both physical and psychological needs. They are particularly adept at dealing with the psychosocial problems of patients, so it is not surprising that they are more popular than medical doctors.

There are three forms of emotional support in Balm. Many patients are truly suffering from a sickness, and the emotional support of healers can assuage the anxiety generated by it. Some patients use a genuine sickness to meet personality needs too. And there are patients who play a "sick role" primarily for the gratification of personality needs.

Jamaican peasants often use illness behavior as a passive, quasi-hysterical means to manipulate others, principally for the disguised gratification of personality needs for attention, affection, dependency, and nurturance. This behavior is learned in childhood and reinforced in adulthood.

Jamaican socialization practices encourage passivity and dependency. Mothers are domineering and restrictive, and children are expected to be obedient and submissive. Independence and initiative are discouraged, and parental discipline is based on nagging, scolding, threats, and occasional "floggings." Children consequently learn to use subtle, passive strategies to meet their needs.

Parents show great concern for the health and conduct of their children, but they generally fail to recognize that children have legitimate emotional needs too. Therefore, children often act rudely to get attention or pretend to be sick to gain affection. Sick children and adults are treated like invalids and receive a great deal of attention, sympathy, affection, and nurturance. Church groups routinely visit sick members and pray for them, and every illness is announced in Revival and Pentecostal services. Given the amount of "secondary gain" from illness, it is not surprising that it is a "cultural focus" or major preoccupation in Jamaica. It seems to be the main avenue for the gratification of emotional needs in the society.

Jamaican Balm exemplifies what I believe to be a basic principle of psychological anthropology, that every culture produces a unique set of personality needs and conflicts and develops institutionalized means for their satisfaction or resolution. Balm is not simply a traditional medical system but also, and perhaps more importantly, a source of psychological support. The psychological processes involved in Balm are not just techniques that facilitate healing but ends in themselves. Patients come to healers not only to be cured of illnesses but to gratify affective needs as well.

One of the dominant concerns of Jamaicans is "love." Many older people remarked to me that Jamaicans were once very "loving," but they are too "selfish" today. The plague of violence that Kingston has experienced over the past two decades is generally blamed on lack of love. Church sermons often dwell on social disorder, and Christian love is put forward as the salvation of society. "Peace and love" and the need for brotherly love and unity are central themes in popular music and in the ideology of the messianic cult of Rastafarianism. Mother Jones is of the opinion that most illnesses are due to "stress" in general and "lack of love" in particular. She says Jamaicans are not close, they fear each other, and they cannot give love to others. So she offers them her love, and tries to teach them to love others, to "make them whole."

What Jamaicans mean by "love" is closeness, caring, and concern for others—unity, sharing, and cooperation. Family ties are strong, and they want community relations to be close and friendly as well. Although there has probably been some erosion of *gemeinschaft* and a weakening of kin ties over the past few decades, I cannot agree with Mother Jones that Jamaicans are unloving. They are at least as "loving" as Americans, but they have a much stronger need for affiliation and place a higher value on interpersonal relations (Jones and Zoppel 1979; Phillips 1973). "Love" is a cultural focus, part of the Jamaican ethos, and one of the principal functions of Balm and Revivalism is to gratify that need.

Women and Healing

As Spiro (1978, xvi–xvii) has noted, "The practitioner of anthropology as 'science,' placing the local setting in a theoretical context, is concerned with the local as a variant of—and therefore a means for understanding—the universal." According to my analysis, the relationship between healers and patients in Balm is modeled on the mother-child relationship, a very strong bond in Jamaican society, and the mothering behavior of maternal figures such as Mother Jones provides emotional support for distressed and demoralized individuals. To what extent can this interpretation be generalized to other cultures?

A pioneering article by Carl Rogers (1957) identified congruence (genuineness and personality integration), unconditional positive regard (warm acceptance and nonpossessive caring), and accurate empathy as personal qualities that a healer must communicate to a patient if psychotherapeutic change is to take place. Additional research has indicated that effective healers are also intelligent, responsible, creative, sincere, energetic, warm, tolerant, respectful, supportive, self-confident, keenly attentive, benign, concerned, reassuring, firm, persuasive, encouraging, credible, sensitive, gentle, and trustworthy (J. D. Frank 1974; Lambert, Shapiro, and Bergin 1986). It should be noted, however, that these conclusions are based on research on American psychotherapists and thus the characteristics may be not be universal.

Many of the personal qualities noted above seem to apply to women more than men. Women are said to be more empathic and have more positive feelings about being close to others, to be more cooperative and altruistic, to share more, to be more accommodative and interested in social relationships, to be more vocal, personal, and superior at nonverbal communication (G. Mitchell 1981), "more sensitive to social cues and to the needs of others" (Draper, quoted in Quinn 1977, 198), and more nurturant or kind and supportive to others (Martin and Voorhies 1975). In a study of kibbutz children, Spiro (1979, 93) found that girls showed more "integrative behavior"—aid, assistance, sharing and cooperation—than boys, and regularly consoled victims of aggression.

These claims about universal differences in adult male and female "styles" of behavior have apparently not been put to the test of a systematic cross-cultural study. However, there are excellent data on children aged three through eleven from the Six Cultures Study (Whiting and Whiting 1975), which found that girls are more intimate-dependent (touch and seek help) and nurturant (offer help and support) and that boys are more aggressive (assault, insult, horseplay) and dominant-dependent (seek dominance and attention).

Characteristics associated with women seem to be closely related to their role as mothers. Although this may reflect an innate predisposition to bond with and nurture infants (Rossi 1977), it can also be adequately explained by socialization practices. Women have the main responsibility for child care in every society, and they are prepared for that role in childhood. A well-known cross-cultural survey on sex differences in socialization concluded that there is "a widespread pattern of greater pressure toward nurturance, obedience, and responsibility in girls, and toward self-reliance and achievement striving in boys" (Barry, Bacon, and Child 1957, 332).

There is a close correspondence between the personal qualities of effective healers and women, and it seems to be due to strong similarities between the roles of healing and mothering. According to Kakar (1982,

59), many psychotherapists claim that "the 'feminine' powers of nurturance, warmth, concern, intuitive understanding, and relatedness . . . are essential in every healing encounter and for the success of the healing process."

If "feminine powers" are essential for healing, then women should, on average, be more effective at it than men. In fact, a review of research on the sex of psychotherapists concluded that "there appear to be some demonstrable trends, under certain circumstances, toward greater patient satisfaction or benefit from psychotherapy with female therapists and no studies showing such trends with male therapists" (Mogul 1982, 1–3).

It might also be reasonable to expect that the majority of healers in the world are, as in Jamaica, women. However, a cross-cultural survey of seventy-three societies by Whyte (1978) found that male shamans were more numerous or powerful in 54 percent; female shamans were more numerous or powerful in only 10 percent. This finding does not necessarily disprove the hypothesis that women generally make better healers. Personal qualities are only one factor in recruitment to a healing role and social, political, and economic factors can be important too. Given what we know about sexual inequality, it would not be surprising to find that women occupy healing roles when these roles are low in prestige or income, while men come to monopolize them when healing is high in prestige or income. It would be worthwhile to conduct a more extensive cross-cultural survey on the sex of healers in a study that would broaden the subject from shamans to include other types of healers and would attempt to identify social conditions associated with a preponderance of male or female healers.

Although "feminine powers" such as nurturance, warmth, and concern may, as Kakar suggests, be necessary for effective healing, they are probably not sufficient. Healers also seem to be firm and often domineering. For example, Raymond Prince (pers. comm.) notes that Nigerian healers, who are almost all male, are "abrupt, authoritarian, and sometimes punitive in their relations with patients, particularly psychotic ones."

It is probably more accurate to say that the personal qualities of effective healers are androgynous. Mother Jones is not only warm, empathic, caring, sensitive, and supportive with her patients but also firm, assertive, and domineering. Male shamans often dress in female clothing and assume female roles (Halifax 1979, 24). I noticed that the husky voice of a Jamaican male healer changed to a high pitch when he entered a trance to treat his patients, and he became warmer and more empathic as well. Torrey (1972, 103) described a male healer in Ethiopia as having a fatherly relationship with his patients and an "underlying warmth . . . partly masked by an authoritarian manner."

The personal qualities of an effective healer may vary with the degree of involvement of men and women in child care in a society. However, the maternal element of healing is probably more constant than the paternal element, because women are always heavily involved in child care and there is much greater variation in the involvement of men. The emphasis on mothering in Balm is a reflection of the strong degree of maternal dependency in Jamaican society, which is encouraged by a high rate of father-absence and a general lack of involvement of men in child rearing. In addition, the androgynous character of Jamaican healers seems to be due to the fact that Jamaican mothers often have to play maternal and paternal roles in child care and family life.

Healing relationship may also vary with, and reflect, the style of parenting in a society. Jamaican mothers tend to be very domineering, restrictive, nagging, scolding, punitive, directive, and even dictatorial with their children. I observed a popular Balm healer who matched this description when I was asked to drive two patients to a balmyard. She was very abrasive and publicly scolded her patients, and I was quite surprised to hear my companions extolling her on our journey home. When I asked them if they would like her for a mother, they enthusiastically replied that she would be splendid.

Notes

A condensed version of this chapter was presented at the annual meeting of the Association of Caribbean Studies in Port-of-Spain, Trinidad, in July 1985. Field-work on Jamaican Balm was conducted during 1975–1976 as part of a broader project on the psychodynamics of Jamaican Revival cultism and was supplemented by shorter field visits in 1985 and 1986. This research was supported by predoctoral fellowships from the National Institute of Mental Health and the Organization of American States and a faculty fellowship and sabbatical leave from Southwest Missouri State University. The methodology was primarily naturalistic and based on participant-observation and interviews, which were supplemented by questionnaire data and psychological tests. I wish to thank Melford E. Spiro and Raymond H. Prince for reading and commenting on an earlier draft.

1. There are only four publications on Jamaican Balm: Barrett 1973, 1976; Long 1973; and Seaga 1968.
2. Successful Revival cults often seek greater legitimacy through affiliation with an American sect. This allows them to register with the state and perform marriages and funerals, and it gives them some protection from prosecution for violation of laws prohibiting the practice of Obeah.
3. In African healing, it is often said that the healer already knows a great deal about a patient's life before he or she comes for healing. In Jamaican Balm, however, perhaps a majority of patients are strangers from other communities. Mother Jones sees patients from throughout the island and often knows nothing about them.
4. I administered, scored, and interpreted the protocols myself. Prior to doing fieldwork in Jamaica, I went through a year's practicum in projective testing under the supervision of Dr. Lowell Storms, chief psychologist at the La Jolla Veterans Hospital, and I went over my Jamaican protocols with him after returning from the field. Mother Jones's Rorschach and TAT protocols and a more detailed analysis of her personality can be found in Wedenoja 1978.
5. Statistical data on church leadership are from a survey I conducted of 120 churches in a sixty-square-mile area in central Jamaica.
6. This was not only polite or honorific but manipulative as well. Kin terms establish special relationships, governed by expectations of generalized reciprocity and mutual support. As a "rich relative," I was often called on to provide transportation and other assistance for my "family."

The Socioreligious Role of the Christian Science Practitioner

To the truism that women gravitate to religion in greater numbers than men, Christian Science presents a supporting case bordering on overkill. The nineteenth-century American religious sect,[1] which incorporates a therapeutic system, was founded in New England about 1875[2] by a woman, Mary Baker Eddy.[3] At the time when Christian Science was getting started, the women's movement in the United States had lost momentum, not yet having recovered from its post–Civil War defeats and disappointments. Perhaps because other social and political outlets were few, and despite Mrs. Eddy's disinterest in feminism, women flocked to Christian Science, expecially to the healing roles that the sect offered. Elsewhere I have argued that Christian Science during its formative years—the 1880s and 1890s—assumed the character of an unconscious protest movement for middle-class women who found the practitioner's role an interesting and socially acceptable alternative to the stifling Victorian stereotypes then current (Fox 1978).

Probably no less important than the hospitable psychosocial milieu that brought women into Christian Science was Mrs. Eddy's influence as a role model. Mary Baker Eddy was sickly and in pain throughout much of her adult life. One of her critical biographers (Dakin 1929) remarks upon the near-miraculous improvement in her physical appearance and bearing when, in middle age, her emergent entrepreneurial skills transformed what had begun as a struggling little sect into a religion of national prominence. Whether religion or material success renewed Mrs. Eddy is difficult to ascertain; certainly both contributed to a personal charisma that played no small part in making her a beacon for other women. Men, too, became Christian Scientists—for, not wanting a "female religion," Mrs. Eddy made a point of recruiting men—but they never joined in the same numbers as women (Bates and Dittemore 1932, 274–277).

Gender Roles

A gender-role asymmetry that sees women universally occupying lesser social roles vis-à-vis men in the world's cultures is one of the consistent findings in the growing anthropological literature on women over the past decade or so (see Quinn 1977; Rosaldo and Lamphere 1974, 1–15). A few cracks appear in this generalization when it is applied to the field of religion, but certainly not of a sort to cause rejoicing among women and their supporters. In some primitive societies the roles of diviner and spirit medium or witch doctor are taken up by people who are blocked from advancing in the secular world; these may include women (Lewis 1971). Women have traditionally been the soothsayers, fortunetellers, astrologists, and clairvoyants of western society, but these roles are not highly valued and indispensable in the West as the Ndembu diviner and the Azande witch doctor are in Africa. There is a historical association of women with millennial movements, and a few exceptional women (in addition to Mrs. Eddy) have been leaders: Ellen G. White founded the Seventh-Day Adventists, Mother Ann Lee the Shakers (Fox 1973; Shepperson 1970, 48).

Until very recently, women seldom moved out of secondary roles in any of the major religions. In some, the roles of missionary and nun are offered to those women willing to undertake them, but these roles are usually subject to masculine authority and control. Women have been active in American Protestantism since the nineteenth century, but again, almost never in major roles. Rather, they have been used as helpers, depended on for their aesthetic talents like flower arrangement or their pedogogical skills as church school teachers in training young children (Crabtree 1970, 19).

On the face of it, a survey of the distribution of gender roles in Christian Science creates the impression that the sect has replicated the gender-role asymmetry of the wider society as well as of other religions.

TABLE 6.1   Ranking and Gender Ratios of Christian Science
Occupations

Position	Gender Weighting	Ratio
Administrator	M+	strongly M
Lecturer	M	5–1 M
Teacher	M/F	1–1
Practitioner	F+	8–1 F
Nurse	F+	strongly F

In Christian Science, women predominate in the therapeutic roles of practitioner and nurse, while the more prestigious, higher-paying administrative jobs in the organization go to men. A crude ranking of occupational roles and their gender ratios in Christian Science would look something like the distribution in table 6.1

It can be seen that women come into their own only as we descend the hierarchy. Male administrators explain the asymmetrical ratio of female to male practitioners largely in economic terms, saying that a practitioner's earnings are comparatively low in relation to an administrator's— or nurse's—salary, so that the practitioner's income must be and usually is a second income, supplementing either a private source of funds or a husband's income.

It would be a grievous mistake, however, to evaluate gender roles in Christian Science solely in terms of our expectations derived from the ethnographic literature or in comparison with current secular values in the United States. As I will point out later in this chapter, the practitioner role is highly respected for its dual attributes of physician and spiritual leader within the sect, which is where things really matter for Christian Scientists. Moreover, the religious doctrine of Christian Science, with its concept of an androgynous deity, is strongly conducive to the ideal of gender equality, and practical support is given to gender equality in the ritual system.

The assignment of gender roles in Christian Science was historically determined when, in her organization of the church, Mrs. Eddy probably imitating what she perceived in her own social milieu, assigned the businesslike, administrative roles to men. Somewhat uniquely, however, she reserved the tasks that demanded persuasive communication skills for women, and dispatched a series of talented female emissaries from Boston to found Christian Science churches in major cities across the country. The more orthodox and influential Protestant denominations would wait another seventy-five years to confer similarly high status and holy missions on women.

This chapter examines social and religious aspects of the practitioner's role that have been generally overlooked in the literature on both Christian Science and gender roles. First, I briefly summarize the belief system of Christian Science in order to relate its tenets to healing practice. There follows an account of the social process of becoming a practitioner and a comparison of the ideology of metaphysical healing versus the actual techniques of healing. Finally, in an overview, I analyze the practitioner's role in the contrasting light of sectarian and secular values to suggest some reasons why relatively high social status inheres in this role within the religious group.

Theology and Metaphysics

Mary Baker Eddy's textbook, *Science and Health with Key to the Scriptures,* which her followers believe to be divinely inspired, is the primary source of Christian Science beliefs and practices. The conception of the deity is the omnipotent, onmiscient, and benevolent Christian God. However, the chief familial metaphor in Christianity, God the Father, is recast as father-mother god; hence the deity contains both masculine and feminine principles. This dual nature is logically reflected in God's creation, in which everything possesses both masculine and feminine properties. The concept of an androgynous universe extends to male and female social roles; in order to qualify as complete persons, men and women are expected to possess a balanced combination of masculine and feminine attributes. Mrs. Eddy states: "Union of the masculine and feminine qualities constitutes completeness. The masculine mind reaches a higher tone through certain elements of the feminine, while the feminine mind gains courage and strength through masculine qualities" (1910, 57).

The founder put this principle into egalitarian practice when she designed the ritual system of Christian Science. The Sunday service, for example, dispenses with the conventional Protestant minister and expresses equality between the sexes in having the ritual led by two Readers, almost always a man and a woman, who are periodically elected from the congregation.

The Christian Science doctrine represents a syncretism of primitive Christianity as interpreted by Mrs. Eddy, which emphasized the healing mission of Jesus, and a metaphysical philosophy that scholars have linked with various nineteenth-century American intellectual currents, from a backwoods Transcendentalism to expansionist optimism and a general belief in human perfectability. The doctrine is based on the opposition of spirit and matter, spirit being of god and the one mind (god's) that governs the universe, therefore good; matter being not of god, therefore evil and false. If material things are evil and god creates only that which is good, it follows that god cannot be the creator of the material universe. That universe is the product of erring human perception; the subjective state of men's mortal minds. From this, Mrs. Eddy derived the opposing concepts of divine Mind, coming from god; and mortal mind, not from god. The opposition divine Mind/mortal mind is used to form a paradigm in which everything on the left side acquires a positive, true meaning and everything on the right side is negative and false.

In this system, individuals are wholly spiritual and perfect, like their creator, and therefore incapable of suffering, sickness, sin, or death. Only the counterfeit, material self experiences those illusions of evil as false claims of the senses, and these claims must be rejected and denied (Eddy 1910, 113, 302, 467–468).

The therapeutic system is an integral part of the doctrine and directly related to Mrs. Eddy's interpretation of Jesus. In Christian Science, the orthodox christian figure of a suffering divinity gives way to the image of an earthly individual so suffused with the divine spirit that he could become, in Mrs. Eddy's terms, the most scientific man the world has ever known—and therefore able to gain mastery over natural phenomena. Healing in Christian Science rests on the belief that through reading and prayer the believer may acquire a spark of the divine mind that Jesus possessed and become similarly empowered to break through the material world of pain and suffering. Mastery over the world is strongly emphasized in Christian Science metaphysics (Wilson 1970).

To the ordinary Christian Scientist, mastery might prosaically connote no more than "doing well" in life. To the religious healer generally, mastery and control presuppose spiritual forces; they emanate from the sacred world, to borrow Durkheim's term. The Christian Science practitioner, the Ndembu diviner, and the Cuna shaman similarly draw their power to heal from sacred sources, and they exercise that power over illness and disability in the secular world (Lévi-Strauss 1967; V. Turner, 1967). Hence, supernatural healers can be viewed as linking figures or mediators between the sacred and the secular. More important for our purposes, the Christian Science practitioner's healing powers are based on the foundation of belief in the sect's religious doctrine.

The Christian Science Practitioner as Healer

The present Christian Science organization is a bureaucracy with central authority vested in the Mother Church in Boston, Massachusetts. Some three thousand similarly ordered branch churches are located throughout the United States, as well as in Japan, Indonesia, the northern countries of Europe, and a few countries in Latin America. The ritual system is controlled from Boston, where weekly texts based on *Science and Health* and the Bible are prepared in advance and published four times a year; this enables the branch churches throughout the world to have identical Sunday services.

Healing work is performed with the guidance and help of practitioners, whose training is controlled entirely by the Christian Science organization. They do not need to meet any minimum educational requirement or pass a standard qualifying examination. State licensing regulations exempt practitioners on the constitutional grounds that Christian Science is a religion, not a medical system. The only formal educational requirement is that would-be practitioners must enroll in Primary Class instruction with a qualified teacher.[4] The course, lasting about two weeks, is based on twenty-four questions and answers in the chapter entitled "Recapitulation" in *Science and Health*. Completion of the course entitles the student to append the initials C.S. after her name and to be listed in the *Christian Science Journal.*[5] Only students who actually become practitioners, however, use the initials, and this is a lengthier process.

The foregoing qualifying procedures constitute the outward form of becoming a practitioner. The pathway to any religious healing role connects the psychosocial terrain between personal character and ability, the supernatural requirements of the role, and social acceptance of the healer on the part of the community.

Practitioners are self-recruited on the basis of several routes to the healing role that Landy (1977) has described. He indicates that these paths are more numerous than those open to Western scientific healers.

Selection by others is of necessity a critical part of the process, which is detailed below. *Self-dedication to a healing cult* applies insofar as practitioners are loyal members of the Christian Science church, but the term healing cult, although it may suggest nonrational beliefs and practices in curing, flies in the face of Christian Scientists' middle-class respectability. We are on sounder ground to label Christian Science a sect similar to American Protestantism. *Miraculous self-recovery,* the founder's own experience, also accounts for some practitioner's recruitment to the role. *Exceptional personality traits* are found variously among practitioners. The church imposes no specific demands in this respect.

Cross-cultural comparisons of recruitment patterns in an American middle-class religion like Christian Science with those of religious healing groups in other cultures are at best merely suggestive. Women who come into Christian Science, for example, could be considered "disadvantaged" to the extent that all women in the United States are disadvantaged relative to men. But specific parallels with groups such as the Somali possession cults that Lewis studied, in which similarly disadvantaged women are the principal recruits, would have to be carefully documented (Lewis 1971).

Practitioners say the practice comes to you, not you to it; they see it as something that unfolds slowly with time. This lengthy process by which the branch church gradually confers practitioner status on an individual through its approval and consent is what makes becoming a practitioner so distinctive a social phenomenon. I have distinguished three phases of the process.

Phase One is an early screening procedure and precedes Primary Class instruction. It attempts to resolve the eternal human difficulty, which Simmel (1950) perceived, of recognizing a priori the personality suited for a given position. The problem becomes pronounced when the requirements of office derive less from the novice's own attributes than from the construction of a ruling personality—in this case, Mrs. Eddy. However, there is room for individuality, and practitioners do not try to imitate Mrs. Eddy slavishly.

During Phase One, which is of indeterminate length, a few members of the branch church congregation begin to approach a particular person with their problems and ask for help. The individual whose help is sought is usually a recent graduate of Primary Class instruction and is felt to be progressing spiritually. She has had some success, known by word of mouth, in healing family members and close friends, among whom all healing work originates. Practitioners insist that there is no fixed route or ideal age for the practice. One of my informants had a personal healing at age twelve and headed in a straight line for her practice. Another did not become a practitioner until she was over forty.[6] Perhaps the most important attribute of a practitioner emerges in the meshing of personalities that is an enduring feature of practitioner-patient relations. This rapport can be based on such nonobjective qualities as an individual's looks, voice, or mannerisms, which will suggest to the prospective patient that the person is "all right."

Phase One is an exploratory period in which the novice can try out her healing skills, discover whether she is suited for the practice, and establish the social bonds that are the foundation of the practice; their persistence will depend on her adeptness in maintaining and deepening them. For someone determined at the outset to become a practitioner, Phase One can be an important confirming or disconfirming experience. Those who succeed in Phase One move on to the next.

Phase Two extends the novice's activities beyong a private circle of family and friends into a more public realm where her goals and abilities become more generally known. How widely she becomes known depends in part on the size of the church, among other factors. An ambitious person might get elected as Reader or appointed as Librarian of the Reading Room of a branch church, and the visibillity of office will put her personal qualities on view. Inquiries will be made. People who do not know her may ask if she is a practitioner, and she will have to decide what to tell them. Thus is her status determined.

Sometimes the results of her work are broadcast via the weekly Wednesday night ritual held at every Christian Science church. At this service, members stand up before the congregation and testify about their healings. The service has the important socioreligious function of publicly affirming the efficacy of Christian Science treatment. Although a testifier rarely mentions a practitioner by name, he or she will usually enter the church with the practitioner and they will often sit together, so that everyone knows who the healer is. During Phase Two, the practitioner's religious role also becomes prominent. In the absence of a trained clergy, it is the practitioner, more than any other person in Christian Science, who brings people "into Science." She answers members' questions about points of theology, bolsters their faith, helps patients do their readings, and generally acts as an information source for the congregation. The materials for the Sunday ritual, prepared in Boston from the Bible and *Science and Health,* are subdivided into daily readings that members are expected to do (Wilson 1970 refers to Christian Science as a "reading religion"). Thus by the time of the Sunday morning service, the congregation is already familiar with its substance.

Most people in this phase are developing part-time practices and are not yet listed in *The Journal*. Some may be waiting for young children to grow up to avoid conflict between work and parenthood; others are postponing full-time practice until they retire from other careers. Phase Two enables the practitioner to nurture a small, part-time practice while her status as a healer becomes validated informally by consensus of the congregation.

Phase Three carries the new practitioner into the formal aspects of the role: meeting the requirements of a listing in *The Journal*. When they are ready, candidates write to the Department of Branches and Practitioners in Boston for an application and typically receive a warm, encouraging letter from the head of that department. The application is designed to elicit the fruitage—a favorite Christian Science term—of the preceding phases: a description of what the applicant's work has been like. The Mother Church tries to discourage practitioners from opening offices and failing. Candidates are required to submit at least three testimonial letters describing "good physical healings." Although Christian Science broadly interprets the concept of healing to include social and emotional problems of all sorts on various levels of magnitude, the sine qua non of a practitioner's competence is the "demonstration"—the Christian Science term for healing—over serious physical illnesses such as bacterial and viral infections, cardiac diseases, and the like. *The Journal* will list the practitioner only after the Board of Directors, the ruling body of the Christian Science Church, has approved the application and supporting documents.

Formal recognition actually means in social terms that a number of people in the branch congregation have made the decision to depend on this person for friendship, comfort, health, and religious instruction and advice. They have entrusted her with the most important elements of their lives.

Healing Metaphysics

In many respects, Christian Scientists speak a language all their own. The point can be made that by placing ordinary English words in unconventional symbolic contexts, Christian Scientist further the creation and maintenance of sectarian boundaries. The special vocabulary of Christian Science is the practitioner's symbolic stock in trade and builds toward a healing rhetoric that all members share. The word "healing" itself is fraught with meaning: one can be healed of cancer, but also of tobacco and alcohol use and of hostility toward one's neighbor; the world's great problems could be healed if only Christian Scientists would "do their work," i.e., pray and read. The ritual of "demonstration" is the Christian Science equivalent of a medical cure, proving that metaphysics can empower the practitioner and her patients to master the material world with its "claims" of pain and suffering.

The image of "light" occurs repeatedly in connection with healing and other mental attitudes. As used in healing, it affords us a starting point from which to explore the practitioner's methods. Success in healing is considered a matter of light that streams into and floods the consciousness. If there are impediments that screen out any part of the light, healing will take a long time; if not, it can be instantaneous. Christian Scientists explain this kind of light by saying it is the light of the mind that reaches the mental need of others. Not telepathy, it is thought to be a metaphysical force by which divine Mind gains entrance to the individual consciousness.

It becomes a matter of first importance that the practitioner learn to "keep her thought clear," to manipulate her thought independently of the patient's, to know that she is always in the presence of a perfect being and to rejoice in that perfection. This is tantamount to seeing people as Jesus saw them, and it imparts a Christlike light to the practitioner's thought. In that light, darkness has no power.

Christian Scientists believe that almost everyone is able to self-heal but that only a few have the talent for helping others. Again, light is the distinguishing element, for when someone does serious metaphysical work that really takes hold, it creates in that person a lilght that radiates and attracts others. Those who cannot heal are inclined to blame their intellectualism, for the intellect is believed to be the medium through which disruptive information slips into the consciousness and contaminates the correct view of mankind. Keeping one's "thought quiet" is a desirable goal. Practitioners are always purifying their own thought, working out their own salvation, in the healing process.

Ideally, Christian Science treatment should be entirely and exclusively metaphysical. Practitioners are not even supposed to listen too attentively to patients' symptoms lest they be tempted to accept them as real; also, they idealize "undifferentiated" treatment that is not directed toward a specific problem. There should be no counseling of patients on a human level, no appeal to psychological processes. In this respect, practitioners share with some non-Western and primitive healers the generalized character of their roles in contrast to the high degree of specialization found in Western medicine (Landy 177, 416).

Healing Techniques

It would seem that in this religio-therapeutic enterprise, neither practitioners nor patients need to perform any actions in the physical world for the system to work; all is metaphysics. This is not quite the case. It is important to point out that in their beliefs, Christian Scientists formally recognize two levels of reality: the absolute and the relative. The absolute is the spiritual level of doctrinal purity, the sacred world; the relative is the ordinary, workaday world in which Christian Scientists play out their daily lives, the secular world. One may reasonably assume that discrepancies between belief and practice are the rule in any religious system. Recognizing two levels helps Christian Scientists cope with the special contradictions their system creates between belief and behavior: for example, aging does not happen, but older women wear wigs and makeup ("we like to look our best"); illness is an illusion, yet there are Christian Science sanitoriums and nurses ("we're not fools—we take good care of ourselves!").

When they are not "speaking in the absolute," that is, describing the healing system in its ideal form as above, practitioners divulge in their unguarded moments many of the practical techniques they actually use in healing, techniques they are not always consciously aware of. The practitioners I have met are impressive in their strength of conviction and forceful personalities, but the single, outstanding quality they all have in abundance is verbal skill. Mrs. Eddy is again the model, her repartee with students having originally made her such a focus for the press during her lifetime. Moreover, since practitioners heal by various combinations of persuasion, cajoling, and good-natured bullying—entirely by talking to patients—a certain eloquence is requisite for the role.

Mrs. B, a practitioner who is exceptionally gifted, uses humor to reach her patients, one of whom is the wife of a concert singer. The patient called Mrs. B complaining about a bad cough, which several previous Christian Science treatments did not cure. Later Mrs. B spoke to the husband on the telephone and asked him how he felt about some caustic newspaper reviews he had received after a recent concert. When he replied that he didn't mind them too much, Mrs. B advised, "Well, tell your wife to stop barking at the critics, then." The patient overheard, laughed, and was "instantly healed."

Use of the psychosomatic theory of illness is widespread among practitioners, although not in any sense of coming to grips with psychology as a discipline. Rather, practitioners look for tension-producing areas in the patient's life that are causing disharmonies; some also believe that damaged interpersonal relations can produce symptoms of illness. This means that, objectively speaking, the practioner is working not on the image of perfect man but on her diagnosis of the patient's emotional problem. The false belief of physical symptoms that the patient has is due to psychic causes that the practitioner has identified.

Still other practitioners are concerned with the causal connections between sickness and wrongdoing and orient their treatment to the moral sources of patients' problems. Practitioners say great delicacy is necessary or else patients become embarrassed and do not return. This approach is more successful with patients of long standing, whose histories are already known; then when the practitioner senses patients are holding back information, as they often do, she can say, "Now *you* know what is wrong. . . ." Chances are the patient will think of some recurrent transgression with which both he and the practitioner are familiar. In theory, he is spared embarrassment but also alerted to the cause of his problem.

The Social World

The Christian Science practitioner stands at the center of a network of patients and patient-friends in what I have described elsewhere as a "star pattern." In this configuration, the central figure interacts with each of the others more than they do with one another (Fox, Gibbs, and Auerbach 1985). The dynamics of this pattern in Christian Science resides in a series of dyads in which the practitioner is always the superordinate member, the patient subordinate and dependent.

To stabilize the dyads, to ensure that they will become lasting and that patients will not stray, practitioners try to make the relationship rewarding in ways other than therapeutic, so that patients get something in exchange for their dependency. Affective ties are an indispensable means of redressing the imbalance of super/subordination, even though

in the realm of affect the advantage remains structurally with the practitioner, who is always the object of the patient's emotional sensibilities.
This is because Christian Scientists are very status-conscious within the
sect and ordinary members look up to practitioners, not vice versa. To
strengthen socioemotional bonds, practitioners employ strategies that
vary according to life style, personal affinities, income, and the like.
One may invite her favorite patients to small dinner parties in her home;
another takes a group of patients regularly to shop in the supermarket;
still another invites certain patients for summer weekends at her house
at the seashore. In their turn, patients usually reciprocate these favors in
such ways as driving the practitioner to meetings or sending her a box of
candy or some other delicacy she likes.

If we are to give credence to practitioners' statements, these methods
of reinforcing affective ties can be seen as nothing more than sound
business tactics, since practitioners say they do not encourage deep
friendships with patients. Practitioners claim that they must be on guard
against demanding relationships growing on the patient's side. Ideal
behavior is an impersonality that leaves the patient always free to go to
another practitioner, but practitioners of course differ in their ability to
maintain impersonality. Usually there is considerable merging of friendship and healing roles. Even so, practitioners borrow the outward accoutrements of physicians. They have offices and they send bills to patients.

Although Christian Scientists claim they cultivate non-Scientist
friends, and "have lots of them," I have not found this to be so. Their
special beliefs and attitudes create barriers that really preclude outside
friendships of any depth or duration. Non-Scientists are always talking
about illness and doctors, and Scientists fear "mental contagion"; non-
Scientists smoke and drink whereas Scientists eschew tobacco and alcohol; the Scientists' habit of denying evil things seems pollyanna-like to
outsiders. Hence, social relations tend to become exclusive among Christian Scientists.

The practitioner's social world is governed to a significant extent by
the nature of number of the complaints—the "claims"—she handles. In
view of the rarity of good physical healings, nonphysical and minor
problems constitute the greater part of the practitioner's work. Nonphysical problems include lesser psychoneurotic disturbances and troubled interpersonal relations. Minor complaints encompass rashes, hay
fever, sore limbs, and the like. The Mother Church has made some
attempts to devalue the latter in answer to past criticism that confidence
in Christian Science treatment is based on the healing of trivial problems
(see England 1954). Although it is true that each day the telephones

hum and the rhetoric flows with backaches, leaky plumbing, falling plaster, itching feet, and recalcitrant in-laws, the astute practitioner recognizes the disabilities these complaints mask: stress, self-doubt, inadequacy, and fear, factors that motivate people to spend so much of their time denying reality.

It would be hasty, even superficial to assume that the Christian Science movement depends for its day-to-day existence on healing trivia and the rhetoric they stimulate. Yet nonphysical and minor problems are essential in maintaining the operation and continuity of practitioner-patient dyads, and therefore they animate that area of social relations in Christian Science. A practitioner builds her reputation and influence as she becomes adept in establishing new dyadic relations and in maintaining old ones. It seems that recruitment of patients and their retention as church members lie at the core of this socioreligious role.

Concomitantly, as her experience with patients deepens, the practitioner is believed to be advancing spiritually. She become in the congregation's eyes more of a holy person, set apart from the rest: on call twenty-four hours a day, always ready with a stream of good thoughts and "right" soothing words. Thus the practitioner's structural position at the center of a therapeutic network does not result in a busy social life. On the contrary, and paradoxically, the morning coffees, afternoon bridge games, showers, and going-away parties are for ordinary people. Practitioners are admired for transcending the ordinary, for withdrawing into the ritual activities that signify their spirituality. For this reason, the practitioner exemplifies one of Simmel's sociological form-types—his concept of the isolated individual: "For, isolation, insofar as it is important to the individual, refers by no means only to the absence of society. On the contrary, the idea involves the somehow imagined, but then rejected, existence of society. Isolation attains its unequivocal significance only as society's effect at a distance" (Simmel 1950, 118–119).

The very nature of the therapeutic work itself is isolating in Simmel's sense, for the major part of the practitioner's therapy is absent treatment that does not require the patient to be present. It merely presupposes the patient. Often there is no face-to-face interaction between practitioner and client, and a great deal of the interaction that does occur is over the telephone.

To be the kind of person who teaches others to deny reality by spiritualizing their thought, the practitioner must struggle to keep her own thought pure; to keep well "prayed up," she must retire alone into her books and do her metaphysical work, usually in the gray, quiet hours of the early morning before the calls start coming in.

Overview

Religious sects possess dual, complementary social characteristics. The first is their position as subcultures within society. The beliefs, values, and behavior patterns of the larger social system cannot fail to influence the sect. The second characteristic is a proclivity for closure from the outside world, and this involves problems of boundary maintenance.

The dynamics of Christian Science and the task of being a Christian Scientist spring in large measure from the tensions of sustaining a sectarian outlook in the wider society. Certain features of Christian Science, apart from doctrine, work almost inevitably to preserve its sectarian boundaries: the secrecy surrounding their educational system; the special vocabulary they use; the exclusiveness of their social relations. Nevertheless, in spite of these boundary-maintaining facets, Christian Science has a major problem in preserving its sectarian identity and doctrine against the world's incursions. The likelihood of these incursions is rendered all the more threatening by Christian Scientists' participation in and interaction with the world at large.

When it comes to women's roles in the church, however, the conflicts present elsewhere in the movement—in the bureaucracy, the ritual system, in concepts of illness and healing themselves—seem to transform themselves into positive attributes for women.

The issue of women's occupational or professional roles can be characterized as one of subcultural appearance versus sectarian reality. As I have indicated, it appears that the Christian Science church mirrors the traditional values of the secular society in regard to the allocation of roles by gender. Most of the prestigious, higher-salaried administrative roles are occupied by men, and women dominate only in the therapeutic sphere, where men are not competing strongly against them. Thus a plausible explanation of women's preponderance in the therapeutic roles is that their low prestige and poor economic rewards do not interest men; these roles are the dregs.

In actual fact, the practitioner and teacher roles are highly valued within the sect. The practitioner is the functional equivalent of the physician on the outside; in addition, as we have seen she is considered a holy person who in the absence of formal clergy acts as religious leader and advisor to patients and other church members. The teacher role is a step above the practitioner's and both these roles carry high presitge in the branch church, which is the principal social field of Christian Science. An outsider cannot fully appreciate the importance of these roles; they must be placed in the sectarian context, for they acquire their meaning in circumstances of closure.

Within its own boundaries, Christian Science gives formal power, that is, legitimate power in Weber's sense,[7] to women in therapeutic roles, conferring on them the legal authority to practice. The secular society also gives women formal power in various professional roles: doctor, lawyer, teacher, and so forth. But the consequences for secular women are often detrimental to their domestic and reproductive roles, as well as disruptive to their socioemotional relations with men and women alike. Powerful women in secular society are often perceived as threatening interlopers and antagonists.

Christian Science women who hold formal power never suffer these disadvantages. Their power roles are considered normative in the sect's organization and essential to the movement's vitality. Reasons may lie in the sect's ideological background: a charismatic woman founder and an androgynous deity. In addition to the prestige of the practitioner role, which its incumbents do appreciate, women become practitioners simply because they enjoy the role, not because they have analyzed its power potential. The instrumental advantages of the role are a short training period, no previous educational qualifications, and no age limit. An exhilarating later-life career becomes possible for women. To the religious-minded, the role offers a variety of challenging interpersonal relationships articulated within a higher order of meaning. The practitioner may elaborate her informal power from the same role elements as the secular housewife, but the practitioner operates under principles that endow her life and work with transcendence. Emotion and the use of affect with legitimate authority is another of the role's satisfactions.

In sum, this religious sect, by means of its healing roles, provides women alternative ways of participating in the social system without incurring the risk that their behavior in the sect will be defined as antisocial on the outside. Whether large numbers of women will continue to exercise the sectarian option will almost certainly reflect the strength, magnitude, and durability of women's social advancement in the wider society.

Notes

1. I follow Wilson's use of the term "sect" in describing Christian Science (Wilson 1970).
2. Christian Science doctrine dates the movement's founding to 1866, the year

Mrs. Eddy claimed to have healed herself of a crippling fall on the ice in Lynn, Massachusetts.
3. Born Mary Morse Baker, Mrs. Eddy took the name of her third and last husband, Gilbert Eddy, for her professional name.
4. Christian Science teachers are graduates of Primary Class instruction who have been practitioners in good standing for at least three years. They have advanced their education in Christian Science by taking the Normal Course, given once every three years in Boston under the auspices of the Christian Science Board of Education. This six-day course, the highest level of training in the system, earns for its graduates the CSB, Bachelor of Christian Science. Little is known about the Normal Course among the ordinary membership.
5. A monthly publication of the Christian Science organization. In addition to articles and testimonials of healing, it also lists practitioners, nurses, and teachers.
6. It will be recalled that Mrs. Eddy was fifty-four when *Science and Health* was first published. From a doctrinal standpoint, Christian Scientists deny aging as false testimony of the senses—yet another example of mortal mind at work.
7. The reference is to Weber's familiar scheme of legitimate authority based on charisma, tradition, or law. These are nonmutually exclusive categories (Weber 1947).

BARBARA KEREWSKY-HALPERN

Healing with Mother Metaphors: Serbian Conjurers' Word Magic

There are elderly women curers in central Serbia (Yugoslavia) who continue to preserve, transmit, and practice a mode of healing based on imagery associations aroused by arrangements of sounds, words, and utterances. These oral charms retain metaphors and other elements carried over from ancient times, and their persistence in contemporary Europe acknowledges the efficacy of traditional practices in a region where, thanks to the paving of a rural road some years ago, a full range of modern biomedical options is now accessible to villagers.

As part of the larger Balkan area where oral genres have long been studied extensively, especially epic (Karadžić 1896; Lord 1968; Murko 1929; Parry and Lord 1954) and to a lesser degree lament and other significant oral forms, relatively little attention has been accorded healing charms (Radenković 1986). To demonstrate the richness of mother metaphors in the inventory of Serbian healing images, the present discussion documents, by looking in on selected healing rituals and listening to fragments of their accompanying incantations, how charms are used. Mother metaphors appear as themes or frames in the spoken charms and through the medium of diverse somatic representations.

Over the course of more than three decades of research in villages in Šumadija, a region that forms the geographic and emotional heartland of Serbia (Halpern and Kerewsky-Halpern 1972), part of my fieldwork has focused on ethnomedicine, including linguistic and semantic interpretations of oral charms and the phenomenology of healing rites (Kerewsky-

Halpern and Foley 1978a, 1978b), role reversal when a male serves as a ritual female (Kerewsky-Halpern 1983), and communicative modes of trust, talk, and touch in patient/practitioner interactions (Kerewsky-Halpern 1985). Mother themes were gradually disclosed to me as villagers began to perceive me as an "elderly woman" and a rightful recipient of (and participant in) women's collective wisdom transmitted orally across generations and through female lines (cf. alternate gender transmission in rural Greece, Blum and Blum 1970, 351). Incantations and healing rituals are inexorably bound here, as elsewhere (see also Leach 1966, 407, quoted in Tambiah 1968, 187–189). Together they present a powerful thematic manifestation, access to which was cunningly withheld from me until village practitioners deemed appropriate.

Entering the Scene

That appropriate time arrives. A rainstorm washes away the August dust and restores to freshness the greens and golds, the hills, the tapestry of colors, contours, and textures. You can smell the earth again. Fields of tall corn and wheat stand out in adjacent rectangles, revived. The swath of potholed road curves through the village with a few raw-looking brick or stuccoed houses alongside it, their newness not yet softened by time or trees grown tall. Most of the village houses are lower, smaller. Whitewashed, built with wattle and daub, and capped with weathered ochre- and red-tile roofs, they fit snugly in a landscape embraced by plum orchards heavy with fruit. Set far back from the road, these houses are accessible via dirt lanes. After heavy rain, the lanes become ribbons of unctuous mud, in recent years somewhat ameliorated by chips of crushed limestone shoveled randomly from the rear of a cow cart. To get from one household to another you can trek down one lane, go out onto the road, and eventually turn into the feeder land leading to your destination. When the lanes are too muddy it is better to go via the fields, skirting the acacia hedges marking fragmented property boundaries and cutting across the final field by gauging the shortest diagonal distance to the household compound to be visited. Usually it is possible to discover a narrow mud footpath that someone's sandaled feet tamped down earlier in the day.

Today a trail is discernible, sticky but negotiable in the wheat field I need to cross, and the grain is already dry. I knot my kerchief more securely under my hair in back and clip together the rims of my peasant-style striped wool bag so that wheat chaff will not fall on the tape recorder inside. I arrange my arms and hands forward, like the prow of a ship, and plunge in. Myriads of tiny white butterflies rise from the stalks as I maneuver through. At the far side I hop over a straggling patch of stinging nettle and blue chicory and disentangle the slim vines of cow-vetch from my ankles before stepping into the muddied courtyard of my friend and mentor, Milena.

Džoni, her husband's mongrel pup, yelps a warning. Milena hears and appears on the threshold. I note that the door frame has been painted a bright bile green since my previous visit three years ago. "Jao, sister, is it you!" she cries, and we run to embrace each other and resume conversation as though time had not intervened. Milena is my age: we were brides together. (I first came to the village as a young bride, and her wedding was one of the first my husband and I participated in as novice anthropologists.) Together we two women have moved through village-defined stages of life, from bride, to young mother, to matron, and now to older woman, a status of some privilege in rural Serbia. Milena has grandchildren. As yet I do not. It doesn't matter; my eldest daughter has come to visit briefly while working elsewhere in Europe, and villagers who have known her since she was a toddler see her this summer as "ripe," a grown woman ready to bear children of her own. Their perception of her entitles me to the status of grandmother.

I come to understand that more important than the kin term is what it represents. To be a *baba,* "old woman" or fictive "granny," is a euphemism for being regarded as ritually clean. This becomes apparent as Milena pats my face and beams. Once again we two are in step along life's way. She adjusts her own kerchief low over her forehead to match the sunburn line on her brow and ties the ends under her chin. She puts her work-worn hands in mine and says, "Remember, sister, when you asked how my mother-in-law stops a colicky baby from fretting?" (Yes, I remember, I first started asking about that decades ago.) "*I* can do it now! Stay until dusk and you can help. I'll teach you," Milena says.

Women in a Patriarchy

According to village ethos, the main function of women is as childbearing vessels. Females past reproductive age are seen as asexual and therefore not in need of having their honor protected. For such older women, it becomes permissible to go about the village unaccompanied, unprotected even after dark. (Additional benefits are behaviors that at younger ages are regarded as unseemly, such as excessive drinking and exuberant cursing.) For the female anthropologist this elevation in status is a gift of freedom of movement (and for village hosts a release from responsibility). Getting around is not too difficult. The road is functional, potholes aside. Electricity that originally was strung only along the road has been brought down most of the lanes. If the mud is not too slick, there is access by foot and thence by bus to an expanded peasant market, manufactured goods, entertainment, and medical facilities in town some nine kilometers over the hill. All these changes have opened village windows on the wider world.

Many village homes have a television set. Most have a radio. These innovations have not worked against traditional communicative modes. Oral tradition, albeit in altered form, remains a vital part of village life. In particular, the persistence of oral charms for healing amply illustrates this viability.

Certain features of social structure also show great constancy. Although the definition is a bit facile, it remains true that rural Serbia can be characterized as largely patriarchal, patrilocal, and patrilineal. The maintenance of such a pattern has direct bearing on a consideration of mother metaphors, for in the villages there exists a kind of complementarity within this still strongly patriarchal society: it is men who have always controlled, and who continue to regulate, the ongoing cycles of secular and ritual life. Women are categorically excluded from active participation in such events except in their prescribed female roles. A widow without a grown son at home may be listed in the village clerk's record book as titular (and temporary) household head, but it would be inconceivable for her to host the celebration of the feast day honoring the household's (i.e., her late husband's lineage's) patron saint. Even for less important events in the annual and life cycles—breaking the Lenten fast, greeting the ritual "first guest" at yuletide, inviting guests to a son's wedding—it is not acceptable for a woman to perform these designated male roles. If the husband is deceased or absent, a male relative is recruited.

It appears, however, that there is an artful balance in the allocation of ritual roles. The regularized activities of daily, seasonal, and annual life carried out by men are performed for a collective good. But there are components of village life that are nonregularized and nonordered, and these roles are fulfilled by women. Women's ritual intervention is personal, on behalf of an individual. It relates to the perceived suitability of women as mediators with inhabitants and forces or orderless realms where men do not venture—the worlds of the past, the future, and the unknown.[1]

Mediating with the past takes the form of funerary ritual and especially lament over the grave, a particular type of direct oral communication with recently deceased persons and, through them, with other long-deceased kin (Kerewsky-Halpern 1981; Šaulić 1929). Intervention with the future is a very different kind of rite, a practice fraught with danger. The process of divining can be a two-way channel and unless arbitrated with utmost skill can turn against both client and practitioner. (One of the examples of mother metaphors described below introduces elements of this danger, where reversals are put in motion and the outcome is not entirely predictable.)

Dealing with the unknown relates to mediating with ill winds that bear diseases and with other chthonic forces that dwell in caves and under rocks. Given the exigencies of everyday village life, with agricultural accidents and resultant frequent infections, plus the fact that modern health care delivery is available in town, it is notable that many villagers prefer the traditional way. Folk healing incorporates the highly important elements of trust and familiarity and, through the charms, the soothing human qualities of talk and sound especially valued in this oral culture. Continuance of complementarity in gender-defined ritual roles merits comment in a society undergoing modernization as rapidly as is the case for rural Serbia.

Being a *Bajalica*

A woman who has received the knowledge of how to mediate with forces of disorder is called a *bajalica,* from the Serbian[2] *bajati,* "to conjure"; her oral charm is a *basma.* (These terms are cognate with an Indo-European root pertaining to use of the voice, to speaking out.)[3] A bajalica is seen in both her biological and her ritual roles as a provider of sustenance and comfort, of nurturing and nourishment, and thus as protectress, healer. The older village women recognized for skills in conjuring are respected as quintessential mothers. Powerful maternal representations resonate throughout the charms they intone, some of the ritual objects they manipulate, and their use of secular gender-related activities combined in inventive variations on mother mimesis to dispel many kinds of maladies.

This kind of sex-specific riutal performance is played out against a background in which women are viewed by men as complex and suspect beings, imbued with contrastive dual powers that may be polluting and dangerous at the same time that they are instrumental in effecting purification (cf. Douglas 1966). Here is woman as mythic Great Mother, embodying the polar forces of evil and good.

When a girl begins to menstruate, she is instructed in a time-honored catalog of prohibitions related to potential defilement of crops and fruit- and nut-bearing trees and to food preparation, serving, and other interventions. This instruction is a rite of passage incorporating temporary isolation, as in many other cultures. For this reason a girl or woman cannot engage in conjuring unless the village community perceives her an nonpolluting. This means that *bajalice* by definition are older women, postmenopausal (although in principle a premenstrual girl may participate; see also A. Petrović 1939, 79).

Milena welcomes me as a cohort, cleared as ritually clean and eligible for the practice of conjuring. Thereby I become part of the informal sisterhood of five or six bajalice residing in three adjacent villages who carry out their work semiclandestinely. Although everyone knows about conjuring, it is rarely discussed openly. Small-scale private business is authorized by the government, but conjuring is a different category of enterprise. Payment is in goods or services; cash is inappropriate. A bajalica's following is based on referral. People know whom to seek for a particular problem. Patients exercise caution, nevertheless, and maintain the attitude that it is best to be prudent and to refrain from conversation about the bajalica and especially about the texts of the basma she composes. One never knows where the evil eye may lurk, spying on proceedings and deflecting them from their intended outcome.

An intriguing cognitive issue is that of the extremely long elapsed time between the period when young females might learn the components of a charm and the point at which they can begin to use this knowledge. For example, a premenstrual young girl may learn frames for a particular charm from an older woman, perhaps a grandmother or great-aunt in her household of origin, but probably would not practice conjuring while her elderly female kin were alive and capable. Or she may hear charms while she is an older girl living at home. A bride might learn from female agnates in her new husband's household. In neither of the latter two instances may she practice conjuring until much later on, when she is ritually clean. For most women, therefore, there is a span of some thirty-five to forty years during which the semantic content and prosodic features may be stored in the mind until the individuals are of appropriate age. During this substantial period a female may be present at or accidentally overhear variations on charms and, at an older age, may selectively recall or forget some sections or elaborate on other. Certain conjurers are more skilled at recollection and others at embellishment. There is no formal text. In an oral culture a charm, in whatever form, is fresh and meaningful each time it is uttered. Each variant is "the charm" on the occasion of its use (Lord 1968, 101).

A healing charm may even be a part of a bride's dowry. My "lane neighbor" Draga tells me how her mother passed one on to her before she moved into her husband's family's house. Draga says, "My mother urged me, "Take it, it will be good for you to have. You can use it as a *sevap* [Turkish for good deed]." So that's how I received it." She adds, "And now I can use it." she received the charm twenty-eight years ago.

Metaphoric Mother Figures

In addition to age-mate Milena and neighbor Draga, my teachers are Baba Vuka and Desanka. Baba Vuka knows about curing distresses as varied as jaundice and impotence. Desanka, who lives over the crest of the vineyard slope, conjures cures for problems brought on by "the nine winds." Draga is skilled in alleviating pain. This evening Milena and I are about to embark on a first session for curing colic. She says, "We go out to the edge of the field when it gets dark. You'll see. *They* [the men in my household] won't worry about you."

A Cure for Colic

Milena's son is a "guest-worker" in Switzerland. He sent a letter complaining that his infant son kept him up all night fretting and crying, and he had trouble doing his job without adequate sleep. Milena is literate, though barely. Carefully she wrote with pencil on pages torn from an old copybook, instructing her son and daughter-in-law in the correct procedure for curing the baby. The first step, she tells me, was for them to find an old woman they could trust. The next was to go out to the edge of a field when it started getting dark, with the old women carrying the infant, and to find a pat of dried cow dung. Then she gave step-by-step instructions for the surrogate mother and wrote out a version of the words of the charm. She explains to me that it seemed strange to write the basma: "I never saw the words. I only hear them in my mind."

The son wrote back that they could find an old woman easily enough, and even coach her in the Serbian words she was to say, but the plan failed because they could not find any dung. "What to do? Milena asks, shrugging her shoulders and sighing deeply. "I told them to put up with the wretched crying until they came home on vacation, and I'd take care of it myself." Holding both hands out in a gesture of frustration she asks rhetorically, "What can you do when there's not a splat of manure in all of Switzerland!"

At twilight the daughter-in-law comes out of the sleeping room with the finicky baby. Milena tells me I am *k'o bajagi majka,* the pretend mother. The infant, swaddled in a Swiss baby blanket decorated with nursery figures of elves and white-spotted mushrooms, is handed over to me. The weary young mother trails behind as Milena with a flashlight and I with the infant make our way to the edge of her husband's pastureland about a half-kilometer distant, to where the lights of Mladenovac can be seen flickering a fair distance across the darkening panorama. Milena tells me to shift the baby to my left arm and removes from her apron pocket a small round yeast cake, which she hands to me. She instructs me to step firmly onto a dung patty (no dearth of them here) and position myself in the direction of the lights. She teaches me her charm in a series of assonating couplets, with this repeated chorus:

> So we thank you all very much.
> For inviting little Marko to your celebration.
> Since he is not able to attend,
> We are sending this cake in his stead.

Now I am to heave the cake as far toward the lights as I can, trying not to lose my balance as one of my heels skids through the dung crust and sinks into the soft center. Then Milena and I repeat the charm twice and softly call out a refrain in unison three times, *"Plač i kolač"* ["the cry and the cake"]. The words for fretful cry and the rounded cake form a rhyming doublet. The cake replicates the dung patty in shape and consistency, with hard crust and soft center. The one representing power is the dung; it comes directly from a cow, a vital milk-giving, nourishing mother. The baby's mother stands by, scratching her arms. She is anxious. The substitute mother, grounded on the dung cake (and thereby also a surrogate Earth Mother?), becomes an extension of that other nourishing mother and the trajectory through which the real cake[4] is sent off, along with the discarded cry. The transference is enhanced by the strength of the acoustical collocation of the doublet. The process is followed on the next two evenings, in keeping with the folk aesthetic about performing rituals three times three.

Shortly thereafter Milena sends word that the baby is "peaceful" and so are her son and daughter-in-law. The next time we meet she nudges her face toward mine and whispers, "*Ej,* now you know how."

Jaundice

Radisav, a village-born young man who works in the Fiat assembly plant in the regional capital and who, unlike peasants, has medical insurance, comes home to the village on sick leave. He looks peaked. His skin is sallow and his eyeballs have a yellow cast. "*Žutica* [jaundice]," his grand-mother diagnoses and directs him, "Go see old Vuka. She knows what to do." Radisav is on medication issued at the factory clinic. He reasons that if the old way and the new both help, how can he go wrong? Together we trek out to Baba Vuka's, making our way slowly across the fields, he straining and wearing his grandfather's straw hat to shield him from the mid-afternoon sun.

Baba Vuka, hunched over her walking stick, raises her eyes to Radisav briefly and signals him to lie down on her bed and rest. She puts down her stick and takes up the distaff propped against her kitchen wall. A fluff of carded wool is strapped to the face of the spinning-board. Deftly she tucks the handle into her left waistband. Hooking her left arm around it, and bringing her hand forward, with left thumb and forefinger she pulls out a strand of wool, twisting and strengthening it with spittle. Simultaneously she winds up the newly created strand on a simple wooden spindle held in her right hand and rotated at the wrist. As she spins she walks slowly about the low-ceilinged dirt-floored kitchen, tell-ing me where to find dried chamomile flowers and a mug to make tea, where to fetch the onion skins and rose hips she is going to need next.

The required length of wool is spun. She breaks it off, laying the strand across her worn oaken table. She measures it into four equal lengths, breaks them, and shows me how to join the ends by twisting and more spit. We make woolen loops. Radisav is attended with tea and lulling, shushing sounds, as though he were a small child, while I cook up dyes in battered pots saved expressly for the purpose. The onion skins make a yellow dye and the rose hips a pleasing red. We dye two of the wool circlets yellow and two red. Baba Vuka lifts them out with a stick. Droplets of dye spatter the dirt floor as the loops are carried out and laid on the grass to dry.

Radisav is moved outside and made comfortable on a pallet stuffed with dry cornhusks. Baba Vuka bends over him, still crooning, and slips a yellow circlet onto each of his wrists. She tell me to take the red circlets and place them on branches of the red rosebush in the yard.

The sun goes down. Baba Vuka, in her seventies, is tired. She eases herself onto her three-legged milking stool, passes her hands over her face and begins to mutter a charm in which she, the consummate care-giving mother, equates red with ruddiness and health and yellow with lack of health, to be passed out of Radisav's body like urine and re-placed by rosiness. Baba Vuka turns to face her patient. She intones the second and third renditions, given power by the repetitions of her hiss-ing sibilants:

Yellow, yellow, pass out of Radisav and disappear.
Disappear into the earth!
Disappear under a stone!
You have no place here!
Red, red, jump onto Radisav and stay.
Come back from your journey!
Come back to this place!
This is where you belong!

The sound contours and flexible ornamentation each of the times she utters the charm imbue the colored cords with a life of their own. I do not remember removing or replacing them. Radisav and I return on the following two afternoons. At the end of the three-day period the yellow cords are left on his wrists to remain until they wear off, and the red ones are removed from the rosebush and burned. Radisav continues taking his pills for a few more days but not until they are used up. His eyeballs and skin lose their yellow hue. He stays in the village until his sick leave is over, feeling more robust and using the time to help his father mow hay and build haystacks. "Which medicine do you think worked?" he asks with a grin. "You know, it's nice to lie down, have someone bring you tea, and fuss over you."

To me Baba Vuka says, when I repeat Radisav's question, "What does he mean, 'which medicine worked?' The words, daughter-in-law, the words. That's the strength."

A Case of Impotence

Baba Vuka says she wants to pass her knowledge to me since "women in the village who are 'clean' aren't interested the way you are." Her great-granddaughter, twelve, comes to summon me one day. Baba Vuka tells both of us unceremoniously, with a wave of her stick, "Just go sit over there and watch. Pay attention and be quiet." We obey, the great-granddaughter and I. We sit on a striped rag rug spread on the grass. (It is dangerous to sit directly on grass or on the ground because mysterious disease-bearing forces can enter the body and cause trouble. This I have been well schooled in, having raised three children in the village.) From beneath the folds of her faded black kerchief Baba Vuka gives me a significant look and lays a forefinger alongside her nose, signaling for silence. A man is approaching, first stopping to scrape mud from the soles of his rubber sandals.

"Good day, Mother," he says. "Good day, *sinko,*" she replies, using the diminutive form for son. Chronologically they are within ten years of each other's age, and this artificial mother/son dyad is his way of acknowledging her as symbolic mother. Baba Vuka invites her patient to sit down on a sheepskin she spreads on the packed earth surface in a corner of her courtyard. She draws a circle around him on the ground, marking it with white string, one end overlapping the other. This completed, she steps into the circle and shakily seats herself next to him. At first I think this is a symbolic earth-womb she has outlined. As the intervention unfolds I come to speculate that what I am observing is a modern day uroborus into which are placed male and female, positive and negative primordial elements (cf. Neumann 1972, 18–19). I wonder if this configuration is my imagination, coincidence, or an atavistic vestige that has filtered down to an old woman in a Serbian village over millennia.

The man's problem is impotence. For several years he has been philandering with a local widow. Village gossip has it that he was able to perform sexually with the widow but not with his wife, and that the wife attributed the problem to his advancing years. The story goes that the widow had visited Baba Vuka and asked her to "fix it" so that the man would have an erection with her only and remain impotent with his own wife. Eventually the wife herself sought Baba Vuka to implore her to reverse the situation. The result was that the man consistently became impotent. This unfortunate scenario had unfolded in the course of our previous field visit; since local goings-on are public knowledge, people joked about it with sympathetic mirth.

This time the man comes to Baba Vuka. With an attitude of earnestness and respect, he tells this specially empowered mother that he is a reformed man who now wants nothing more than to satisfy his wife. Baba Vuka replies equally earnestly that because he is doing the right thing, all will go well.

He listens and nods gravely. Baba Vuka takes hold of his elbow, supporting it with her hand, and alternately flexes and extends his arm, uttering words I cannot discern and concluding with a ritual closure I have heard her use on other occasions. She calls on the wolf, that denizen of the underworld, to be her co-mediator. With a play on words that equates "speaking out" with "responsibility" (as in English), she ends the charm with a near-rhyme (rep/lek) in which the trouble passes through the wolf and is banished, and her speaking out is the ultimate cure. Her magical words augment a hypnotic ebb and flow while she manipulates the man's forearm like a symbolic penis. A source of particularized power is that Baba Vuka's name pairs the twin forces for resolution—Vuka is the feminine form of the proper name Wolf (Vuk).[5] At the market that Friday I observed the wife confide to a friend, "*Ovoliko!* This big!" using more than a bit of hyperbole as she joins thumbs and forefingers to delineate a circumference.

"The Red Wind"

For a decade I have been studying Desanka's charms. Her ability to conjure fantasy worlds and introduce them into real worlds has been reported in detail (Kerewsky-Halpern and Foley 1978a). On this visit I am particularly interested in her skills with animal mother metaphors. She uses these to banish the common skin infection erysipelas. Unlike the situation with Baba Vuka's treatment for jaundice, where red is the healthy color to be reinstated, in Desanka's conjuring to dispel erysipelas red represents the disease—the hard, red, inflamed skin lesion to be banished. She accomplishes this by recollecting or inventing animal mother metaphors, in which red animal mothers provide their red young with red nourishment in the unknown world of *otud* ("from out there"), where such redness (erysipelas) is appropriate. In the real world, *tu* ("here"), red is undesirable, and so she extends the paradigm to include herself, a nonred mother who nurtures her red (ill) patient with nonred charm nourishment. Here is the age-old opposition of good over evil in which strength of her nonred mediation is victorious over the red illness, and the trouble is cured.[6] One of Desanka's favorite mother metaphors is a red mother hen:

From out there comes a red hen,	*Otud ide crven kvočka,*
She leads nine red chicks.	*Vode devet crvenih pilića.*
She fell upon a red dung heap,	*Pokupiše crveni bunjak,*
And gathered up red worms.	*Pikupiše crveni crvići.*

Using similar prosodic elements, including the established but loosely fixed trope, and verb tense switches (present tense in the first couplet and archaic aorist in the second), she creates animal mother frames about a red cow who gives birth to a red calf, a red sow with red piglets, a red ewe with a red lamb. In these she elaborates on suckling as nurturance, a feature not possible with her mother hen. The special strength of the hen frame, which is the mother metaphor she usually starts off with is phonological patternings based on rhyming palatalizations.

Desanka's charms for banishing erysipelas through the agency of her red mother metaphors are enhanced by her purification refrain, in which she appeals to the forces of disorder to heed her intercession and leave her patient "light as a feather" (here she waves a feather), "pure as silver" (she holds up a silver-colored coin), and "gentle as mother's milk" (she cups her hands under her breasts). The last gesture is reminiscent of representations of Minoan goddesses. Along with the charm she applies sensible nostrums, often with motions matching the cadence of her recitation. She cleanses the infected area with home-brewed plum brandy, an all-purpose highly effective village disinfectant, seals the lesion with a pharmacologically apt camphor-based balm she prepares in advance, and bandages the area with sterile rags. The infection begins to subside after the ritually prescribed days of treatment, and her reputation is maintained. People from town come to see her too, despite their ease in obtaining manufactured ointments. They say her calming voice, the confidence she engenders, and her gentle touch are more attractive than waiting on a bench to be seen at the clinic in town (Kerewsky-Halpern 1985).

Aches and Pains

Frequently piercing shrieks are heard coming from the direction of Draga's house. Sometimes I stop in the lane and listen. If the timing seems right, I drop by to observe. Draga has a busy practice treating

reuma, a colloquialism for aches and pains that may include rheuma-
tism, arthritis, bursitis, sciatica, and general muscle aches. She pre-
scribes bed rest. She massages aching joints with a warming aromatic
unguent made from beeswax mixed with pulverized spearmint and incense. For painful knee joints a favorite treatment is cabbage leaves
soaked in brine, an effective compress to draw out the swelling and pain.
The aspirin Draga sometimes administers is brought to her in large
quantities by a daughter who works in Stuttgart (Draga says Bayer is
best because it is German). Before a treatment Draga exorcises the pain
with a charm that curses the nine ill winds responsible for bringing it.
She ends each stanza by emitting a series of shrieks exhorting the winds
to retreat and be gone. Her performance is dramatic and confident. It
appears to heighten the patient's predisposition toward a positive outcome (see also J. D. Frank 1961, 53).

I strain to catch the words Draga whispers as her voice gets progres-
sively hoarser and lower after each shriek series. I cannot make out all
the words. One day I simply ask her to tell me what she says. She laughs
and explains that she says "what comes into my head (*ono što mi uidje u
glavi*).[7] She walks me to the edge of the pigsty marking the boundary of
her husband's property and says, "Well, I say something like this, but
I'm not going to shriek truly for you at the end":

Over the hill a pure mother,	*Preko brda bistra majka,*
Escorting nine industrious young girls,	*Prati devet vrednih devojaka,*
Carrying nine stout brooms	*Nose devel dobrih metala,*
To brush away the nine ills.	*Da izbrišu devet boljki.*
Nine evils, nine evils, nine cats, nine winds,	*Devet zlica, devet mica, devet vetrova,*
Brushed,	*Brisaše,*
Brushed off,	*Odbrisaše,*
Brushed away . . .	*Izbrisaše . . .*
I curse the nine ills! Retreat! Retreat! Retreat! Retreat!	*Ja uk'nem devet boljki! Stuk! Stuk! Stuk! Stuk!*

This charm, retaining the prosody with introductory present tense and
verb of banishment in the aorist, is faithful to other mother metaphor
structures. What is new is that the mother figure Draga conjures is not an
invented mother from the netherworld, but a mother who is from this
world, in fact from just over the hill. By using the adjective "pure" (not a

usual modifier of mother), she appears to be summoning the Holy Virgin. This is an epithet Draga has created, for in ordinary speech the Virgin is always referred to as "Mother of God (*Bogorodica*)" (see Herzfeld 1986, 110, for the Virgin in another guise in a charm from Crete). Thus Draga is calling upon a nonmythic, ultimate, clean, and familiar mother assisted by a bevy of nine equally clean girls. They are of particular interest as they are meant to be very young girls (*devojčiče*), but Draga uses instead the term for maidens, which allows the pleasing tones of the old-fashioned genitive plural ending (*devojaka*) to assonate with a similar type of ending for brooms (*metala*). Her aural acuity stimulates her selection of words. The "*Stuk!*" shrieks are achieved with expulsion sounds, /s/ followed by a loud, slow /u/ enunciated deep within the oral cavity, combining to form a forceful sensory and physical emission.

In Serbian folklore, as elsewhere, brooms are associated with witches. In this instance they are introduced as instruments of purification. In local folk curing, brooms or brushes are often placed under an ill person to protect against witches (P. Ž. Petrović 1970, 202), and Draga extends their function as ordinary and commonplace tools for cleansing.

Explanatory Approaches

From these selected vignettes of healing rituals it is clear that mother metaphors take many forms. The metaphors connect the semantic networks interwoven in states of illness and healing identified by Kleinman (1980, 364): "cognitive categories, personal experiences, physiological states, and social relationships." The bajalica herself becomes a caring mother. Baba Vuka turns herself into an archetypal Great Mother. The healer may enlist the aid of a surrogate mother, as in Milena's banishment of crying from a colicky baby. The bajalica can marshal an array of recollected oral metaphors or invent new ones that "sound right." She can call on her womanly skills to prepare requisite ritual trappings, as in Baba Vuka's colored wool circlets spun on her own distaff (the origin of the expression "the distaff side"). Milena bakes an unadorned version of the same kolač she normally prepares for a saint's day feast; Draga is concerned with brooms, with brushing out and brushing away related to everyday connotations of household (women's) work and rendering clean.

Baba Vuka, the eldest of my mentors, often opens an incantation by summoning an ancient litany of winds: "*Aloviti, viloviti, orloviti, šaro-viti, plikoviti, ...*" Usually she recollects these winds formulaically, with their spellbinding rhythm of alternating initial vowels and conso-nants and the repetitious lulling endings. According to an archaic classifi-catory system most villagers no longer remember, the terms represent characteristics of disease-bearing winds—biting, sprightly, soaring, capri-cious, gusty. Baba Vuka herself cannot recall the full magical catalog, and I hear her complete the list to nine with the names of colored winds matched to specific ills. The color terms lack the acoustical power of the old ones. (As illustrated above, the erysipelas Desanka treats so effec-tively with her red mother metaphors is "the red wind.")

By initiating a charm with the droning, hypnotic sounds of the ancient inventory, Baba Vuka's success is well under way. The patient, seated on a low bench or a ground cover or if bed-ridden, lying very close to her as she bends and sways to the rhythm of her incantations, visibly begins to nod off and slip into an altered state of consciousness when the recitation is barely launched. The unconscious mind takes over as the bajalica proceeds to conjure the metaphors needed to banish the prob-lem. Sometimes Baba Vuka brings her patient back to a state of alert-ness by reverse counting: "From nine, eight; from eight, seven; . . . from two, one; and from one, not one!" This kind of inversion often marks the end of a session by effecting closure, reducing something to nothing and returning the patient to a conscious state. The parallel with techniques in hypnosis is obvious.

Conjuring is always done after noon, when the sun begins its down-ward journey across the sky, a descent that is felt to carry off with it the disease or disorder. Milena waits until dusk because she needs the lights in the distant town as symbols of the party to which she banishes the cry. Despite flexibility and innovation in the oral creativity of the charms, an invariable rule is that a charm is repeated three times on each of three successive days. In ritual interventions that are part of Serbian folk healing, power resides in acts performed three times three. The number nine appears time and again, in the nine winds, the nine maidens, the nine brooms, and the reverse counting starting with nine. The power of nine matches a system prevalent in many cultures throughout antiquity and later into the Middle Ages.[8] Villagers today tell me that the three on which nine is founded stands for the Father, the Son, and the Holy Ghost, and that three times three is *kako treba,* the only possible right way. Conceptualization of the worth of three times three antedates Christianity and is yet another example of contemporary villagers func-tioning according to rules from the collective past.

The mandatory three days allows for patient/practitioner
"child") bonding, the trust relationship on which effective tr\
founded. Concurrently, the temporal dimension may encoura\
tion of psychological stress and an opportunity for physiological\
to begin. It has been established, for example, that biochemic\
cesses mediated between mind and body respond to forms of syn\uolic
healing (Dow 1986, 59; Prince 1982, 409–423). Endogenous substances
like endorphins release to act as pain reducers. Serotonins are neuro-
chemical tranquilizers. Field observations (of course without claim to
clinical testing) appear to confirm that the three-day series of sessions
generally induces in the patient a feeling of serenity conducive to further
positive biochemical response.

The use of mother metaphors for ensuring well-being is a widespread
phenomenon with an ancient history and an abundance of expressive
forms (Neumann 1972). Their preponderance suggests a universality in
recurring themes as a kind of underlying structure in symbolic healing
systems (Dow 1986, 56). The mother metaphors created by the bajalice
of Šumadija from their immediate life experiences and recent and
mythic pasts and their special inheritance of oral artistry combine to lend
strength to a system grounded in aural affect and visual perception. The
visual aspect is the bajalica as symbolic mother, going about her ordinary and ritual tasks right there next to the patient in whatever variant
she chooses to assume or perhaps assigns to another woman.

The sounds and meanings of the oral mother metaphors evoke mental
imageries. From out there comes the red hen, her chicks clustered about
her, pecking and scratching for worms. Just over the hill, the same hill
villagers climb to go to market, comes the pure mother and all the maidens with their sturdy brooms. The images are three-dimensional; everyone can picture them instantly. These associations function in consonance
with the real, the visual ones. There is evidence that seeing and "imaging"
share many neural processes (Finke 1986, 88–89), and the skills of the
Serbian bajalica thus facilitate mutual metaphor reinforcement.[9]

The oral metaphors are in effect miniature tales, and the taleteller's
competence in associating sounds and imageries is similar to that of the
trained psychotherapist. Baba Vuka, Desanka, and the others have
much in common with healing techniques of the acclaimed hypno-
therapist Milton Erickson, who employed embedded metaphors, star-
tling shifts from conscious to unconscious levels, creative word play, and
instructive tales to effect both direct and indirect suggestion. The "scram-
bling" and reframing methods by which these techniques are introduced
into a healing session are identical to those of the bajalica (Rosen 1982).

At the heart of this verbal mastery, whether by innovative hypno-therapist or rural folk healer, is the power of sound. In healing the most effective sound is that which is articulated in alternate ways: novel, creative, and monotonous-repetitious.[10]

What is new in psychotherapeutic approaches in our own society turns out to be analogous to the oral tradition "right way" long known in rural Serbia. Women and men in the healing professions have a nourishing mothering model in the person of the kerchiefed village bajalica.

Notes

Continuity in research is thanks largely to the friendship of villagers among whom we have lived and to ongoing cooperation with the Faculty of Ethnology of the University of Belgrade and the Serbian Academy of Sciences, with support over the years from the National Science Foundation, the National Endowment for the Humanities, and the International Research and Exhanges Board, all appreciatively acknowledged.

1. It has been suggested that these ritual roles are features carried over from polytheistic times and maintained into the present due to the more conservative nature of women (as compared to men) in nurturing ancient beliefs (P. Ž. Petrović 1970, 16, my translation; his use of "nurturing" is worth noting in this context).
2. The main language of Yugoslavia is Serbo-Croatian. Throughout rural Serbia people generally refer to their language as Serbian.
3. Derivation is made from the Indo-European form *bhā-* (Pokorny 1969, 105–106). In some parts of the English-speaking world a cognate is the term "banns," an oral announcement.
4. Similar round ritual cakes, adorned with sprigs of basil, an apple, a candle, and female symbols in addition to later religious symbols, are prepared by ritually clean women for the patron saint's feastday and at Christmas.
5. For "wolf" she uses the archaic term *kurjak*. See Kerewsky-Halpern and Foley 1978, 917–918, for analysis of this closure frame in another healing intervention.
6. In an instructional book for psychotherapists, a section called "Building Your Metaphor" diagrams an isomorphic paradigm that parallels precisely what is going on here. Desanka's ancient charm could have been the prototype for that contemporary therapeutic model (Gordon 1978, 40–41, cf, diagram in Kerewsky-Halpern and Foley 1978, 921–922).

7. This is reminiscent of a comment on oral process related to me years ago by another bajalica:

> *Što, ovaj, upamtim, ja upamtim.*
> *Što ne upamtim ja sasnim noći*
> (Well, what I recollect, I recollect.
> What I don't recollect, I dream [up] in the night.)

8. Cf. the Old English "Nine Herbs Charm" (Dobbie 1942, 119–121).
9. Some of the outstanding Serbian *guslari,* or singers of epic tales, were blind, "seeing" every minute detail of a hero's garments or a steed's trappings and reinterpreting them orally.
10. Commenting on Erickson's originality and attention to detail, Margaret Mead contrasts those features with the nature of monotonous tones in hypnosis. She describes an incident in which a repeating tape of Erickson droning "Go sound, SOUND asleep" caused the secretaries trying to transcribe it to go into trance (Mead 1978, 4).

PART THREE
Women as Ritual Specialists

The three chapters in this section are life histories of women who are ritual practitioners. Yongsu's Mother, in Kendall's paper, is a Korean shaman or *mansin,* a female ritual practitioner who through possession by powerful gods reverses the misfortunes of the living. Kendall's analysis draws attention to an aspect of healers' lives that is made more accessible by life history than by sociological interpretation: how healers retrospectively construct their past experiences into both personally and culturally acceptable pathways to the sacred specialist role. Yongsu's Mother's personal history is filled with disharmonious domestic relationships, primarily with her affinal kin. It is through reliving the painful details of these past sufferings, termed the "lunatic season" by Kendall, that Yongsu's Mother justifies and explains, for herself and to her listeners, whether clients or anthropologist, why she was destined to become a shaman. It is through the repeating of these personal narratives, sometimes contradictory in detail but consistent in theme, that Yongsu's Mother makes at once a cultural and a personal statement. Although her experiences are unique, they are intelligible to others who share her social and symbolic worlds (for a more extensive discussion of how possession integrates the personal and the cultural, see Obeyesekere 1977).

Kendall does not claim that Yongsu's Mother represents the "typical" mansin. Neither is establishing the representativeness of the ritual practitioner the objective of singer and Garcia in their chapter on the Puerto Rican *espiritista* Marta de Jesus, or of Green in his chapter on the Xhosa diviner-medium Thoko. Representativeness is an issue for commentators on the life history as method, who have concerned themselves with, among other issues, how well life history material informs us about whether an individual is typical of or deviates from prevailing cultural norms (Crapanzano 1984; Langness 1965). But as Geiger (1986) has pointed out, a feminist response to this concern argues that it begs the question of how much we know about prevailing cultural norms to begin with. Insofar as traditional social science research has failed to "encompass women's experiences and perceptions" (Geiger 1986, 337), we can say little about cultural norms without repeating received distortions. In this light women's life histories at a minimum bring to view new ethnographic detail and at a maximum correct existing misinterpretations.

Kendall makes explicit in her text the subjective agendas of the ritual practitioner as narrator and the anthropologist as recorder. Singer and Garcia also call to the foreground the narrator/recorder relationship, though their comment is set apart from the text in an endnote. Here we learn that the espiritista has collaborated with the authors in the telling of her own story by having reviewed and slightly revised an earlier version of the manuscript. In both chapters, the disclosure of the relationship between the subject and author reduces representativeness to a moot issue. The healer may or may not be representative of an ideal type. What is important is that the healer's story be told in a form meaningful to the healer herself. Defining their relationship with their informant enables the authors to accomplish this requirement as far as is possible within the limits of the life history genre.

In their narrative, Singer and Garcia trace the development of the espiritista through both the "extraordinary and ordinary, exceptional and common" aspects of being a woman in a social context in which men are dominant. They present the ordinary side of Marta's life by recounting events, relationships, and aspects of her childhood and adulthood that she feels to be significant but that are also common to many poor Puerto Rican women in U.S. cities. These include poverty, family disruption during childhood and marital discord later in life, and discrimination in employment and other encounters in the wider society. But they also emphasize Marta's idiosyncratic responses to these modal experiences, responses of an extraordinary kind that included first an involuntary and later a deliberate turning toward spiritism. Through interweaving both the common and the unusual parts of Marta's life, and by further placing these in the context of Puerto Rican and U.S. ethnic and gender relations, Singer and Garcia make accessible the personal and the cultural significance embodied in the role of the espiritista.

In relating the personal history of the apprentice *sangoma* Thoko, Green explores a mix of hypotheses to explain the predominance of women as diviner-mediums in the modern political, economic, and social context of South Africa. The functionalist interpretation of possession cults as "cults of affliction," most notably articulated by Lewis

(1971, 1986), is one of these. Green notes that Thoko's sense of deprivation may have been intensified because of her nursing education and her exposure to people socially and economically better off than she. Lewis, too, maintains that spirit possession seems to correspond closely with circumstances in which women's aspirations expand at a greater rate than their actual options, circumstances particularly characteristic of development in the Third World (Lewis 1986, 112; see also Hafkin and Bay 1976; Leacock and Safa 1986). Like Marta de Jesus, Thoko is doubly deprived, by the traditional gender relations of the indigenous culture and by the ethnic and gender oppression of the hegemonic culture. Diviner-mediumship is an avenue for escaping, if partially, the stresses that impinge most heavily on women experiencing the burdens of both worlds.

Green puts forward an alternative explanation for Thoko's sangoma apprenticeship, which, although not incompatible with the functionalist interpretation of possession cults, redirects the analytic focus to individual motivation. To the extent that all cultural actors can be viewed as strategic decision makers, Thoko, in this capacity, selected diviner-mediumship as the best possible "career choice" for herself. On the surface, such practicality may seem incongruous with the remarkably consistent pattern of recruitment to the sacred role found in many cultures, in which individuals destined to become ritual healers suffer grave and lengthy illnesses and experience dramatic visions that precede, sometimes by years, their conscious pursuit of ritual healing (Eliade 1946; L. Paul 1978b). At first glance, such prolonged and involuntary suffering would suggest that strategic planning plays little part in recruitment to the sacred role. But as Green points out, however practical the decision to become a ritual healer may be, it does not require that individuals reject or question deeply held cultural values and explanations that make ritual healing meaningful. This would include reinterpreting past events and experiences as culturally appropriate preludes to the status of ritual specialist.

The authors in this section transcend the functionalist explanation of possession as a conduit for women to protest their subordinate status and escape from gender role confines. They make accessible through life history the personal and shared meanings underlying misfortunes in general, and those of women in particular. They make clearer the relationship between what individuals do and the social and cultural patterns and variations that result from combined individual action. The creative as well as the limiting dimensions of culture become more apparent in the process.

Old Ghosts and Ungrateful Children:
A Korean Shaman's Story

In this chapter, a Korean shaman, a female healer, tells two autobiographical tales and an anthropologist describes the ethnographic context in which these tales were told. Through her tales, the shaman presents ancestral affliction as a lived experience with both social and ritual implications. She musters evidence from her remembered past to validate her understanding of present suffering much as she would probe her clients' past during a divination session. This two-tiered presentation—of tales and the telling of tales—illuminates dynamic notions of cause and effect, of affliction and curing that the shaman and her clients hold in common but realize as personal history. The account also suggests how the shaman uses biographical information, mediated through her knowledge of gods and ancestors, to heal.

Garbed in the red robes of an antique general or wielding the Spirit Warrior's broadsword as she drives malevolent forces from her path, the Korean *mansin* claims an imposing presence. Even in everyday dress and sprawling comfortably on the heated floor of her own home, she speaks with authority. By virtue of the powerful gods who possess her, she can summon up divination visions and probe the source of a client's misfortunes, exorcise the sick and the chronically unlucky, remove ill humors from those who have difficulty finding mates, and coax a reluctant birth spirit into an infertile womb. The professional shaman makes the gods and ancestors a vivid presence in the home; she spots them in her visions and gives them voice in trance. In *kut,* her most elaborate ritual, she garbs herself in their costumes and, in their person, scolds, banters, advises, and commiserates with the mortal members of household and community. Most Korean mansin are women and they minister most immediately to a female clientele. The few men who claim the shaman's powers perform in women's clothing, down to the long silken pantaloons that they wear under their slips.

There is logic, or at least convenience, in the shaman's gender, since women are the ones who represent their households at the shaman's shrine when they suspect that angry gods or restless ancestors are the root cause of serious or prolonged misfortune. Their visits to the shrine are an extension of other sacred duties. Within the home, women make offerings to the household gods (*kosa*) and, although men conduct the formal rites of ancestor worship (*chesa*), women deal with the restless and potentially dangerous dead. Despite this complementarity in the religious functions of shaman and housewife, Korea is a society where, traditionally, "good women stay home." Among moralists who invoke Korea's Confucian tradition, the mansin is disdained as a woman who sings and dances in public and demands cash in the name of greedy spirits. The mansin, for their part, emphatically distinguish their performances from those of equally important female entertainers (*kisaeng*). Both in her calling and in each appearance of the ever-demanding spirits, the mansin is compelled by the gods and ancestors who possess her. No woman claims to have willfully embarked upon this career. Rather, the gods torment the destined shaman with visions, voices, mysterious illnesses, and general ill luck. A "god-descended" woman and her family may deny the signs, but only for so long; those who resist the calling die the deaths of crazy women whose thwarted destinies yield ominous ghosts. But once a woman is initiated as a mansin, the spirits that tormented her become allies who send her divination visions and the power to cure. As in other societies where shamans practice, there are some doubters among the populace and many skeptics. Thus in retrospect, the mansin's suffering as a god-descended person, her emphatic but ultimately futile efforts to resist, and the tales of that lunatic season, told and retold throughout her career, testify to the power and authority of her gods and the sincerity of her calling. Once she has been initiated, clients will visit her, initially out of curiosity but subsequently for the accuracy of her divination visions, the efficacy of her rituals, and the perceptiveness of her advice (Kendall 1985).

The anthropological literature is replete with examples of women who engage in ecstatic religious practices, often uncountenanced by the ideologies that men codify. A common interpretive theme threads through the ethnography of women and spirit possession, a theme that has been synthesized and most boldly stated in the work of Lewis (1966, 1969). Lewis contends that women everywhere use possession trance as a means of getting back, of claiming power and prerogatives otherwise denied them. This theory can be but gingerly applied to the Korean mansin. Analyzing mansin biographies, Harvey does interpret the experience of divine calling as a reaction against constraints imposed upon Korean women by Korean families. Possession propelled these women out of stressful domestic situations and into reasonably satisfying careers as practicing shamans. Moreover, in telling of their lives the women retain a profound sense of having been wronged as women, as daughters, wives, and daughters-in-law (Harvey 1979, 1980). This theme will also emerge in the tales recounted below. There is, however, a wrinkle in the easy linkage of spirit possession and women's oppression. The Korean shaman is fundamentally different from the possession cult devotees that Lewis describes, women who, though they may manipulate possession for their own ends, are generally perceived to be the passive vehicles of the spirits. The ritual activities in which women attain personal satisfaction are often orchestrated by a male priest or holy man (Lewis 1966, 1971). By contrast, the Korean shaman is a recognized professional practitioner who, ministering to the afflictions of client households and communities, uses her powers for socially beneficial ends. Harvey's informants attained something more than a vague catharsis; indeed, the professional status of the mansin is crucial to Harvey's analysis. She describes the mansin as extraordinarily intelligent, articulate, perceptive women who apply these talents to the shaman role and thereby make a good livelihood (Harvey 1979, 235–240; 1980). If the Korean case seems to contradict received scholarly wisdom concerning what Lewis calls "the sexual bias of the spirits" (Lewis 1966, 309), it is not unique. Other ethnographic examples suggest that women can be the acknowledged custodians of various sacred attributes even when they are denied a public voice and secular prerogatives (cf. Bell 1983; Falk and Gross 1980; Lebra 1966).

As I have suggested, the Korean mansin's role is consistent with and complementary to the religious life of ordinary Korean housewives. Although these activities exist outside the Confucian sphere of patriarchal ideology and male-enacted rites, women and their rituals are not at odds with men and their goals. Shaman and housewife subscribe to the common values of a Confucian society. Children should respect their elders, elders should be benevolent and understanding, the living should honor the ancestors with appropriate rituals, sons should be born, and parents should live to a ripe old age, having seen their children successfully married and established in life. This is often not the case, however, and shamans provide not only explanations but therapies (Kendall 1985).

In 1976, I went to Korea to investigate the ritual activities of women and female shamans (mansin). Early in my research, I was introduced to a vivacious and witty mansin, Yongsu's Mother, who became my teacher and confidante. With few exceptions, I spent some portion of each day that I was in the field in Yongsu's Mother's company, either accompanying her to rituals in client households or observing divination sessions and minor rituals in her own home. I would often ask her to clarify points or answer the multitude of questions that had occurred to me while I transcribed my most recent batch of field notes. Yongsu's Mother loves to talk and has the knack of a gifted storyteller; her language is clear and fluid, accompanied by graphic gestures and tragicomic expressions. The book that I eventually wrote is better for her sharp observations and her sense of humor.

Because I was more immediately interested in what shamans do than in who they are, I did not initially seek a detailed account of Yongsu's Mother's life. Nevertheless, in our many discussions Yongsu's Mother would often use bits and pieces of her own experience to illustrate a point: why she unfailingly makes a mountain pilgrimage or scrupulously honors the death anniversary of her husband's first wife. Her accounts were vivid and entertaining, sometimes melodramatic, and often humorous. Sensing my growing interest and curiosity, it was Yongsu's Mother who seized the initiative, announcing that she would give me the full story of her life, "so that when you read it in your own country, your tears will flow." True to her word, she told her stories gradually, over the next year, sometimes providing me with several accounts of the same incident. Undoubtedly, I was the most consistently engaged audience that she had yet enjoyed, and the spinning cassettes on my tape recorder vested her performance with a new aura of significance. I soon realized, however, that I was not the only beneficiary of Yongsu's Mother's stories. She tells her life to edify her clients (as she would edify me) and to entertain her casual quests (as I was entertained). I heard most of her stories in both public and private renderings. As a professional shaman, she makes cautionary tales of the auspicious and inauspicious circumstances that have befallen her, her family, neighbors, and clients. With the force of personal history, she illustrates the power of a particular god, the baleful force of ancestral anger, or the danger of a ritual lapse. As a woman among women she seeks sympathy for the misfortunes and cruelties that she has experienced and wonder at the evident hand of the gods in her destiny. Like all autobiography, Yongsu's Mother's tales are necessarily subjective, often exaggerated and sometimes contradictory. They gain in ethnographic value precisely because she has told and retold them to clients and neighbors for a variety of personal and cultural reasons.

Social scientists have long recognized the value of personal histories in rendering comprehensible the life and times of men and women in different cultural and historical circumstances. Because of their narrative form and intrinsic human interest, life histories are perhaps more easily consumed (and enjoyed) than other forms of ethnographic writing, and as near-primary documents, they have enduring scholarly value (Davis, Black, and MacLean 1977; FWPWPA 1975 [1939]; Kluckhohn 1945; Langness 1965; Langness and Frank 1981). Nevertheless, contemporary anthropologists have suggested that there is something dishonest, or at least distorted, in the business of recording an informant's life history in the field. They argue that, at worst, life material is forced into the ethnographer's a priori (and Western) notion of biography or overdetermined by the ethnographer's categories of inquiry (Crapanzano 1977, 22; Crapanzano 1984; Dwyer 1982; Little 1980; R. Rosaldo 1976). They remind us that the truth of an informant's life history, like autobiographical truth, is shaped by the circumstances of the telling, and that memory and self-presentation are selective and sometimes self-contradictory processes (Crapanzano 1980; cf. Boaz 1943, 334–335; G. Frank 1979; Langness and Frank 1981). We have only recently begun to ask why it is that people tell about their lives and how it is that they fashion the tales that they tell (J. Berger 1981; Crapanzano 1980, 1984; Obeyesekere 1981; Zempleni 1977).

To appreciate the social and spiritual dimensions of a Korean Shaman's life as it is lived among neighbors and clients and realized in events and conversations, I am presenting Yongsu's Mother in her own words and setting. Rather than presenting a racing overview of her career, I shall describe a specific set of circumstances that evoked a specific set of tales and a ritual response.[1] The ethnographic present is a rapidly modernizing Korean village on the periphery of Seoul in the autumn of 1977.

It was the tenth lunar month, November by the Western calendar. The harvest had been gathered in, the farmer could rest, it was again the mansin's busy season. Clients would come to mansins' inner rooms, sit on the hot floor, and receive divinations; some clients would sponsor kut, and some would call the mansin to sing kosa invocations when the family honored the household gods with rice-cake offerings made of the newly harvested grain (Kendall 1985, 114–121). But Yongsu's Mother sat at home; business was off. No one called her to preside at a kosa, no one tapped on the door seeking a divination, and three regular customers canceled scheduled kut, even after she had pulled out her charts and found them lucky days to match their horoscopes. She heard later that one of these women has held her kut with another mansin. A year ago, Yongsu's Mother had spent the entire tenth month going hither and yon to kosa and kut, and just last month she had been busy. Her present inactivity was strange, ominous, and Yongsu's Mother was worried. "My fortune is blocked [*uni maegyŏtta*]." She was sleeping badly and brooding.

When she thought about it, her luck had not been good since her stepdaughter's wedding, not since she had given *yŏt'am* offerings of wedding feast food and cloth to the ancestors in her shrine to settle and appease them lest they follow the bride and bring ominous influences to her new home. Yongsu's Mother was particularly wary of her own dead husband and his first wife, the ancestral shades of the bride's parents. Because Yongsu's Mother is a shaman and holds numerous spirits in her shrine, she felt obliged to hold a particularly lavish and expensive yŏt'am, and called on one of her colleagues to assist her. Instead of offering the customary scrap of a handkerchief that most of her clients provided, she had given her dead husband lengths of silky synthetic fabric for spirit clothes. Yongsu's Mother grumbled about this, though with a touch of pride, as she itemized her laments over the cost and bother of marrying off a daughter. But even after making such a good show of the yŏt'am, something had gone terribly wrong.

Like the women who seek her services, she considered her present misfortune so unusual, so inexplicable as to suggest supernatural causation. Like her clients, she substantiated her hunch by tracing the onset of her misfortune to a ritual event, and like her clients, she sought out another mansin who could give her a divination. At a break in a kut that they were performing together, Yongsu's Mother told her troubles to the apprentice mansin, Okkyong's Mother, who confirmed Yongsu's Mother's fears with a vision of something aqua-blue that had been brought to the house. The vision was not surprising, the diagnosis common; meddlesome ghosts often ride into the house on cloth, clothing, or bright objects (Kendall 1985, 101).

On the day after her divination, Okkyong's Mother called on Yongsu's Mother while I was visiting and determined that the inauspicious piece of cloth was somewhere in the inner room. Yongsu's Mother unlocked her large wardrobe cabinet and fished through the clothing piled within. She drew out a white Korean blouse and long aqua skirt and threw them to the floor with a vehement curse.

This must be it, the only aqua clothing in the chest, the Korean dress she had purchased for her eldest stepdaughter. Yongsu's Mother was angry. She spoke quickly. The whole family should wear new clothes in the wedding hall, and she had bought this because she had known that this was beyond her eldest stepdaughter's means. The woman had thanked her for the gift, but she had never come to take the dress away. Yongsu's Mother said, "I'll take it to the outhouse." Okkyong's Mother mentioned throwing salt and chanting. I was confused, and curious.

After Okkyong's Mother left, Yongsu's Mother continued to mutter, "It must be that. The dress and the cloth are the only new things that have come in." And then she announced in a loud voice, "I'm going out to take a piss." She carried the dress, still in the dressmaker's plastic bag, out with her, but returned with her arms full of laundry. She had left the bag behind.

I asked her what was going on, and she told me how Okkyong's Mother had seen a vision of aqua-blue clothing, how she had thought it was the cloth for her husband, and how she could not fathom her stepdaughter's having left the dress behind, "That fucking woman! Why is she such a slut? Last year I went to so many kosa, and now . . ."

"What happened?"

"A restless spirit is active."

"Which one?"

"An *ancestral* restless spirit." (Didn't the anthropologist understand that much?)

"Which ancestor?"

"That woman's mother, of course. It's because she died young."

Yongsu's Mother told me that she had "thrown the dress away in the outhouse," and giggled. This was a feint to put off the troublesome shade. Later, she asked me to bring the bag and its contents back inside. She had set them inside the shed but a safe distance from the foul pit. She washed her face and feet, performed an exorcism, and then we took the bag to the market and sought out the eldest stepdaughter. She was not at her usual place among the hawkers of rice cake, but Yongsu's Mother recognized a woman from the stepdaughter's village. She handed the bag over, asked the woman to deliver it, then walked away with a decisive step and an air of having settled something.

The stepdaughter's oversight was probably a rebuke; she would not accept her young stepmother's charity. The two women, never on good terms, had mustered a brave show of cordiality for the younger step-daughter's wedding, but I had been thoroughly informed of Yongsu's Mother's many tribulations as a stepmother and of her profound dislike for her eldest stepdaughter. In recent years, the stepdaughter had encouraged her brother to run away, telling him: "That woman isn't your mother. She's just your stepmother (*somo*), so why should you stay with her?" Yongsu's Mother smarts at this remembered injustice, claims that she nursed the little boy at her own breast, that he had always thought of her as his own mother, that he had never really known otherwise. "Why should that one come and and tell him these things to make him run away?"

For more than a year, she had refused to let the first son come home. "I was so mad, I told him, 'I took your shit and piss and raised you as though you were my own son, but you said that I was just a stepmother, and left.' He cried and cried and said that he wanted to see his mother so much he could die. Now he comes by and hangs around." The stepdaughter, possibly anticipating her younger sister's inevitable marriage and the major role that Yongsu's Mother would be expected to play, also asked her for forgiveness.

Yongsu's Mother claims that the woman approached her in the market saying, "Mother, forgive me, I'm so sorry, I didn't know what I was doing." But this did not keep Yongsu's Mother from having her say: "I went to your family and I raised you all. I didn't do you any wrong, but you ran away and caused your father to die of drink ['How he drank!' she interpolates in the retelling, 'He smashed all the plates in the cabinet and bashed in the door.'] What do you mean by coming over and telling your brother to run away? What right have you to return to your natal home?" The stepdaughter promised to visit during the New Year holiday and pay her respects, but Yongsu's Mother told her not to come. What if she started encouraging Yongsu, her own child, to run away? "There's no use in raising other people's children," was Yongsu's Mother's summation. "If you do ten things right and make just one mistake, they say you've done badly by them because you're just a stepmother."

The eldest stepdaughter made trouble almost from the beginning of Yongsu's Mother's married life, and this story, told to the anthropologist to win sympathy, was told and retold to women who visited the house in the winter of Yongsu's Mother's bad luck.

At first, Okhwa and I shared the housework. She cooked when I did the housework and when I cooked, she did the housework. She was twenty-one years old then. I was married on the nineteenth day of the last [lunar] month, and on the fifteenth day of the New Year, they celebrated the end of the mourning period in the main house [the *k'ŭnjip,* the senior brother or uncle's household]. I pressed my husband's formal jacket and he told the daughter, You go on ahead and help them out."[2] When I got to the main house, Okhwa wasn't there. I said, "This is strange, she went out early." When my husband arrived, she was still missing. "Where did they say she's gone?" "She hasn't even been here."

He said, "I'll go back home and look for her; you stay here." I stayed and helped in the kitchen and he went back home but then neither he nor the daughter returned. He hadn't returned by evening when they set up for the chesa offering to the ancestors. Finally, my husband arrived. I asked, "Was Okhwa there?" She wasn't. The other children had seen her leave the house carrying a big white bundle. The men were doing their chesa bows, but this gentleman, my husband, just stood at the side staring off into space. His soul had taken flight. Until that time, no maiden in the Yun family had ever run away. They were so concerned with proper behavior that in the past the women couldn't even go outside the big gate; no matter how hot it was, they could only mope around inside. It was a disgrace for the daughter of such a *yangban*[3] house to run away. From that moment, my husband seemed to go crazy. . . .

By the time I arrived back home, he was up to his neck in liquor. [She raises her eyebrows.] He was so drunk he didn't even recognize me. I went into the kitchen and started to light the fire, but he accosted me, "Who are you? What do you mean by coming into someone else's kitchen and lighting the fire?" He was that far gone. I was dumbfounded. Good grief, his pockets were stuffed with *soju* bottles. I stood by, speechless, while he kicked in the door and broke the one forlorn little shrimp-paste dish in the empty cabinet. He lambasted me and pissed, shhh, shhh, like that, all night. He didn't know what he was doing, he couldn't tell one thing from another. And all night, I went back and forth between crying, and trying to reason with him, and crying some more.

At dawn, my senior sister-in-law came over with the nieces and nephews. Having been reviled all night, I was so relieved to see her that I ran outside in my bare feet and cried on her shoulder. Even if it was the death of me, I could not go on living in that house! I had never said a harsh word to Okhwa, what did she mean by running away? Since she'd taken off, it was unendurable to stay there. My husband had drunk all the bottles of soju that were in his pockets. When I counted them, there were sixteen bottles. He'd drunk them all down, so what could one expect? He was shivering and shaking, his chest was heaving, his face was drained and white, he kept saying, "I'm so cold, I'm so cold." . . .

We took him to the hospital and he had an injection. They told me to watch out for him because if he kept on behaving this way, it would be the end of him. I said, "Do you really think he'd stop drinking on my account?"

The very next morning, just as it was getting light, he went out again. He came back drunk and announced that he was going to throw himself in the river and drown. All the nephews and nephews' wives, all the grandchildren tried to hold him back so that he couldn't throw himself into the river. He was living on liquor. But then sometimes he was very subdued; he wouldn't say much at all. Sometimes he would just sit with a glazed look on his face. He was so ashamed because in all the Yun family there had never been a daughter who had run away like Okhwa. He was tense, always anticipating people's talk, the gossip that a daughter of the Yun family had run away.

When he wasn't drunk, he'd say that he had done me a great wrong in bringing me to his house and making me suffer these hardships. "What's the use?" he would say, "I brought you here to satisfy my own needs, and now my daughter's gone." But even as he said these things, he'd get all worked up about it and start drinking again, and soon enough the drinking broke his health.

After he'd gone on drinking like that for a few years, didn't that wretch of a daughter come back! Words can't express [her brazenness]. I said, "When you see the state your father's in, you'll really regret what you've done." He was cutting weeds in the rice field when someone told him, "Your daughter's here." He ran to the house, waving his knife and shouting, "I'm going to kill her!" He was about to strike but I grabbed the knife and ran out of the room with it. . . . The senior mother said, "This fucking woman, he'd just begun to settle down again, and now she's come back and caused all this commotion."

After three years of marriage, I was finally able to go and visit my own family. While I was back in Willow Market, I received a letter from the senior mother saying that Okhwa couldn't stand it at home any longer and had gone off again. If they mentioned this to the father of my children, he'd fly off and say he was going to kill her. The senior mother had sent me Okhwa's address and I went right off to find her; I didn't even take the time to eat breakfast.

I saw Okhwa strolling alongh the path with a baby on her back. "What baby is this?" I asked. She was a maid-of-all-work and the baby belonged to her employers. I told her, "I'm not going to say anything more about it. Either you come with me or you don't and that's that. Your father is sick and there's nothing that can be done to change it."

Okhwa said, "I'll go with you even if it's the death of me. I'll go with you, Mother, and you can marry me off to anyone you choose, even to a common laborer."

And here the story breaks off. Having related all of Okhwa's infractions, Yongsu's Mother tells her audience in a low but emphatic voice, "That woman raised the wind, she fooled around." This is Yongsu's Mother's story; Okhwa would undoubtedly tell a different tale, perhaps of a wicked stepmother who drove her out of the house.

Okhwa did have a respectable wedding. The family photo album holds a portrait of Okhwa masked in white bride's makeup with red dots on her cheeks and forehead. She looks glum but this tells us nothing, for brides in those days were not supposed to smile. To highlight her later difficulties in single-handedly planning the younger stepdaughter's wedding, Yongsu's Mother once conjured an image of herself and her husband cozily discussing Okhwa's wedding preparations across their common sleeping pallet. I noted, at the time, that this picture jarred with her usual portrayal of her short and fractious married life.

Throughout the winter of her discontent, Yongsu's Mother grumbled about her stepchildren. Clients came to see her, but now her health was bad.[4] She had "used her nerves so much" over the younger stepdaughter's wedding, and then, in the thick of things, her stepson had an attack of acute appendicitis and she rushed off to Seoul to spend several days nursing him with yet more worry, more bother, more expense. And inevitably, when she launched into this topic, some long or short fragment of the story of her eldest stepdaughter would tumble out. The younger stepchildren had worn her down, she had "used her nerves," worried, fretted, brooded, and this was the cause of the diarrhea and indigestion that plagued her all January. More generally, stepchildren are nothing but trouble, which led her to the story of the one who ran away and drove her own father to drink. But how was the eldest stepdaughter responsible for Yongsu's Mother's professional dry season? How was the intrusion of the first wife's shade in any sense the stepdaughter's fault? The connection appears in another of Yongsu's Mother's stories, one she told me in bits and pieces to illustrate the power of restless ancestors. She related it at length to pass the time that winter, and yet again in the summer of 1983 on the night of the first wife's chesa.

I saw her when my husband was sick, no, even before he was sick. It was when I first married into that house. Every night, a woman with a child on her back would come and sit on the porch just outside the inner room. Since I was newly married, what did I know about these things? She was always there, sitting on the porch. I thought, "This isn't a good dream." You see, it was my husband's first wife who was sitting there on the porch.

Then my husband was sick and my stepson was sick. The boy was her son, wasn't he? If the father wasn't sick, the son was sick, and if the son wasn't sick, the father was sick. We did exorcisms [*p'uda-kkŏri*] and more exorcisms and then kut. When the stepson was five years old he caught the measles. The red blemishes came out and blossomed, but they didn't go away. They're supposed to go away. The boy's fever was over 40 degrees [Centigrade; 104 degrees Fahrenheit]. Such a frightening fever! He was a ball of fire.

We took him to the hospital and they have him an injection. It seemed as though the fever was going down bit by bit. But then the next day, the senior mother and father had a look at him and said he was dying. . . . I went to the boy's father and I said, "We've gone to the hospital and that didn't work. I want to go somewhere and see if I can get a divination." The boy's father jumped up, "He's all but dead already, and you say you're going for a divination. We don't do that sort of thing here." I told him not to be so stubborn, but he would't let me go.

The senior mother went to him and said, "Brother-in-law, don't be this way when your child's on the brink of death. Won't you do anything possible to save him? Let her go and try."

I went, and the shaman said we should clean up the measles' influences (*hongyok subi*). I went back and told my husband, but he just said, "What beggar's talk is this?" I was young. What did I know? I went to the senior mother.

"What shall we do?"

"What did the shaman say?"

"She says that if we do an exorcism, the boy will live. It's because of his mother's death. There are [inauspicious] things that must be cast away."

My husband said, "This is stupid talk, the boy's all but dead, what do you mean by saying that you want to hold an exorcism?" But the senior mother coaxed him and I coaxed him, and then we set up two offering trays and I set out the exorcism rice, some vegetables, and the wine. The shaman sat there with a winnowing basket, the kind they used to use. She sat on the veranda chanting a little bit of something, and scratching the basket. . . .

"What foolishness was that?" What was the point of it?"

"Husband, we've spent the money, and now it's done. We did it so that even if the boy dies, there won't be any resentment. (His soul won't carry a grudge since we've done everything we can for him.)"

We'd brought it off, and that night the child slept. But how could I sleep? I was so anxious. At dawn the child mumbled something, "Mother, let me have some water." I brought in some boiled water and gave him a spoonful. He'd swallowed a spoonful of water. He hadn't died.

I knew that I wouldn't be able to sleep, so I told my husband, "You watch the child. I'm going to fix the rice." He was still sleepy. [She yawns in the telling.] He was surprised that I would think of fixing breakfast so early in the morning. I was cooking the rice when he called me back in. "The boy's asking for something." He wanted more water. By that time, the rice was boiling away. I took some of the rice water, put in some sugar, and took it to him saying, "Here, try this." He drank about half a cup and I said, "Well, this kid's going to live." I felt ill at ease, though. I was glad that the child would live, but it was strange. [And she describes how she nursed the child back to health, carrying him on her back to the doctor for a daily injection.]

The boy lived and got better, but then his father got sick. He had nightmares. He was exhausted. He took Chinese medicine, but his digestion was always off so he took medicine (*wijangyak*) for that. One night we were sleeping with the baby on the warm spot, then me, then my husband. All of a sudden and still in his sleep, my husband raised his fist and struck the floor. I was startled. I woke up and asked him what he meant my pounding the floor with his fist. He said "Don't think badly of me."

"Badly of you?"

"Okhwa's mother, my dead wife, came into the room."

I was here, and my husband was there, and she came right in between us. He had yelled, "Vile woman!" and tried to strike her.

He had flailed at her and flailed at her, but his fist just struck the floor.[5]

I said, "This is strange. This is no ordinary dream. I often dream of a woman with a child on her back who sits on the porch. I feel uneasy when I have these dreams."

He said, "Can a dead person come back to life? Don't fret over it," but his condition went from bad to worse. He went to the hospital. Our senior cousin's wife went to a *posal* [inspirational diviner], who said to do an exorcism. I asked his permission and went to the posal's house, but even though we held an exorcism, my husband's health did not improve.

He went from bad to worse. We would try this hospital and then try that hospital. At one place they would say his digestion was bad. At another place, they would say it was his liver. At still another, it was his bowels. They'd say this here and they'd say that there. You think that wasn't frustrating? And he just got worse and worse. My husband's stomach was bloated way out to here. We went to a Chinese doctor for a pulse reading, and they said he had to take his medicine diligently. Just one tablet was expensive, but still he took it, and that seemed to make him even worse. The senior mother told me not to give him any more of that medicine.

Then we went to Seoul, to some big hospital way out to the east of the city. What was the name of that place? At that hospital, they said his problem was parasites! I thought, "If he takes the least bit of food, he runs to the outhouse. Parasites aren't like that. I don't think that's what it is." Next I took him to my old home in Willow Market. There was a hospital for Chinese medicine (Hanyak) nearby where they read his pulse every day and gave him herbal tonics. The doctor in charge said, "This is difficult, very difficult to cure." So then didn't my children's father ask for a kut!

We held the kut in my mother's house. My mother sold a pig that she had been raising. On the day of the kut, my husband sat up and said, "I think I'm going to live." We did the kut and I thought to myself that he seemed better, but the next day he was even worse. The senior father and mother and the nieces and nephews came and took him to the university hospital in Seoul. At the hospital, they said that it was all because he had drunk so much, and they said that he would have to stay in the hospital.

He was so sick. What could I do? My two-year-old Yongsu was still nursing at my breast, so I took him on my back and went to tend to my husband in the hospital. There I was, nursing my baby, and I fell asleep. Didn't that woman come back again! That ghost (*kwisin*) came right into the hospital with her baby on her back.

It was the sixth day of the fifth month, her chesa day. Of course since we were at the hospital we hadn't held a chesa for her. She said, "I've come to eat."

"What do you mean, 'Come to eat?' We haven't fixed any rice."

"I'm going to stay right here. I'm going to the kitchen to get the rice measure." She went to the kitchen and came back in again.

In my dream, I had some of the sweet cake we call "Costella bread." I had some of that sweet cake in my hand and was about to eat it when I thought to myself, "Why should I eat this? I should give it to the patient." I went over to my husband and said, "Dear, here's some cake. You'll take some won't you? It's that Costella bread that you like so much. Try a little, won't you?"

"Cake?"

"Yes, have some. You have to eat and gather your strength."

He reached up for it, but that woman snatched it away. She said, "No! I'm going to take it away and eat it," and grabbed the cake just as my husband reached for it. [In another version of the story, when the dead first wife returns from the kitchen with the rice scoop, the ailing husband wakes suddenly, screams, and turns his face to the wall.]

I was startled awake. I was muttering to myself, "Such a strange, strange dream. Why should that woman come all the way to the hospital like that?" . . . He brushed it off, but even in the hospital, his health got worse. He went back to the hospital on the sixth day of the second [lunar] month but by the fourteenth day of the fourth month, they said that they could not cure him, and he came back home. After five nights at home, he died at four in the morning. After he died, I never again saw that woman in a dream. She had come to take her husband away with her. That woman took him away.

To corroborate this accusation, she told me the story of her sister-in-law's dream on Yongsu's Mother's wedding night.

They kept me up past midnight on my wedding night bowing to all the relatives. I was so exhausted I could have died. One of my sisters-in-law kept dozing off because it was so late. My sister-in-law dreamed that it was summer. Why should it be summer? I had married in the last month of the year. [In her dream] the whole front courtyard was in flames, so high that no one could get through it. But there, in the midst of the fire, was someone clearing a path through the flames with the big broadsword we use in kut. The dead woman was clearing a path from the front gate, the flames rose up on both sides of her. My sister-in-law called out to her, "You should cut down all the flames. Why are you just making a path?"

I was sitting in the inner room with all the grandfathers' [gods' and ancestors'] costumes on a line above my head, the way we hang them at a kut. Rice and vegetables [offerings] had been set out, and I was sitting there hitting the hour-glass drum [like a shaman]. [The dead woman said], "What does your new sister-in-law think she's doing, this bride who has just come to her husband's house? Day and night, she just eats and hits the hour-glass drum. The cucumbers have all ripened in the field. Even though they're spoiling, she neither pickles them nor sets them to soak in brine. She just hits the drum."

My sister-in-law said, "Elder sister-in-law, please take care of things."

"Me? Why should I do that for her? Younger sister-in-law, you gather up the cucumbers and set them to soak."

"How can I do that? What if the new elder sister-in-law who arrived yesterday makes a fuss?"

"No, she won't."

My younger brother-in-law shook his wife awake, "Dear, dear, what were you dreaming?" and my sister-in-law saw that it was a dream. That woman came to take her husband away with her. She had even cleared a path. I married very badly.

Her closing comment ties together the stories she told in her winter doldrums. She married badly because she married into a house with an ominous restless ancestor, a dead first wife who returned to claim her husband. She married badly because she was married to an impoverished older man, was burdened with ungrateful stepchildren, and was soon widowed. She married badly because a stepdaughter's transgressions drove the mortified husband to destructive drinking. In Yongu's Mother's world, stepchildren tend to misbehave, elderly widowers tend to predecease their wives, and dead first wives vent jealousy and spite (Kendall 1984). Okhawa ran away, and her father drank himself to death in shame; the dead wife returned, cleared a path, and carried her husband away. The stories are not contradictory; their common end result, Yongsu's Mother's early widowhood, is the most dire conse-quence of her having "married badly," a fusion of social and spiritual circumstances.

The remembered, retold, and possibly remolded past casts its shadow on Yongsu's Mother's present. Her tales make sense of experience; how things came to be this way, why things continue to be this way, and how one might deal with adversity. The eldest stepdaughter refused to accept her gift of a holiday dress, a slight and not intentional sorcery, but the stepdaughter's ill-humored act drew in the dead first wife's restless spirit and precipitated Yongsu's Mother's season of ill luck. Yongsu's Mother was vexed with her stepdaughter for both past and present infractions and for, however unwittingly, stirring up the dead first wife, Yongsu's Mother's old nemesis, the most salient symbol of her disappointing mar-riage. In Yongsu's Mother's world, it is perfectly logical that a spiteful stepdaughter should act in concert with a dead mother. These are com-mon complaints among Yongsu's Mother's clients. Although Yongsu's Mother has never (in my hearings) attributed Okhwa's early "raising the wind" to her mother's influence, she frequently blames a dead first wife for the unruliness of a client's stepchild and the jealousy of a dead first wife for illness or death of a client's husband (Kendall 1984).[6]

In her own adversity, memory confirmed suspicion and justified com-plaint. Yongsu's Mother could again deal with her old adversary and cast out the ghost with a pelting of course grain and the slashing of a kitchen knife. But though she can hold the dead first wife at bay, she is stuck with this old ghost, just as she is stuck with her ungrateful step-children. With the stepdaughter's wedding and the stepson's appen-dectomy, her stepchildren had worn her down, both financially and emotionally. They were also responsible, indirectly, for the depletion of her spiritual resources. The tales "explain" on several levels: why busi-ness was off and Yongsu's Mother indisposed, why she continued to suffer the consequences of her bad marriage, and more generally, how it is that the dead impinge upon human destiny.

The spiritual traditions that shaman and housewife share are realized in the stories they tell each other—of the grandmother who prayed on a sacred mountain, the brother who was killed during the war, or the aunt who should have been initiated as a shaman but died a raving lunatic. From such histories come the ancestors and gods that hold a particularly marked presence in the pantheons of shaman and client households. The stories women tell in consultation with a shaman are both familiar and varied, just as every client family's history is both typical and unique and every kut is an improvisational drama wherein the client household's own particular gods and ancestors say their piece within an established ritual frame.

As propitiators of household gods and placators of restless ancestors and ghosts, women are the primary custodians of these traditions and stories. As a female practitioner among women, the shamen must divine the source of her client's affliction—conjure a vision of "someone who died young, dripping blood," "someone who prayed on the mountain," "someone who was the same sort of person I am"—and extract the story that confirms her diagnosis.[7] Where the conjured symbol is shared, deemed consistent with client memory and with more general notions of supernatural causation, then the propitiation of old ghosts and angry gods can take place. As a woman among women, a professional shaman, and a gifted storyteller, Yongsu's Mother offers her own life in affirmation of some common assumptions: the meddling of the dead, the ingratitude of stepchildren, and the outrageousness of fortune.

Notes

This paper was originally prepared for a symposium held in memory of Youngsook Kim Harvey and owes its inspiration to her work, both to her anthology of six shaman lives (Harvey 1979, 1980) and to her professional interest in the use of biographical material in the social sciences.

My research in Korean in 1977 and 1978 was supported by the Korean-American Educational Commission (Fulbright), the Social Science Research Council, and the National Science Foundation. A grant from the Eppley Foundation for Research made it possible for me to return to Korea in 1985 to collect additional life history material. Some of the material contained in this paper appears in my book, *The Life and Hard Times of a Korean Shaman: Of Tales and Telling of Tales* (Honolulu, 1988) and appears here with the generous permission of University of Hawaii Press.

1. For a complete rendering of her story, see Kendall (n.d.).
2. Although men perform the chesa, the day of an ancestral offering is particularly onerous for the women of the family, who must prepare the offering food and the feast that will be served to all of the assembled family members.
3. In Korea, only the members of yangban lineages were eligible to take the civil service examinations and hold public office. Those who claimed yangban ancestors constituted the local elite and saw themselves as the exemplars of Confucian social virtues.

4. For an account of how Yongsu's Mother dealt with her health problems, see Kendall (n.d.).

5. In 1985, she told me this story yet again, but in this version, her husband was too ashamed to tell the young wife of his dream. She heard about it later from a senior sister-in-law who described how the dead wife had puckered her lips for a kiss.

6. Husbands' first wives appeared in seven of the twenty-five kut that I observed and recorded in 1977 and 1978. More than a quarter of the women who sponsored a kut had joined widowers' households and now dealt with ghostly first wives. I also noted five village households where, during the period of my field study, shamans exorcised the baleful influences of dead first wives (Kendall 1984, 222).

7. For a description of the specifics of shaman divination in Korea see Kendall 1985, 71–79. Note Yongsu's Mother's horror at the idea of a mother who allowed her married daughter to live overseas without first giving her necessary information about the family ghosts (Kendall 1985, 73).

MERRILL SINGER and ROBERTO GARCIA

Becoming a Puerto Rican Espiritista: Life History of a Female Healer

In their cross-cultural discussion of the role of women, Hammond and Jablow (1976) analyze the importance of women's participation in religio-therapeutic cults focused on trance-possession experiences. Following Lewis (1971), these writers interpret the prominent place of women in these cults in terms of women's "exclusion from the mainstream of religious life, and probably from other aspects of social participation as well" (Hammond and Jablow 1976, 125). According to Hammond and Jablow, the cults serve as avenues for the expression of resentment and the ventilation of hostility borne of sexual oppression in the wider society.

Other writers have similarly discussed the ways in which religio-therapeutic cults serve to palliate structurally imposed suffering and oppression (Baer 1981; Crapanzano 1973). In addition, however, these cultic phenomena may help to create opportunities for some of their members that would otherwise be unattainable. As Finkler (1981, 494; see also Lawless 1983) has argued: "while women may initially gravitate to the movement because of lack of power in society, or because of afflictions, or because females predominate in the movement, a number of such women subsequently are able to covert their powerlessness or affliction to authority and to transfer any influence they may possess in the private sector to the public sphere."

This chapter examines the life of one such woman. Her name is Marta de Jesus, and she is the founder and leading practitioner in a Puerto Rican spiritist center in Hartford, Connecticut. Utilizing life history materials, this essay will explore how she has skillfully used the healer role as a vehicle to overcome numerous hardships and challenge both dominant and subcultural constaints on women.

Marta is the type of "extraordinary and ordinary; exceptional and common" Puerto Rican woman that Hidalgo and Hidalgo Christensen (1979) have described. Although she grew up in a relatively poor family that was subject to racial discrimination, had a father who was an alcoholic and two siblings who were heroin users, dropped out of school in the eighth grade, acquired only limited ability to read and write, was married to one man who beat her and another who is now in prison, and along the way had five children, Marta has used her role as a spiritist healer as a route to social achievement, public recognition, and self-assertion—in short, as a pathway to a degree of social power. As the *madrina* (godmother) of an active and growing *centro de espiritismo* (spiritist healing center), Marta has attracted a following of several dozen spiritist trainees, both male and female, and a large clientele in the Puerto Rican community and beyond. In this position, she possesses a level of authority unusual for a woman of her background. She has been able to use this position, moreover, as a base from which to advocate for her community. Thus Marta's case illustrates the importance of the healer role as a culturally constituted avenue for social mobility for women in otherwise male-dominated social settings.

A brief discussion of the history, beliefs, and practices of Espiritismo (spiritism) will be followed by a detailed life history of Marta as a folk healer and community leader in light of the social role of women in the United States generally and in the Puerto Rican community specifically. Materials for this account were collected during approximately twenty hours of life history interviewing as part of a much larger and ongoing ethnographic study of Marta's centro (Singer 1984; Singer and Borrero 1984); Singer and Garcia 1984; Garcia, de Jesus, and Singer 1987).

Espiritismo: An Overview

From the black spiritual churches of the American South (Baer 1984) to Candomble, Batuque, Umbanda, and Macumba of Brazil (Leacock and Leacock 1975); and from Mexican Espiritualismo (Finkler 1985; Kearney 1978) to Vodun in Haiti (Metraux 1959) and Santería in Cuba

(Sandoval 1979), the circum-Caribbean region supports a rich diversity of spiritist cults. These religio-therapeutic movements, primarily and traditionally centered among dominated populations, urban and rural poor, and the descendants of slaves, share a common belief in communication with and possession by an array of incorporeal spirits.

Initially spiritism (in a primarily nontherapeutic form) was embraced as a purported science of the nonmaterial world by the intellectual and social elite of France, which in the mid-nineteenth century was the center of the international intelligentsia, including the privileged classes of Latin America. Individuals from this strata, who were attracked by the progressive and inherently utopian character of this "anti-clerical, anti-catholic but profoundly Christian religion complete with revitalistic overtones" (Koss 1976, 32), brought spiritism to Puerto Rico in the 1850s and 1860s. As in other dominated countries of Latin America and the Caribbean, spiritism was at first in vogue in Puerto Rican high society, but it soon diffused to the urban poor and peasantry. These sectors "borrowed those pragmatic aspects of the system which were useful in solving daily problems of life, illness, and death. These they transmitted in the oral tradition as well as in family and neighborhood curing and cultic rituals" (Macklin 1974, 393). Through this process, spiritism was transformed from an intellectual pastime into a folk-healing system and popular religion with a diverse and dedicated following.

The focus of ritual activity in Espiritismo is the intersection between the shade world of the spirits and the material world inhabited by living people. Interaction between these two contrasting realms ranges from the marvelous to the malign. Spirits have the power to cause all manner of misfortune, including financial reversal, interpersonal conflict, physical and mental deterioration, and even death. Especially noteworthy in the realm of calamity are low-ranking spirits known as *espíritus intranquilos* (intranquil spirits). These wayward entities departed the world in a disrupted condition because the body they were in suffered an untimely death due to murder or suicide, for example, or because they failed to achieve their full spiritual potential while incarnate. Unsettled and confused, believing they are still embodied, they cling to the material world. To aid these troubled spirits in escaping from limbo, *espiritistas,* the practicing mediums of spiritism, perform special rites involving the offering of prayer, fruit, flowers, and candles. If not thereby elevated to a higher spiritual plane, these spirits may be ensnared by *brujos* (sorcerers) to serve as proximate causes of illness and misfortune.

Unlike biomedical practitioners, espiritistas "view the client's symptoms as a gift or quality" (Ruiz and Langrod 1976, 397). Consequently,

clients commonly are invited to undergo *desarrollo* (spiritual development) to cultivate their innate *facultades* (spiritual abilities) and become
mediums of the centro. Spiritual development involves the acquisition of
new degrees of power by expanding one's relations with increasingly
more potent spiritual beings. Mediums "win" a spirit by adhering to the
centro's code of behavior, serving the spirit realm (e.g., by making
offerings and saying prayers), and exhibiting proper respect to the leading medium.

Currently, Espiritismo is undergoing important changes as it comes
under the influence of the Afro-Cuban spiritist tradition known as
Santería. For Espiritismo, this syncretism involves the adoption of Yoruban deities into the highest ranks of its pantheon of possessing spirits and
the incorporation of associated rituals and music to appease these colorful
spirit personalities. The contemporary evolution of Espiritismo reflects
the versatile and adaptive character of indigenous religio-therapeutic systems as they strive to meet the changing needs and experiences of their
target populations (Press 1971; Singer and Borrero 1984). Espiritismo's
"eclectic sponge-like quality," argues Koss (1976, 43), "is perhaps its
greatest asset in the struggle to survive . . .; it seems to attach to its
system, and popularize for its adherents, whatever social and philosophical new ideas have greatest appeal to some of the more troubled segments
of Puerto Rican society."

The appeal of spiritism has provoked opposition from other religions.
As Koss (1980, 256) writes, "given [its] cosmology of the spirit world and
the denial of the role of intermediaries in one's spiritual life, it is not
surprising that the Catholic Church and many Protestant denominations
have waged war against Spiritism." Despite this opposition, Espiritismo
probably has increased in popularity in recent years, especially among
Puerto Ricans who have migrated in large numbers to New York and
other cities in the United States (Singer n.d.).

Hartford, for example, which is now the third major entry port for
Puerto Rican immigrants (after New York City and Boston), has experienced a dramatic 400–500 percent jump in its Puerto Rican population
in recent years; Puerto Ricans now make up 25–30 percent of the city's
total population (Backstrand and Schensul 1982). Recent changes in the
character of the city, including its transformation from an industrial hub
to a white-collar insurance and banking center, and the minimal level of
government or corporate efforts to provide training and assistance to the
migrants, have combined to create high rates of unemployment and
other expressions of social distress among Puerto Ricans in Hartford
(Backstrand and Schensul 1982; Meswick 1982). Further, few social

service agencies in the city have any significant number of Hispanic staff, and most indigenous agencies are underfunded and have quite limited service-delivery capacity (Schensul and Schensul 1982). Under such circumstances, it is not surprising that Espiritismo, a profoundly instrumental religion that "promises direct, immediate, day-to-day support" to its adherents (Leacock and Leacock 1975, 328), is able to attract a growing clientele.

The appeals and effectiveness of Espiritismo in providing culturally appropriate services to the Puerto Rican population have been documented by a growing number of researchers and clinicians (Comas Diaz 1981; Delgado 1977; Garrison 1977; Gaviria and Winthrop 1976, 1979; Harwood 1977; Koss 1975, 1987; Rogler and Hollingshead 1961; Ruiz 1976; Salgado 1974; Singer 1984; Singer and Borrero 1984). In making its services highly accessible and responsive to clients' needs, in maintaining minimal social distance from clients, and in creatively utilizing and adapting a shared ethnic heritage, Espiritismo has developed a socially sensitive treatment system for the many psychosocial and health problems faced by Puerto Ricans.

Marta's Life History

The following pages will examine in some detail the important phases and events in Marta's life as she traversed the road to healership, and will then describe the activities and organization of the spiritist centro Marta founded and Marta's community efforts beyond ritual healing.[1]

Earlier Generations

Marta's heritage reflects the diverse roots of the people of Puerto Rico and includes a long family involvement with Espirtismo. On her mother's side, her relatives were poor farmers of mixed Indian ancestry. Her maternal grandmother married into a wealthy Spanish family and gave birth to eighteen children. The fifth was Casimira, Marta's mother.[2]

Marta remembers her maternal grandfather fondly and believes that he was a major influence on her life: "When I was little and my parents were going to hit me, he protected me. He would curse at my father for hitting me. . . . He said we should always be proud that we were Puerto Ricans. He understood me a lot, my way of acting and my temper. He used to look at me and say I reminded him of my mother." Like their father, the children born to this side of the family were known for being high-spirited and strong-willed.

When Casimira was twelve years old, she eloped with a pharmacist named Augustín. He was from a wealthy family that disapproved of the marriage. Marta recalls that her mother

> had her first child, Nico, when she was fifteen and her second child when she was sixteen. . . . His family did not like my mother and the mother-in-law was very very strict. He used to fight with his mother because he loved my mother a lot. But his mother had power over him, she controlled him, and after a while she took him back and my mother was left with two kids. Her own mother had recently died. And then one of the children, the younger one, died too.

Over thirty years later, Marta was to marry Carlos, a son born to Augustín by a subsequent wife.

Casimira turned for comfort to a young cousin named Valeriano Vazquez, a troubled young man trying to overcome a difficult childhood. Born of an adulterous relationship, he always resented his father. When Valeriano was eight, his mother died and he went to live with an aunt, and later, after his father died, he was raised by his father's wife. In an expression of his undying anger toward his father, Valeriano took his mother's surname, de Jesus.

Casimira and Valeriano were able to acquire a small wooden house with dirt floors in the countryside, where they eked out a meager existence by farming the land. One day, Augustín came and took his daughter, Nico. Because of the wealth and social standing of Augustín's family, there was little Casimira could do. Instead, she and Valeriano began a new family of their own. Casimira bore nineteen children with Valeriano, but most did not survive infancy. Marta relates: "My mother went to a spiritual healer in Puerto Rico and they told her witchcraft had been done on her and all her children born in Puerto Rico would die; her children would only survive if she crossed water. And it was true!" The couple decided to leave the grinding poverty and tragic losses they had suffered and join the migrant flow to the United States.

Migration

The first significant migration of Puerto Ricans to the United States began in the 1920s, and the biggest push came after World War II. The postward relocation of Puerto Ricans stands as "one of the greatest exoduses registered in contemporary history" (Vasquez Calzada 1976, 224). The focus for most migrants until the 1970s was New York City, which by the early 1950s already had over two hundred thousand Puerto Rican residents (Backstrand and Schensul 1982). It was to the burgeoning Puerto Rican community in Brooklyn that Casimira and Valeriano moved in 1946. Seventy thousand of their countrymen migrated to New York the same year.

New to U.S. society and to urban life, Valeriano had great difficulty gaining employment. Unskilled and uneducated, he was only able to find manual labor. Eventually he began working as a janitor in an appliance factory. A fellow worker taught him to draft blueprints, which enabled him to be hired as a draftsman. Casimira sewed clothes to sell in the neighborhood. A few months after arriving, she gave birth to a baby girl. Over the next decade, she had five additional children, three girls, and two boys, as well as two miscarriages. The third child, a girl born in November 1950, was named Marta.

Coming of Age

Marta remembers her parents as strict disciplinarians with a strong bent for privacy. "My mother was the type of person who always stayed in her house. She would visit her family or her husband's family. In fact, she would hit us and punish us if we would go in a neighbor's house. My mother and father were very demanding of us. If we wanted water, we had to ask her. If they had company, the kids had to go to their room."

Despite Casimira's strictness, Marta felt that she was her mother's favorite. They developed a strong emotional bond.

> She used to look at me with pity. I was the black sheep. She didn't want me to get married or have kids because I had a temper. . . . She was my teacher. . . . She was like a friend. She used to protect me because I was the skinniest. No one really understood me except her. . . . I used to lock my feelings inside and I won't tell nobody but her. She was always watching over me to make sure

that I didn't lose my strength and she gave me vitamins and all kinds of teas.

But when Marta was eleven, her mother developed tuberculosis and Marta's insulated world began to crack open: "They put her in a hospital and they took us away for three months. They put us in a home, a place where they put children whose parents were sick. While I was there I changed a lot. I didn't want to be in there, so I was very bad. I used to get in a lot of trouble and fight with everybody."

In high school, Marta was seen as an incorrigible troublemaker. She used marijuana and alcohol and had a brief relationship with a boy named Carlos whom she was later to marry. During this period she began a girl's gang.

I was the head of the gang and when a new member would come in, she could challenge me and fight me. If she would win, she would be the head of the gang. . . . We were always looking for trouble. Once . . . I pulled out a knife to a lady because she hit my brother. She pulled the knife on me and I picked up a snow scraper and she dropped the knife and I took it. Then the cops came and they threw me on the floor. . . . We had to break up the gang and give up our colors because they were going to throw me out of school.

Marta today explains her early rebelliousness in terms of an increasingly unstable home environment, a situation that began when her father lost his job after the appliance factory where he worked moved out of the state. At the time, her father was in his mid-forties, and despite his efforts he was never again able to locate steady employment. At first he received unemployment benefits, but when these ran out, the de Jesus family was forced to go on welfare. This greatly embarrassed her father, who began to drink and act abusively.

A big cloud came over us and everything kept getting worse and worse in the house. This was 1964, 1965, 1966. . . . The pressure would work on him and he used to drink and then beat my mother. But my mother wouldn't hit him back. . . . I went a year and a half without speaking to my father. He would say that I wasn't his daughter. We respected our father, but he lost our respect 'cause of the way he used to treat us. He would beat me and I would curse at him. One day I couldn t take it any more and I drank 150 pills,

pills they gave my mother for her lungs. I almost died. I was in semicoma for three days. That hurt my mother a lot. When I was fifteen I did it again. I took 40 sleeping pills. When my mother couldn't take the pressure any more, she would drink too. She'd go inside the bars and take us with her. Her personality changed when she drank; she became hostile. My parents would get into fights and we had to get in between. Once they had a fight and my father moved out. My sister and brother went into drugs. My sister did it for a long time and went to jail.

Adulthood

Because of the tensions at home, Marta dropped out of school at age fifteen with only a rudimentary ability to read or write. She found an assembly-line job, the first in a long series of low-paid, labor-intensive jobs she was to hold over the next ten years. She remained at home during this period but continued to fight with her father.

My father was getting too much on my case. Sometimes, I would get dressed to go out and he would say "no." The only way to get out was to run away. When I ran away my father had my mother check to see if I was still a virgin. That got me very upset. When I left home to live with my first husband at age sixteen, I didn't even know him. I knew him only as a friend, a neighbor. His name was Hernando. One evening I went to my cousin's and Hernando wanted to ride to Philadelphia to see his father. So we drove down there but the car was leaking oil. . . . We stayed on the highway until 5:00 A.M. Since it was closer to Philadelphia than to New York, we went back to Philadelphia. I stayed with Hernando for two weeks. For three days I didn't do anything with him. Then I decided, what the hell. I started living with him. I went back to New York to get my clothes. I was pregnant, but I didn't know it. When I got to New York, the police were looking for me. When my father met Hernando, they became good friends.

Valeriano's relationship never improved with Marta, however. They had not reconciled when he died in 1971.

After a year in Philadelphia, Marta and Hernando moved to New York and he enrolled in a course to get a tractor trailor driver's license. Although he completed the course, he got a job at the airport filling gas tanks, where his new skills went unused. Eventually he lost this job because he was caught smoking. He began driving a taxi, and did this sporadically for several years. The couple had three children. By age nineteen, working and caring for her children, Marta began to feel overwhelmed.

> I wanted the first child, but not the other two. I was very young when I had the first one. When I had the second, I told the doctor I didn't want her if she was a girl. I always told God not to send me a girl because I didn't want her to suffer like I had suffered. Hernando was happy about the first two children, but for the last, it was just another baby. He had been a whole year without working after our daughter was born. We lived on welfare. Hernando had a lady friend out in the street. He didn't care about the family. Sometimes I didn't have no food for the kids.

When Marta's third child was seven months old, she went back to work in a factory and Hernando began driving a truck. With their joint income, they were able to buy a condominium. But the conflicts in their relationship began to take their toll.

> I had always thought that the lady of the house should stay at home and be respectful and the man could go out and come back when he felt like it. That's the way my mother taught us. But it was a big mistake. One day, I remember, I had twenty dollars and it was close to Father's Day. He asked me for money and I told him I didn't have any. But then I went out with the lady next door and bought him a pair of sandals and some T-shirts for Father's Day. He met me on the street and asked me where I'd been and started arguing with me. We got into a big fight, a fistfight. I took the kids and ran upstairs and he ran after me. That day I wound up with two black eyes and everything was broken in the house. After that things started changing. Before that I had to do everything in the house, even though I was working. And if he brought men home to drink, I had to get up and cook for them. He would accuse me of a lot of things, having affairs. . . . He was drinking a lot and using a lot of amphetamines and cocaine. Then one of his mistresses had a baby. . . . It got to be lady after lady, beating after beating. So it got to the point where I was just living with Hernando because of the kids. That's when I got involved with Carlos. He had been my boyfriend from when I was fifteen. My husband accused me of

being with Carlos, but I denied it. He didn't hit me then because I got a gun. I threatened him with it. The next day I left for Puerto Rico.

During this time, she decided that her relationship with Hernando was over. When she returned to New York City, she moved in with a girlfriend and later found her own apartment. But the pressures of the last several years had broken her confidence, and her self-esteem had plummeted. She began to consume alcohol, and following her parents' footsteps, quickly lost control of her drinking.

I couldn't face my family. I was very proud. So I hit the bottle. Day and night I would drink. I was three months drinking. . . . One day I left my girlfriend's house . . . and my kids had to take me home because I didn't know where I was. When the kids took me to the house, I couldn't even go up the stairs. That's how drunk I was. When I got up in the morning, the kids had gone to bed without food. That hurt me. . . . I found my youngest son sleeping next to me with his sneakers on. I said, "What am I doing? I'm ruining them and I'm ruining myself."

When Hernando found out where Marta was living, he went to her apartment and in a fit of rage threatened her with a knife. She responded by calling the police, the first time she had done so in ten years of periodic physical abuse. The police removed Hernando from the apartment. He retaliated by telling the Welfare Department that he was still supporting the children and that Marta did not need assistance. Marta was subsequently notified that she would have to attend a hearing to evaluate her application for aid. She decided not to wait for the hearing, and instead she packed her clothing and left for Hartford, where her uncle lived. Carlos, whom she had continued to see after leaving Hernando, went with her.

At this point Marta, believing that her relationship with Carlos would not last long, did not take this involvement seriously. She knew that he had serious personal problems, including a tendency to abuse alcohol and a history of arrests for burglary and drug use. Still, Marta's life was topsy-turvy, and Carlos offered support and companionship. His personal problems did not diminish, however, and ultimately contributed to the demise of their relationship.

Hartford provided a stark contrast to the life Marta had known in New York. The Puerto Rican community in Hartford was relatively new

and lacked many of the institutions and cultural amenities available in
the older, more populated Hispanic sections of New York City. The
pace of life was slower and less exciting than in the larger metropolis.
Moreover, Marta lacked the social support network that she could count
on in New York. Despite their desire to start a new life, she and Carlos
faced serious difficulties after their relocation.

> When we first came, we went through a lot. There were a lot of
> times when I had nothing to feed the kids. . . . I made friends with
> a girl named Annie. She was young and she was pregnant. One day
> it got to the point . . . where we had nothing, but nothing, to eat at
> the house. Carlos was in jail. He got arrested for assaulting a
> woman. . . . My friend had nothing for her kid either. Everybody
> that we knew was broke. My friend knew this guy and she went out
> with him and came back an hour later with twenty. I asked her
> where she got the twenty and she said she sold her body in order so
> the kids could eat. That hurt me 'cause it was for my kids too. I
> told her never to do it again. I said that I'd rather steal first. She
> said, "if they catch you for stealing the punishment is greater than
> if you lay down with a man for money."

When Carlos was released on bail, he convinced Marta to move back
to New York so he could avoid imprisonment. Marta's friend, Annie,
also came along. A small, three-room apartment in Brooklyn became
the home for ten people: Marta, Carlos, Marta's three children, Marta's
brother, Annie and her boyfriend, and Annie's two children. Marta
applied for welfare but did not receive payments for several months. In
the interim, the crowded household had no regular means of support.

> I went through hell. . . . We didn't have no food for the kids.
> Sometimes Carlos would go out and steal food. I used to get hand-
> outs. Because the welfare wasn't helping much, me, Carlos, and
> my brother went out looking for a job. I found a job working in a
> factory that made shower caps and shower curtains. . . . I started
> working on a Monday. On Tuesday, my friend Annie ran to where
> I was working and said, "Run, Marta, run. The cops are at the
> house. . . . Carlos got inside a bus to rob it and they arrested your
> brother." I ran home and they had the SWAT team there. Carlos
> had cut the bus driver. He had a knife. They arrested two of my
> brothers and my cousin but they didn't catch Carlos. But Carlos
> kept getting in trouble and things got worse. Carlos started drink-

ing heavy. He just kept drinking. And he was doing a lot of acid [LSD]. . . . I did it with him about three times, but I didn't like it because it seemed to screw up your brain.

On a visit to Hartford, Marta decided to leave New York. On August 7, 1978, she and Carlos returned to Hartford in yet another attempt to start a new life together. They moved in with Marta's cousin until they could find an apartment of their own. Marta applied for welfare, and Carlos worked briefly in the tobacco fields north of the city. Over the next several years, the couple had two children, in addition to Marta's three children from her previous marraige. A year after their return to Hartford, Carlos was rearrested on the earlier charge and imprisoned for four months. In the meantime, Marta, in a culmination of her life-long flirtation with Espiritismo, began to direct her energies into spiritual development.

Involvement with Espiritismo

As is the case for many Puerto Ricans, the beliefs and practices of Espiritismo were woven into the daily fabric of Marta's cultural experience from birth. Her mother, grandmother, and great-grandmother had all been active participants in the tradition, and her father, thought not a steady adherent, was nonetheless a believer and also a folk healer, specializing in bone setting. These relatives taught Marta about the spirit world and enculturated her into the spiritist world view.

They used to tell us stories about witches, about things they used to find. My mother used to see spirits when she was small. One day, she told us, when her grandfather died they could still see him. They would see a man on a horse. These are all stories we know because they told us about the spiritual ways. . . . My mother told me that this lady once had cursed her daughter. She told her daughter that she hoped the devil would take her. That girl started raising in the air, flying around and hitting against the bushes. Everyone started screaming. . . . The girl's godmother had to pull her down and pray. A priest sprayed the girl with holy water. They got her down, but the devil almost took her.

Beginning at age five, Marta experienced visions of the spirit world. Her initial visions were of the Yoruban deity known as Chango, the god

of fire and lightning. A central figure in the spiritual pantheon of
Santería and other Afro-Caribbean possession cults, Chango is commonly portrayed as a large black male wearing a golden crown. He is
said to be a very powerful, if somewhat playful, spirit. In Santería,
Chango is syncretized with St. Barbara, a Catholic saint. She is usually
depicted as a young girl with a golden crown. In one hand she holds a
sword and in the other a large chalice. Because both of these spiritual
beings are linked with lightning and the color red in their respective folk
traditions, Chango and St. Barbara have come to be identified as expressions of a single spirit, despite differences of age, sex, and race.

> When I was small, around five, I started seeing Chango. He came
> toward me one day while I was crying because my father beat me. I
> heard somebody telling me, "You're going to see me, don't get
> scared. I'm going to be your spiritual guide to help you." When I
> looked toward the door, I saw this black man. He was very big. I
> kept looking and I didn't get afraid. He had a lot of rings on him.
> He had a big medallion on his chest. He had a rag on and he wore a
> crown. He came toward me, but not very close. He threw some-
> thing at me. It was a litle rock and it hit me in my forehead. Then
> he disappeared. . . . When I told my mother,. . . she told me not
> to get afraid, if I got scared he would go away and not play with
> me. . . . After that day, every day I would lock myself up in my
> room after kindergarten. But he didn't come and I was very disap-
> pointed. I thought it was because I told my mommy. . . . Around
> three months later, I was standing on a bench washing dishes and I
> heard somebody laugh. When I looked, he was there. I asked him
> his name and he said Chango. . . . He would talk to me in an
> African language and I would understand what he said to me. He
> would also talk to me in Spanish and English and I would under-
> stand everything he said to me. . . . I used to see him on and off,
> every two weeks or so. Some people told me I was daydreaming,
> that it was a fantasy. But I'd say, "No, he tells me that he is my
> spiritual guide." One day when I was around nine, I had to do a
> small report and I did a report on Chango. I put, "I have a friend
> and nobody sees him but me. He brings me all kinds of colored
> rocks to play with. He takes me to the jungle and I climb on top of
> an elephant. We go all around Africa and see a lot of native peo-
> ple. This friend is named Chango." They took the report to the
> principal. A couple days later, a doctor came to the house to talk
> to me. He asked me a lot of questions . . . and I would not answer

him. I told him, "I wrote what I wrote and I see what I see and if you don't believe me, then drop dead." But I got an A on my report. I don't know how, but I did.

By the age of eight, Marta realized that she could spiritually influence events around her.

I used to wish things would happen and they would. I never wished anything like for somebody to die, but one time I wished a boy would break his leg and . . . a few hours later he did break his leg. . . . One day, I wished on my first husband that the police would lock him up and they did because of a stolen taxi he was driving. I told him that I wished the police would lock him up and . . . five minutes later the phone was ringing. He was arrested. Since then, I haven't done anything to nobody. I don't do it anymore.

Marta remembers going as a child to the spiritist center where her mother worked as a medium. The center was located in the basement of the home of its founder, a woman named Diosa who was Casimira's spiritual leader and close confidante.

The centro was called La Purísima Concepción, the Purified Conception. My mother belonged for years and years, until Diosa moved back to Puerto Rico in 1965. They were like kinfolks. They were from the same town. My mother knew her for a long time, ever since my mother was a little girl. She helped my mother . . . and fed us when we needed help. They made the service there on Friday nights. I used to go all the time and we went to other centros too. There were seven mediums including my mother and my sister and the *presidente* [Diosa]. All the places my mother took us to were *mesa blanca* [i.e., Espiritismo], not Santería. A lot of mediums came to our house. They'd bring their kids for *santiguar* [treatment for stomach problems]. But after Diosa left for Puerto Rico, my mother stopped working mesa blanca.

Marta's visions continued for several years. They became more intense and at times were accompanied by convulsions. By age fifteen, during the period of greatest conflict and disorganization within her family, these experiences began to overwhelm her: "When I was fifteen, I almost went crazy. I used to black out. I used to go into a rage, kick and bite myself. I couldn't stop it . . . because spirits used to throw me on the floor. My mother took me to a psychiatrist and the psychiatrist said I wasn't crazy, to look for spiritual help. . . . Then my mother took me to a Santero [practitioner of Santería]." The Santero ritually "sealed" Marta's *camino espiritual* (the pathway of her spiritual development), thereby removing her visions and other symptoms. He told her that these abilities would remain dormant for a period of ten years, after which, when she was emotionally mature enough to handle them, her spiritual powers would return. Although Marta continued to have periodic contact with Espiritismo during her teen years, she no longer experienced trance states. During her first marriage, Marta's participation in Espiritismo remained fairly limited because of Hernando's vehement opposition. As that relationship deteriorated and Marta asserted her independence, however, she began to get more involved in spiritist activities.

> I used to go to spiritual healers and Hernando didn't like that. He didn't want me to burn candles. He wouldn't even let me put an altar in the house. . . . But the last couple of years we lived together, I didn't pay no mind to him. . . . With Carlos, I used to speak about spiritual ways. He accepted it. Maybe that was why I got involved with him. . . . But with Hernando, I would do it without him knowing about it. The first time I passed a spirit [experienced possession] was when I was with Hernando. There was a *botánica* [religious goods store] where I would buy candles. They introduced my to a *padrino* [godfather, a leader in Santería]. He invited me to his house for a *fiesta santera* [celebration for a Yoruban diety]. He told me to dress in red and white. . . . When we got there, I stood way in the back next to the stairway. . . . The godfather went into the spiritual trance and Chango came. I got nervous. I felt a vibration in my body that I never felt before and my heart started to beat real fast. Chango's spirit appeared in the godfather and he came up and called me. He said, "The girl dressed in red and white, come forward." But I was sacred, I told him so. Then he called me by my name, "Marta come forward." I told him no. But then something strange happened because that black man that I used to play with used to call me by a name, a name that I cannot say, and that day Chango called me by that name. I had never seen Chango passing through nobody's body. Chango pointed at me and called me by that name. I went three steps back. That's the only thing I remember, I blocked it out. They tell me that I just jumped. I flew over everybody and fell

right at the feet of Chango. When I opened my eyes, they told me that I had danced, and I had passed St. Barbara. But I didn't believe nothing that was going on.

After moving to Hartford, Marta had another spiritual experience. "We were walking back from the Welfare office and we went through Bushnell Park. That was the first time I saw the fountain there. I said to Carlos, 'You know what, I seen that fountain before in my dreams.' " This dream signified to Marta that her spiritual powers were returning and that her spiritual development would take place in Hartford. From this point on, Marta's visions occurred more frequently, often foretelling future events:

I started to feel something inside me that wanted me to help people, wanted me to do something. . . . I kept having these visions and I said to myself, if I avoid it things are going to get worse and worse for me. . . . One day I saw a vision with my neighbor's little daughter where I saw her falling and breaking one of her legs. I went to her house and told her. Two days after, my neighbor came to my house crying, saying that the little girl had fallen and broken her leg. When they removed the cast, her leg looked bent. That day we just kept talking and I felt cold all of a sudden. . . . I felt this vibration all through my body and I saw this Indian lady walking in the apartment. She was very beautiful, with dark skin and long hair and she wore something covering her breasts and a little skirt and moccasins with bells. She kept coming closer to me and when she touched my forehead I blanked out. The Indian woman grabbed the leg of the girl and cleansed it. . . . When I woke up the little girl's leg was better and she was walking. After that I was positive that I was going to keep on with Espiritismo. Seeing that girl running around and playing gave me a good feeling inside me. To me it was a miracle. The doctor had told her that she was going to limp all her life and she doesn't. Two days before this happened, I had an experience at home with Carlos. He told me that I passed a spirit in my body. The spirit was bent backward and talked in a mumbling saying, "ba ba ba ba." Carlos didn't understand it. That was my *madama* [African guardian spirit]. The spirit asked for a broom and swept the whole house. Then one day, it was a Tuesday and I got up very early. I wanted to do a spiritual cleaning of the apartment before noon. After I finished cleaning, I started to feel sick. By noon that night I was admitted to the hospital. They said I

had a gall bladder attack. But something in my mind kept telling
me, "Don't operate, don't operate." I was never so sick in my life,
but the next day the pain was gone. They took a lot of X-rays.
They couldn't find anything. So they sent me home.

Following this series of events, Marta began to perform "spiritual
works." These consisted of spiritual cleansings and consultations with
her neighbors and friends who recognized and appreciated her budding
spiritual talents. Word spread and people beyond her immediate circle
began coming to her home seeking help.

I talked to Carlos about working in the house. Before I began, we
went to Puerto Rico. I felt I had to take that trip. I knew I was
going to get something, what it was I didn't know. . . . Carlos'
mother is a Santería. When we got to Puerto Rico we went to see
her. She told me, "You didn't come here because you wanted to
come but because the spirits brought you. When you leave Puerto
Rico, you are going to be leaving with a big knowledge and a big
force surrounding you. . . . You are going to take a bath in the
river and a bath in the ocean." And I did. I went and took two
baths. . . . When we came back to Hartford, we brought my sister's altar and all the saints [i.e., statues] back. . . . I brought
candles for the altar and I kneeled and prayed to God. I promised
God if he would help me I would never cut my hair. I asked God if
he was sending me as a messenger, someone who was a nobody
who didn't know how to read and write, with no education. . . .
The next day there were around twenty people in my apartment
asking for help. I don't know how the word spread. I started doing
the seance and *consultas* [consultations]. . . . Word spread that
there was a new medium. . . . Meanwhile, Carlos made a promise
to St. Lazarus that if his mother would be cured of a sickness that
she had he would stop drinking. . . . I had this vision then in which
I went to Puerto Rico and I was digging in back of his mother's
house. I took out a little box made of tin and there was a little doll
in it. The doll was his mother and the same way that the rust from
the box would stick on the doll, that was how the sickness stuck on
her body. I saw myself running and throwing the box in the river.
Two days after, Carlos' mother called from Puerto Rico and said
that in her centro the spirits had notified her that a spiritual person
had broken the work [i.e., witchcraft] that had been put on her.
Her powers told her that I was the one that broke the work and I

told her that I had the same vision. But Carlos didn't stop drinking. Shortly after I had a vision that Carlos would get arrested and he did. When he came out, he didn't drink and he put on a sack, a burlap sack, as a sign of repentance and as a promise to the saints.

Centro de Nuestro Padre Lázaro

By 1980, Marta and Carlos were prepared to open a Centro de Espiritismo. This move was prompted by several spiritual occurrences. Most important of these was a vision Marta had of a small wooden house with a thatched roof. Inside the hut there was a sign that read "Centro de Nuestro Padre Lázaro." In subsequent weeks Marta continued to see St. Lazarus in her visions. In this way she came to realize that she would be "baptized in the spirit" by this powerful saint in the Espiritismo pantheon. Sacrificing oneself to a saint is a focal developmental rite in the process of becoming a healer in Afro-Caribbean possession cults. Because St. Lazarus is syncretized with the Yoruba deity Babalu-aye, patron of the sick, Marta realized that she would help the sick when possessed by her patron saint.

Marta and Carlos rented a small storefront in the high density Puerto Rican commercial and residential area of Hartford known as Park Street–South Green. Later, the centro was moved a few blocks to its current location. At first, Marta and Carlos served as madrina and padrino of the apprentice mediums that were attracted to the centro. But it became clear to the mediums that Marta possessed the greater spiritual force and organizational ability. As one of the early participants in the centro explained:

> The madrina was the madrina and you have to obey her words. But Carlos didn't want to. He thought he should be the man of the house. . . . He was seeing the relationship materialwise and not spiritualwise. . . . But it was the madrina who really went out of her way for him. She only made him the padrino, I think, because he was her husband. She went through hell with him, but she held it inside herself. . . . He started messing up. He would walk out in the middle of a section [reunion or seance], argue with the mediums, and take drugs. . . . He gave me LSD without telling me what it was. Then he dropped out of the centro and a month later he went to jail.

These events convinced Marta to end her relationship with Carlos. Her involvement with the centro, in contrast, began to blossom. The centro quickly became the focal point of her life and a landmark in the emerging Puerto Rican community of Hartford.

For passersby, the centro is a highly visible and accessible institution. In the windows, there are statues of spirits, which signifies to the initiated that a spiritist center is located within. During the warmer months, the rhythmic beat of Santero music can be heard through the open door. Just inside the entrance, Marta and her fellow mediums have arranged a small botánica, containing many of the items used in healing, including herbs, oils, colognes, baths, candles, printed prayers, incense, talismans, and statues of saints and Yoruba deities.

At the opposite end of the main room is the mesa blanca, a long wooden table covered with a white cloth. In the center of the table there is a large glass bowl, filled with water, called the *fuente* (fountain). Water is used in cleansing a person of harmful spirits. It symbolizes spiritual purity and clarity of thought and purpose.

To the left and right of the fuente, respectively, are large statues of St. Lazarus, patron of the centro, and St. Barbara, Marta's main spiritual guide. Also found on the table are various fruits, flowers, candles, and other offerings to the spirits, as well as a large rosary and a donation basket. Typically, the table is cluttered with other objects too, such as cigars, bottles of Florida water, packets of incense, photographs of clients, pens and pencils, and other items utilized during healing rituals. On the wall behind the mesa blanca, there is a plaque representing the all-seeing eye of God, and below it a crucifix, symbolizing, as in Catholicism, the suffering and material death of Christ. Pictures of numerous saints hang nearby. Higher on the wall are two shelves, which hold statues of the most important spirits active during healing rites. Another large set of saint statues, as well as bowls of water and various offerings, are located on a second cloth-covered table.

A partition erected behind the mesa blanca creates a small kitchen area at the back of the centro. Food is prepared here for special feasts that fill the calendrical cycle of ritual activity at the centro. This room is also used for healings that require the client to remove articles of clothing, such as the treatment for *empacho* (clogging of the stomach or intestines), which involves the application of oils to the client's stomach.

Upon walking into the centro, the visitor is struck by a barrage of sensations. A small stereo regularly replays a small number of Santero records owned by the group. A dense fog of incense, cigar and cigarette smoke, and various scents and colognes clogs the air. Candles in an array of colors, symbolizing particular spirits, flicker on the tables and shelves and add their illumination to the numerous colorful statues and saint pictures decorating the room. On weekdays, when the centro is open for drop-in clients, the area between the botánica and the mesa blanca is occupied by five to ten clients waiting in randomly scattered chairs to be called to the front for a ten- to thirty-minute consultation with one of the mediums or for a spiritual cleansing at the table to the left of the mesa blanca. Children of these clients play quietly around the room and are an expected part of group activities. On Sundays, during the weekly reunion, the middle area is packed with rows of chairs facing the mesa blanca. Between twenty-five and fifty or more men, women, and children of all ages crowd in sitting on the chairs or standing in the back. When the session begins, the doors are locked to keep out evil influences, not to be reopened for seven or eight hours. Visitors are asked to drop their keys into a small brown paper bag, because metal blocks the flow of spiritual energy. Crossing one's arms and legs is discouraged for the same reason. The session passes through a number of stages, during which diverse spirits possess the mediums, who are arranged in a semicircle facing the audience across the front of the room. For the visitor, the high point of the ritual comes when he or she is called to the front to be diagnosed by the mediums with the aid of the spirits and is perhaps given a written prescription for items to be purchased from the botánica.

When she is present in the centro, Marta usually occupies a rocking chair behind the mesa blanca, immediately behind the fuente. In this central position, she not only can see the entire centro but is the focus of visitor and medium attention. The degree of participation in the ritual activities of the centro by the other mediums is determined by their level of spiritual development.

Almost all mediums first come to the centro as clients seeking help for health, social, or spiritual problems. A recent study of fifty clients at the centro (Singer n.d.) found they report a high number (an average of ten per client) of stress-related symptoms, including frequent nausea, body pains, stomachaches, headaches, sleeplessness, loss of appetite, and dizziness and commonly feel anger, sadness, and depression. The most common presenting complaints of centro clients were found to be emotional problems (31 percent), family conflict (25 percent), general ill health (8 percent), ill health in a child (8 percent), and spiritual problems (8 percent). Approximately half of the clients in the study feared that witchcraft or sorcery was contributing to the problems they were experiencing. Users of the centro apparently feel they benefit from the services offered to treat these conditions, because many become regular visitors and tell friends and relatives about the centro. Continued participation commonly leads to home use of religious paraphernalia of Espiritismo, including burning candles, saying special prayers, spiritual cleaning of floors, and displaying the pictures and statues of powerful spirits, as well as social involvement with mediums and other clients. For some participants, this involvement leads to the decision to undergo training to become a medium.

Mediums go through a protracted period of training—often lasting more than three years—during which they learn to "pass the spirit," identify their spiritual guides, gain control over their lives, and diagnose and spiritually treat centro clients. Mediums are organized into a hierarchy of spiritual ranks, reflecting degrees of ability, learning, and discipline as a medium. These ranks are symbolized by the number and type of *collares* (beaded necklaces) a medium is entitled to wear. At the pinnacle of the hierarchy is Marta. As the mardina, she functions as a teacher, confessor, and counselor for the other mediums. As the most spiritually developed and powerful medium, she is due respect and obedience from her followers. Marta runs the centro with a firm but supportive hand. Those who challenge her command or exhibit disrespect discover that her sympathetic and often jocular demeanor can quickly give way to a devastating verbal assault that is bolstered by a strong sense of self-assurance and rightful authority.

Below Marta, there are five grades of mediumship, occupied by a somewhat fluctuating group of adherents. A census of the centro conducted by the lead author in May 1983 found that there were forty-seven mediums (thirty-eight females, nine males). A second census sixteen months later revealed that there had been a drop to thirty-two mediums (twenty females, twelve males), only seventeen of whom (twelve females, five males) had been mediums during the earlier census. It is important to note that these statistics do not suggest shrinkage in the appeal of Espiritismo, but rather a regular process of passage through the centro as problems arise and are solved in people's lives or as they undergo personal life changes that necessitate enhanced social support (e.g., loss of employment, residential relocation, marital disruption, illness). This interpretation is supported by a third census conducted in January 1985. At that point the number of mediums had risen to its highest level since the founding of the centro (thirty females, twenty-one males).

The top-ranking mediums below Marta hold the title of *palo prenda* (literally "jewel stick," but connoting the beauty of jewels and the power of a club or other weapon). In addition to Marta, there are two of these fully developed mediums (one female, one male). Like Marta, they are believed to have "access" to the high-ranking spirit Olofi (syncretized with Christ) and other very powerful spirit beings. *Prenda* (jewel) is the next rank. Prendas are also fully developed (i.e., capable of founding their own centro), but they lack access to Olofi. There are currently three prendas (two females, one male). All of the palo prendas and prendas are longstanding members of the centro. In addition, most are close personal friends of Marta. One is a regular resident in her apartment and another resides there occasionally. The remaining mediums are distributed into three ranks: santeros, *muertos,* and espiritistas. Used in this context, terms like santero and espiritista have a more specific meaning than that of practitioner in a particular Afro-Caribbean possession cult, and they refer to levels of accomplishment within this centro. Mediums that fill the lower three ranks tend to be newer members of the group and also tend to maintain a somewhat more formal and less intimate relationship with Marta.

As noted earlier, there is considerable variation in belief, practice, and social organization among different centros. Consequently, the hierarchy described above appears to be peculiar to Marta's centro. This particular arrangement has evolved slowly over the last several years as Marta has struggled to shape the centro to meet both her own needs and those of the community she serves. In this sense, Marta functions as a religious innovator, borrowing elements from diverse sources and weaving them into the fabric of centro life. She believes she is guided by the spirits in this process.

For example, during 1983, an autistic child was brought by her parents to the centro for help. The child did not speak or interact, and would sit on the floor screaming. Marta had never treated such a case before. Her approach involved crawling under the table where the child liked to sit and imitating her yelling noises. Marta explained that this strategy was designed to make contact with the child. Within a few weeks, Marta's efforts had some result. The child learned to pronounce Marta's name and showed other signs of progress. Interestingly, when asked about the origin of her treatment approach, Marta revealed that it did not come out of established Espiritismo tradition. Rather, in pragmatic fashion, she was replicating treatment she had seen in a television movie.

An important influence on the centro over the last three years has been Marta's relationship with the Hispanic Health Council, a community-based research, training, and advocacy institute concerned with the health and social problems faced by Puerto Ricans in Hartford. Since its inception in 1978, a central goal of the Council has been to lower the cultural barriers that divide health care providers and institutions from the Puerto Rican community. In this regard, Council staff have sought opportunities to present educational programs on Puerto Rican history, culture, sociodemographics, and health status to careproviders and policy makers. Marta often has played a key role in these presentations. Over the last several years, she has given talks about Espiritismo at community health clinics, regional mental health centers, medical schools, psychiatric hospitals, university social science departments, and state and national health conferences. For example, in February 1988, Marta and the lead author presented their work at a medical and surgery grand rounds at a local Catholic hospital. At presentations like this, Marta not only has an opportunity to explain the beliefs and practices of Espiritismo and to discuss its efficacy in the treatment of particular health and social problems but is also exposed to the concerns, practices, and terminology of biomedicine. Having experienced cultural and linguistic problems in the treatment of Puerto Rican patients and their families, some physicians have recognized the potential advantage of a cooperative relationship with an indigenous healer. In recent years, moreover, Marta has had an opportunity to work with several medical students who have undertaken short-term studies at the centro in partial fulfillment of their primary care clerkship responsibilities. In these ways, Marta has developed mutual referral relationships with several physicians, she is periodically consulted by health care providers with Puerto Rican patients, and she has been invited to treat psychiatric in-patients at a local hospital.

Marta's healing activities have come to the attention of the news media. Long articles on her and the centro have appeared in the major daily and weekly newspapers in Hartford, and she has been interviewed on several radio stations. Involvement with the Council has also exposed Marta to anthropological research and made her the subject of several social science articles.

Community Activities

Marta's concern for the well-being of the Puerto Rican community goes beyond the immediate realm of ritual treatment of health and interpersonal problems. Although her ability to address the larger issues facing the Puerto Rican community has been enhanced through her position at the centro, her involvement with social advocacy predates her move to Hartford and her "development" with Espiritismo. Marta's social activism began while she was married to Hernando, as an outgrowth of her praticipation in a local chapter of the Parent-Teacher Association.

> I used to get involved a lot in the PTA, looking for funds and for other things needed at the school, coordinating projects. I directed the meetings, me and three other ladies. Then the city decided it was going to take out the guards that cross the kids at the streets. . . . They said they didn't have the money. After they took them out, the same week there were two accidents and a little boy died, hit by a car. A lot of parents from all the schools got involved. I was one of the leaders, a spokesman. We marched to City Hall to protest. We'd lay down in the streets with carriages and strollers and blocked the traffic. It came out in the news. They had to put policemen to cross our kids until they got the money for the crossing guards.

While still living in New York, Marta also helped to organize a block association in her neighborhood. Although its initial goal was community beautification, this group soon began assisting new arrivals from Puerto Rico to cope with life in the United States. Marta participated in such activities despite Hernando's insistence that she remain at home and not involve herself outside the domestic sphere.

> We had block parties and we'd clean the streets. We tried to maintain our neighborhood. We gathered funds to take the kids for picnics. We'd take them to the park or the zoo or whatever. Sometimes we'd have fifty kids. We'd help people that came from Puerto Rico. Sometimes if a new family came and they didn't have nothing for their apartment, we'd throw a block party or sell cakes to get money to help start them off. . . . I'd get hit from Hernando for doing it, but I did it anyway.

After moving to Hartford, Marta continued her activism. Once again her involvement began with school-related issues.

> The Board of Education wanted to take out the bus that picked up our children to take them to school. We didn't think it was fair because it was very cold. I talked to other mothers and we made three meetings in my home. . . . Then we had a meeting at La Casa de Puerto Rico [a local community agency]. We had a meeting with the Board of Education. We had to take the kids out of school and we all went to City Hall. They put us in an auditorium.

When they counted how many kids were involved . . . they decided that rather than taking a bus away, they had to add a bus. So
instead of losing a bus, we gained one.

When Marta returned to Hartford in August 1978, she found that the
apartment she had rented was infested with rats. Her effort to force the
landlord to eradicate them developed into an active participation in a
number of community struggles.

I had holes in my apartment and big rats were coming inside. I
complained to the city. A man from the city came and said it was
suitable to live there. But there were rats and the pipes leaked. I
called the news and they came to my apartment and took pictures
and wrote a newspaper article about it. . . . After that, the city
condemned the apartment and made the owner fix it. A group
called the Comité Vente-Cuatro [Committee of Twenty-Four] that
was involved in protesting the rats contacted me. I got a flyer that
they were going to have a *marcha* [protest march] to City Hall. We
took a bunch of dead rats to show them what we were living with.
People got very angry at City Hall and some people got arrested.
But it was very helpful. After that they started fixing up some of
the apartments. Before that nobody gave a damn about how
Puerto Ricans were living. After the march to protest the rats, we
had another march when four Puerto Rican guys were burned to
death in a fire in a building next to the fire department. The fire
department didn't do anything. They claimed the firemen were
someplace else. Then we had a march when a little boy was killed
when the roof where he lived fell in. Then I got discriminated
against by the Housing Authority. They wouldn't let me get an
apartment, [they said] that I was part of a street gang. So we got
involved around that.

Most recently, Marta took an active role in a series of militant demon-
strations in the Puerto Rican community after the hit-and-run death of a
medium's child several blocks from the centro. Several large marches
and vigils were held, including a stormy meeting with the City Council,
to protest the city and Police Department's handling of the case against a
prominent local attorney accused and later convicted of the crime.

In addition to these more public efforts in the fight against poverty and
discrimination, Marta regularly plays an advocacy role on behalf of her
clients and fellow mediums. This commonly involves helping them to link

up with community agencies or assisting them in receiving legal or financial aid. Through her contacts at the Hispanic Health Council and other Puerto Rican agencies, Marta is able to aid her clients in overcoming bureaucratic red tape and the institutional racism that futher complicates the lives of impoverished Puerto Rican families.

Marta views her advocacy activities as part of a struggle for justice and human rights for the Puerto Rican community.

> I think if we don't fight for our rights, no one will. And it is worth fighting for. Everyone should have a fair chance. If we have to walk and talk, we will do it. For instance, in the hit-and-run case, that guy didn't care. Nobody cared. Even though I am a religious person, if I have to go out and scream, I will scream. Even though we pray and fast, to me it is not enough. We have to be out there and scream so they can see us. Some people are afraid of getting involved, afraid they . . . will get in trouble. We had one lady that was discriminated against and I said, "Let's have a march." But she was afraid of losing her welfare. But I don't think we should just stay inside the *templo* [temple] and not help people.

Marta sees her political advocacy efforts as natural extensions of her healing role in the centro. In all of these arenas, she defines her goal as extending aid to people like herself who have long endured the consequences of injustice, prejudice, and poverty.

Conclusion

As Pelto and Pelto (1978, 75) remark, "the richness and personalized nature of life histories afford a vividness and integration of cultural information that are of great value for understanding particular lifeways." Unfortunately, despite a longstanding anthropological interest in the healer role, there is a paucity of detailed biographies of female healers. Notable exceptions include Leacock and Leacock's (1975) account of a Batuque healer from Brazil, Jones's (1966) monograph on Sanapia, a Comanche shaman, Snow's (1973, 1977) work with a black healer in Tucson, Russell's (1984) analysis of the career development of a Philippine curer, Buss's (1980) report on a Mexican-American midwife, and Braden's (1955) book on Mary Baker Eddy, the founder of

Christian Science. But, as the foregoing account of the life of Marta de Jesus demonstrates, life history materials can provide a rich corpus of data for understanding the pathway to the healer role within a particular sociocultural context.

It is evident that in Marta's social world, Espiritismo exists as a culturally constituted religious system capable of providing support and fellowship during times of personal and social crisis. Yet clearly it is an avenue traversed by only a minority of potential participants, and only a tiny portion of those who get involved do so to the degree that Marta has. An examination of the life history presented here indicates that Marta's earliest visions were coincident with a beating administered by her father. As her relationship with her father fractured and her family's economic and social life worsened, Marta's visions and accompanying fainting spells increased in number and intensity, only to diminish after she moved out of her family's home. Her involvement with Espiritismo blossomed anew in the midst of problems with her relationship with Hernando and escalated again as her living conditions and relationship with Carlos deteriorated. In sum, it would appear that Espiritismo offered Marta both an escape from the painful realities of her often turbulent and difficult world and an anchor in an otherwise unwieldy and often unsupportive social environment. Espiritismo offered a concrete set of beliefs, a stable setting, an expanding network of significant others, a mechanism of social support, a route of self-expression, and an arena for personal development and recognition.

In his psychocultural account of the founder of the Levite religion, a modern offshoot of Mormonism, Baer (1979, 193) maintains that "the Levite religious system to a large extent evolved as a projective system which served to resolve or *at least alleviate* various tensions and conflicts experienced by its principle formulator." In Marta's case, these conflicts and tensions were not only psychological but also social: they were rooted in being a female raised in a working-class Puerto Rican family; they were problems of sex, race, and class (Miranda King 1979). In all of these social categories, Marta was cast into the most oppressed position and suffered the consequences of being on the bottom of all social indicators. Buoyed by perhaps unknowable forces, Marta took one of the few paths that presented itself and followed it past numerous obstacles and hardships to a level of public recognition and stature uncommon for a woman of her background. Whatever else its functions, pyschologically, medically, and socially, the healer role within Espiritismo offered Marta not only a solution to many of her personal problems but a creative arena in which to find herself. Moreover, it offered her a social role in which to advocate for her community in an ongoing battle with forces of injustice and oppression and to minister to the wounds suffered by her *compañeros* in that battle.

Notes

The authors would like to thank Maria Borerro, Lani Davison, and Jean J. Schensul for their helpful comments on an earlier draft of this paper, and Zoraida Cotts for her extensive secretarial assistance. As for expressing appreciation to Marta, we can only hope that this chapter embodies the warm affection and sense of graditude we feel.

1. Like others of its genre, the life history text presented here strives to span two often treacherous chasms: between science and literature, and between research and friendship. Consequently, this essay has been a product of negotiation, collaboration, and construction at a number of levels. These factors were operative in the elicitation of materials, their selection and organization for presentation, and finally in Marta's comments on the slight revisions of an earlier draft. Moreover, because of the close personal and collegial relationship that has emerged through several years of interaction, the authors and other members of the Hispanic Health Council staff have had some direct impact on the course of Marta's life, including: (1) the development of opportunities for Marta to interact with the medical and anthropological worlds; (2) the provision of opportunities and perhaps accompanying pressures to enhance the organization of ideas and practices current at the centro; (3) the provision of moderate but occasionally timely access to economic and other resources; (4) the extension of support and approval for Marta's role within and outside of the centro; and (5) the facilitation of contact with the mass media. Whatever the weaknesses of the life history approach (Crapanzano 1984), the life history remains a viable form as we hope the text presented here helps to demonstrate, because there are few alternative bridges between the abstract and the personal—between, so to speak, rigor and vigor.
2. Pseudonyms have been provided for living individuals except, at her request, for Marta. Real names are used for deceased individuals.

EDWARD C. GREEN

Mystical Black Power: The Calling to Diviner-Mediumship in Southern Africa

This chapter sets forth a description and analysis of the *sangoma* diviner-medium healing cult in Swaziland, an independent kingdom in southern Africa. Healing cults, cults of affliction, "peripheral possession cults," or "corporate healing orders" have been described as "bringing together into one corporate organization or network individuals who have suffered a common affliction, been possessed by a given spirit, or have joined because of a common difficulty. . . . Most of these therapeutic orders have in common the feature that the sufferer, once initiated and healed, becomes a healer of the same affliction" (Janzen 1986, 20).

Diviner-mediums are predominantly female in Swaziland, and cult participation can be viewed in part as an adaptive response to institutionalized male-dominance/female subordination in the wider society. However, I will argue here that attraction to diviner-mediumship involves complex conscious and unconscious motivational factors that defy single-level explanations. I will support this argument by using evidence from a case history of a Xhosa woman from Transkei, a South African Bantustan, who journeyed to Swaziland to become a diviner-medium, as well as by a discussion of the psychological, social, and economic forces that together account for her calling to diviner-mediumship. I will also draw on literature describing neighboring Nguni-speaking societies like the Xhosa and Zulu, because Nguni speakers exhibit considerable cultural homogeneity and because there is little recent literature on Swazi indigenous diviner-mediums.

Variants of the Nguni root word *twasa,* such as *intwaso* or *thwasa* in Xhosa or *kutfwasa* in siSwati—all referring to spirit possession—stand as linguistic evidence of similarities in spirit possession found among Nguni peoples and among neighboring Sotho- and Tswana-speaking groups. Linguistic similarity should not, however, obscure the considerable variation among these groups in response to the call of the ancestors and in the resulting cults of affliction.

The ethnographic material that follows derives from fieldwork in Swaziland between 1981 and 1985, during most of which time I worked as Social Science Advisor to the Swaziland Ministry of Health, under contract with the Academy for Educational Development in Washington, D.C. Fieldwork included a survey of 144 traditional healers (including 58 diviner-mediums) in 1983, as well as participant-observation research and in-depth interviews conducted between 1981 and 1985 (Green 1985; Green and Makhubu 1984). The interviews forming the basis of the life history were assisted by an interpreter and took place periodically between February 1984 and March 1985 at the homestead where the diviner-medium was trained.

Diviner-Mediums in Swaziland

There are two basic types of indigenous health practitioners in Swaziland today: the diviner-medium (sangoma) and the herbalist (*lugedla, inyanga yemitsi*). A third type, the Christian or "Zionist" faith healer (*umprofeti*), arose in southern Africa early in this century during the development of Christian sects whose adherents reinterpreted more orthodox Christianity in ways that were compatible with traditional African beliefs and practices.[1] A household survey I conducted in 1983 indicates that roughly 50 percent of healers in Swaziland are herbalists, 40 percent are diviner-mediums, and 10 percent are faith healers. About half of all healers in Swaziland are female (Green and Makhubu 1984, 1072–1073), including at least 70 percent of sangomas.

Sangomas are consulted when illness fails to respond to home remedies or other treatments, or when there is mystery or disagreement concerning the cause of illness or other misfortune. Sangomas divine the cause of illness, either through interpreting the casting of bones and other objects (*kushaya ematsambo*) or through direct spirit possession and interrogation of the spirit, with the assistance of one or more categories of spirits. At the ideal level, sangomas restrict themselves to divining or diagnosing the cause of illness or misfortune; herbalists cure or ameliorate the diagnosed problem. In practice, however, most sangomas also treat clients with herbal and other traditional medicines (e.g., animal fats). But unlike herbalists, who in all cases learn about medicine from teachers, nearly half of a sample of fifty-eight sangomas interviewed reported learning about medicine directly from ancestor spirits. The actual proportion claiming instruction from spirits is probably higher; some sangomas are reluctant to discuss this subject in the context of a formal interview. Through dreams and visions, sangomas learn which specific medicine to use for a particular therapy, where to find the ingredients, and precisely how to prepare and administer the medicine.

Sangomas nowadays tend to have at least two or three, and at times as many as fifteen or more, spirits that guide and assist them in their healing practice. Sangomas describe a division of labor among such spirits whereby each tends to have a specialized purpose, ranging from guidance in diagnosis to help in collecting overdue patient fees.

In an analysis of Zulu sangomas, Sibisi (1975, 50) takes the position that "the special and very close contact with the spirits is reserved for women only" and that "if a man becomes possessed he becomes a transvestite." These requirements appear not to be the case among the Swazi. Although male sangomas may have trained along with women under a female guide and they sometimes resemble women in superficial attributes such as hair style, and even though most sangomas are women, male sangomas—and certainly male guides—have the same deliberately cultivated close relationships with spirits as do female sangomas.

Sangomas are called or coerced into their profession by an ancestor-sent illness (*kwetfwasisa*) believed to be untreatable by either modern or traditional medicine. Submission to the calling is the only way to survive or to be cured. Kwetfwasisa may take nearly any form of physical or mental affliction; its hallmark is its chronicity. In-depth interviews with women undergoing sangoma training revealed that many had status problems and role conflicts in addition to a self-described chronic illness prior to training. Examples include infertility and loss of children through death (in an especially pronatalist society), divorce or separation (in a society where a woman's role and status are defined and legitimized by marriage), and domestic disharmony caused by conflicts between co-wives or between husband and wife.

Sangomas study under an experienced diviner-medium, senior adept (cf. V. Turner 1969), or spiritual guide (*gobela;* 'guide" will be used here), who is usually the same person who diagnosed the sangoma's chronic illness as a call to diviner-mediumship. Although selection of the cult initiate is divine, it is clear that guides also exercise judgment in recruitment of apprentices. Ngubane (1981, 362) observes of the Zulu that the candidate for training must be insightful and able to enter a state of trance. Janzen (n.d.), also in reference to the Zulu, notes that "the sangoma therapist . . . must identify the rehabilitative or reintegrative potential of a client before moving that client through initiation into a healer role."

Trainees (*ematfwasa*) apprentice for an average of three years and pay a training fee of about U.S.$200–250 (in 1983 dollars) in cash, plus one or more cows and goats for sacrifice to the ancestors. The trainee must also observe strict rules of behavior during apprenticeship, such as abstinence from sexual relations, avoidance of certain foods, avoidance of pollution through contact with death, observations of silence, and unquestioning deference toward the guide. Violation of taboos during the training period may cause the trainee to die during the ceremony that marks the transition from trainee (*litfwasa*) to sangoma. Clearly, considerable sacrifice and commitment are required in order to become a sangoma. Sibisi (1976, 56) notes: "all such ascetic abstinence is calculated to achieve a desired contact with the sacred realm."

A sangoma often goes into debt to her guide in order to obtain her training fees, in which case she will work without pay for the guide for a period of at least several months after completion of training. She may also generate income for her guide during the later stages of apprenticeship, by performing routine divination, for example. In other cases a sangoma's husband or parents may lend the money and sacrificial animals for training payment or may simply donate these as an investment in a more secure future for the family, since sangomas usually earn enough to support others once they become established in their healing practice.

The end of formal training is signified by two ceremonies: an *intfwasa* held at the guide's homestead and a *litjembe* held in the home community of the new sangoma. In the former, the initiate eats raw meat and drinks blood from a ritually slaughtered goat. She also purges herself with medicinal infusions in great quantity, a procedure that has been known to result in death. The highlight of the ceremony is when the initiate demonstrates to all assembled—the guide, other trainees, friends, family, and sangomas who previously trained with the same guide—that she has truly developed her spirit-assisted divining powers.

This she does by finding a small object that the guide has hidden, often a ring. The object may then be woven into the sangoma's hair and worn for a number of years.

If the newly qualified sangoma has paid her training fee to the guide in full, she is soon returned to her home community for a litjembe ceremony. In this, another goat is slaughtered and the guide presents the sangoma to her family and neighbors in her new role as diviner-medium. There follows a period of internship during which the newly qualified sangoma continues to turn to her guide for advice. Once the sangoma has built up her own clientele and gains confidence in her own abilities, she may begin to diagnose kwetfwasisa and to sponsor apprentices herself.

The guide-apprentice relationship is highly structured and authoritarian. To show obedience and deference, the sangoma trainee typically kneels before her guide, claps her hands together, and intones the word *Thokosa,* the praise name of a certain class of spirits (*emanzawe*) whenever she comes into her guide's presence. Several especially well known female guides, because they are possessed by a male spirit, are called *babe* (father) by those they have trained.

The training of sangomas has become more institutionalized, standardized, and empirically based in recent years, due to direct and indirect Western influences that have led to increasing professionalization among Swazi healers. Last (1986, 10–11) describes the current growth of professionalism among indigenous African healers as a reaction to the postcolonial rise in the biomedical professions. African physicians, for whom professionalization has meant decolonization, Africanization of jobs, and meeting the European on equal terms, have tended to regard traditional healers as something of an anachronism, a throwback to a time when Europeans believed that "second best" was good enough for Africans. In short, traditional healers have been regarded by African physicians as a threat to their own professionalism; therefore physicians have often opposed initiatives that would result in increased power or official recognition of indigenous healers.

Traditional healers are nevertheless continuing to organize themselves into regional and national associations in Swaziland. Sangoma training as well as practice has developed several parallels with Western biomedical education. Previously, those called by the ancestors would go off on their own for extended periods and acquire healing knowledge largely through personal visions and dreams (Kuper 1947, 164; Makhubu 1978; Marwick 1966, 245). Today, sangoma trainees apprentice together in groups under the same guide and receive extensive empirical instruction in herbal medicines. Sangomas who study together also retain social and professional ties with the guide and with fellow "graduates" long after training is completed. They may wear special adornments or insignias that show where they trained. Since sangomas come to a particular guide from all over Swaziland and from beyond its borders, the "old girl" network tends to be extensive and to transcend in size and scope the kinship and local community networks that define social boundaries for most Swazi women (Ngubane 1981, 363–64, makes a similar observation about Zulu sangoma networks in South Africa, as does Janzen 1988 about sangoma networks in southern and central Africa).

Before turning to the life history, it should be noted that Swazi guides attract many aspiring sangomas from South Africa, especially Zulu and Xhosa speakers whose languages are mutually intelligible with siSwati, the language of Swaziland. This pattern may have emerged because Swaziland's traditions have been less disrupted and transformed by European influences than is the case for other societies located within or close to South Africa's borders. Moreover, South African blacks tend to respect Swazis for being independent and black-ruled. It is also characteristic among the black societies of southern Africa that healers from other ethnolinguistic groups are believed to possess special powers not found among local healers.

The Call of the Ancestors

I began interviewing a young Xhosa woman, who will be called Thoko here, just before her completion of sangoma training in Swaziland. She was about to return to her home in Transkei, a Xhosa "homeland" forcibly created by South Africa, and establish herself there as a diviner-medium. The story of her calling to the Swazi sangoma cult sheds light on one way in which subordinate and powerless people have adapted to the particular forms of economic and political oppression that characterize South Africa today.

Thoko was born in East London, South Africa, in 1953. Her head was covered with a caul at birth, a sign among Xhosas and in other cultures that a child is endowed with special psychic abilities. Because of the circumstances of her birth, including the fact that it was unplanned, she was given a nickname meaning "the gift" by her mother.

Thoko was raised by her mother, a nurse at an East London hospital. In spite of her mother's biomedical education, Thoko was often taken to traditional healers when she became ill. Her mother was "troubled by spirits," manifested in part by dreams and visions, and she eventually gave up her nursing job. Thoko's father maintained a weak relationship with her mother, although they were never married and lived apart. The father was also visited by spirits; in fact his condition was diagnosed by a sangoma as a call by ancestors to become a diviner-medium. He chose instead to become a Zionist faith healer.

Thoko graduated from secondary school in Qumbu District, Transkei, then followed in her mother's footsteps and entered a two-year nurse training course at Livingston Hospital, Port Elizabeth, in 1974. During her training she, too, experienced visitations from spirits, although these episodes did not prevent her from graduating. She married early and gave birth to six children spaced closely together. The accompanying domestic responsibilities prevented her from pursuing a career as a nurse.

In addition to the frustration of not realizing her chosen vocation, Thoko was not particularly happy in her marriage, even though she had a husband she described as caring and securely employed with the Transkei police. During the early years of her marriage, she became increasingly disturbed by dreams and visions. At times she would burst into tears for no apparent reason. At other times, her head would "heat up" and she would lose control over herself, sometimes becoming destructive. Although Thoko had little contact with her father while growing up, she turned to him for help.

In his role as a Zionist healer, Thoko's father prescribed a ceremony to appease Thoko's ancestor spirits. The ceremony took place at his house and though it was largely Christian in content, a sheep was sacrificed in concession to traditional Xhosa religious custom. That night Thoko stayed at her father's house, but she could not sleep. She heard unnatural sounds of whistling and scraping on the ceiling above her. She ran to her father and woke him, telling him about the sounds. He interpreted the disturbances as the work of an evil spirit, and bathed her in holy water. Thoko returned to her room to sleep, but the strange sounds persisted until she finally fled to another room to await the dawn.

The following day Thoko felt very sick. Her body seemed partially paralyzed. She wondered if by mixing Christian and traditional rituals she had not approached her ancestor spirits properly. She decided to remedy this possible affront by going to the ocean to call upon the spirits in strict accordance with Xhosa custom. In Xhosa and Swazi cosmology, certain categories of spirits have an affinity with the sea, and seaside rituals are common, even among Zionist Christians. Interestingly, Thoko's clan name means "those of the sea."

Following the appeal to her ancestors for guidance, Thoko went back to her husband's home and, with the help of friends, sacrificed a goat. That night she had an amazing dream that was to change her life. She later related that she seemed to fly through the air to a distant place. She descended upon a homestead that she had never seen before but that she was able to observe in detail. There were thatch huts without windows and black people with "strange reddish, stringy hair." She could clearly see the face of an older woman and noticed a grain storage tank in a particular position relative to nearby huts.

Thoko had no idea where this place was. However, upon awakening— or return to normal consciousness—she found herself singing that she was about to go to Swaziland. In view of her increasingly erratic behavior and her tearful pleas, her husband agreed to take her to Swaziland as soon as he could manage some time off from his job. All either of them knew about Swaziland was that it lay to the north of Durban, South Africa, and so the first step would be to take a bus to that city.

Thoko agreed to wait until her husband could leave his job, but during the next three nights she found herself waking in her sleep and wandering out of the house, her suitcase in hand. Each time her husband intercepted her and forced her back inside. He began locking her in at night. On the fourth night, Thoko once again flew through the air in a dream. She descended near a heavy gate guarded by police with fierce dogs. She knew this must be the gate of the royal *kraal* (homestead) of King Sobhuza II of Swaziland.

Upon awakening, she knew she had to go straight away to the king's kraal in Swaziland. She recalled, "there was no way I could resist. I was being commanded, it was just like *lihabiya* [a spell whereby a man hypnotizes a woman at a distance and summons her, usually for immoral purposes]." She added that the spirits were making her hate her husband.

Eventually, Thoko and her husband boarded a northbound bus. After changing buses in Durban, they passed through unfamiliar towns— Vryheid, Peit Retief, Gege—until finally they crossed the Swaziland border and stopped at Mahlanya. Soon after arrival, a truck from the Swazi Broadcasting Services pulled up and the driver asked the couple where they were going. Thoko found herself replying "to the king." Amazed at encountering people who had not heard of the death of King Sobhuza II months earlier, the broadcasting crew took the couple to the home of a prince who lived in the nearby royal village of Lobamba.

Because the prince seemed sympathetic, Thoko related to him her detailed visions of the king's kraal and the people with the stringy red hair. The prince was intrigued and pressed for more details. One of the prince's sons who had been listening began to suspect that the old woman in Thoko's vision was actually a well-known Swazi sangoma. The homestead where she trained apprentices was only a forty-five minute drive from Lobamba, and the prince insisted on transporting Thoka and her husband there in his truck.

As I learned in separate interviews, Thoko's guide had been training diviner-mediums for years at her homestead not far from Mbabane. Unlike most other Swazi guides, she did not instruct male sangomas, nor did she wear her hair in the customary long, ochre-reddened style of sangomas signifying a relationship with emanzawe spirits. On special ritual occasions, the guide wore a red wig, but otherwise she dressed like an ordinary, mature Swazi woman. At the time I first interviewed her, she had eight female apprentices.

The guide described Thoko's arrival at her homestead:

I was sitting outside with some friends when a truck pulled up. A woman got out and ran straight to my *indumbe* hut [the abode of the spirits where ritual paraphernalia is kept and where sangomas dance]. She started to sing and shout. I was alarmed and thought, "Who is this mad woman who is disturbing the spirits?" I rushed into the hut just as the noises stopped and found the woman collapsed on the floor with foam on her lips. I thought she was crazy, or maybe dying. I shook her and then began to suspect that this woman wasn't crazy, that the spirits had sent her to me. So I began to beat a drum and seek guidance from my spirits. My spirits told me the story of this woman. I learned that she was from the Transkei and that the spirit troubling her was called Gebani. Gebani then spoke to me directly and told me the woman's whole history. Gebani asked me to cure her and allow him to dwell in her. He then said farewell, but promised to return after she was cured.

By this time Thoko was revived, so the guide asked her to account for her behavior. Thoko proceeded to tell her story, which the guide interpreted as a confirmation of what the spirit had already communicated to her. Thoko also insisted that she had previously visited the guide's kraal in some spirit-assisted manner while still in Transkei. As proof, she claimed she recognized the windowless huts and the ochre-treated hairstyles of the sangoma trainees. The only thing that seemed wrong was the absence of a grain storage tank. Upon hearing this, the guide admitted that her storage tank had recently been moved to another part of the homestead, which removed any doubts that may have lingered in either's mind that guide and student had been spiritually led to one another—although Thoko insisted that when she first saw the guide's face, she knew at once she had found the place encountered in her vision.

The guide convinced Thoko to remain and apprentice with her. Thoko's husband was not happy at the prospect of being without his wife for an extended and indefinite period. But the guide was firm; unless Thoko became a sangoma, the troubling spirit would never be appeased and Thoko's condition would never improve. She also informed him he must pay his wife's initial training fee and then leave quickly, since men were not allowed to stay overnight at the guide's homestead. She also reminded him of the strictly enforced requirement that sangoma trainees abstain from sex until completion of training, a requirement extended to married as well as single apprentices. Thoko's husband paid the required fee and accepted a lift to the nearest bus station.

Thoko had already conceived her sixth child when she arrived but was not yet aware of the pregnancy. The pregnancy did not interfere with her internship. She completed training in fifteen months, somewhat faster than most sangomas who train in Swaziland. Throughout her pregnancy, she participated in ritual dancing and singing and strengthened her spiritual powers with medicines. Thoko delivered her child at a mission-run hospital in the town of Manzini. She named her son Ma-Swati ("the Swazi") in honor of the location of his birth.

By the end of Thoko's training, the guide identified the spirit who initially called her to become a sangoma as Gebani, a *lidloti* or personal ancestor spirit in Thoko's lineage. Gebani and another spirit—a *linzawe* (a foreign avenging spirit)—were appeased through Thoko's "submission" to her calling and then activated through the rituals and taboos of the apprenticeship. The guide identified a third spirit, a *sithunye*, or "angel," as also assisting Thoko. Although an unusual spirit ally for a sangoma, Thoko's sithunye represented and affirmed the Christian element in her personal cosmology. Many Swazi sangomas now regard themselves as both Christians and specialists in traditional Swazi religion and, along with their clients, see no conflict or inconsistency in doing so.

Near the end of her apprenticeship, Thoko believed that in addition to the three spirits "brought out" by her guide, one or more *balozi* spirits (foreign avenging spirits) also seemed to be seeking manifestation through her. However, she concealed this suspicion from her guide since the guide had not trained her in balozi spirits. A knowledgeable Swazi colleague of mine later commented that though balozi spirits are not common in Swaziland, it is also true that guides do not want their apprentices to have as many or more spirits than they themselves have, lest the student become more powerful than the teacher.

Thoko's husband visited her a few times during the months of training, but was denied marital relations both because of the trainee's requirement of abstinence and also because of Thoko's feelings toward him at the time. She believed he had earlier angered her spirits because he stood between her and her divine calling. However, as she came to be at peace with her possessing spirits, she began to feel more positive about her husband.

Diviner-Mediumship as a Personal Solution to Cultural Problems

Why did Thoko leave her family to train to become a sangoma? Lewis (1969, 1971) was among the first to suggest that certain spirit possession cults attract people who are socially marginal, subordinate, underprivileged, or otherwise deprived. Because women are subordinate to men in many traditional societies and "excluded from full participation in social and political affairs," they are found in disproportionate numbers in what Lewis terms peripheral possession cults. These associations are "thinly disguised protest movements directed toward the dominant sex. They thus play a significant part in the sex-war in traditional societies and cultures where women lack more obvious and direct means for forwarding their aims" (Lewis 1971, 31). Such cults, Lewis goes on, 'also commonly embrace downtrodden categories of men who are subject to strong discrimination in rigidly stratified societies."

Messing observes that Zar possession cults in Ethiopia are particularly attractive to "married women who feel neglected in a man's world in which they serve as hewers of wood and haulers of water, and where even the Coptic Abyssinian Church discriminates against females" (Messing 1967, 286), although he adds that people of either sex who have "melancholy natures or weak personalities" are attracted to the cults.

In an analysis of case histories of Xhosa-speaking diviner-healers in Transkei, O'Connell interprets ancestral calling to the healing role as an adaptive response to acute stress, which is in turn related to "an inability to meet role expectations" (O'Connell 1982, 36). He notes that the calling "occurs among women more frequently than men because women are exposed to more stressful situations and have fewer ways of relieving stress." He further suggests that since the illness complex associated with ancestral calling occurs more often among married than unmarried women, married women must be more subject to role-fulfillment stress than unmarried women (O'Connell 1982, 28; cf. Hammond-Tooke 1962). Examples in the life of a married Xhosa woman include meeting expectations of marital fidelity when the husband is absent for long periods, and achieving motherhood if the woman is infertile.

Thoko's personal history is not incompatible with these interpretive frameworks. As a black South African woman she is subordinate both to men of her own group and to all people of either sex outside her own group in a class- and race-stratified society. As a woman in a patrilineal, virilocal society, she occupies a marginal position—that of a jural minor, to use Lewis's term (1971, 32)—with regard to her husband's household and kin group. Such marginality can also mean in Bantu-speaking societies that female affines are not fully constrained by the husband's ancestral spirits from practicing sorcery within the kin group (Ngubane 1977, 91). Further, though Thoko fulfilled the requirement to bear and raise children for her husband's patrilineage, she failed to achieve other, newer gender-related aspirations increasingly sought by black South African women—in her case, the goal of achieving employment outside the home.

Other elements of Thoko's personal history add depth and complexity to the functionalist conceptualization of cults of affliction. Thoko was not especially poor by either birth or marriage, by black South African standards. However, her nursing education and exposure to socially and economically better-off people may have made her feel more deprived than if she had been less exposed to other social worlds. Her relatively high level of formal education and early goal of becoming a nurse did not interfere with her accomplishing the traditional role expectations of adult married women. But these expectations had become constraints once she wished to do more than bear and raise children and manage household affairs. Marital disharmony and enmity with affinal kin, common sources of domestic stress for women elsewhere (see, e.g., Kendall, this volume) are major but not exclusive forms of dissatisfaction that prompt women to seek personal meaning outside domestic contexts.

A psychodynamic perspective would seek significance in circumstances and experiences in Thoko's childhood, particularly their influence on key choices she made as an adult, such as turning to her father for help during her illness and later choosing to place herself under the authority of a powerful woman in exclusively female company. Some psychodynamic analyses focus on "functional nervous disorders," suggesting that women predominate in cults of affliction because they are more inclined to hysterical behavior than are men (Hunter, cited in O'Connell 1982, 28). Sibisi (herself a Zulu) distinguishes between ancestral and alien spirit possession among the Zulu. Ancestral spirit possession leads to initiation into the *isangoma* priesthood, whereas alien spirit possession is "closely related to the extreme form of depression or nervous breakdown which may be coupled with hysteria and suicidal tendencies" (Sibisi 1975, 56). Although the Swazi have somewhat different notions about what Sibisi terms alien spirits, they themselves certainly make a distinction between ancestral calling and psychiatric disorder.[2]

A requirement of Lewis's peripheral possession cults is that the possessing spirits be of foreign origin, often from hostile neighboring societies, and that they be "amoral" in the sense that they are not thought to choose victims on the basis of shortcomings in the victim's character or behavior (Lewis 1971, 31). He adds that these alien spirits play no direct part in upholding the moral code of the societies where they are found. Thus, for Lewis, alien spirit possession characterizes corporate healing orders, whereas for Sibisi, alien spirit possession serves to separate the mentally disturbed from those inducted into healing orders through ancestral spirit possession. My own findings on Swazi sangoma cults suggest that both ancestor spirits (*emadloti*) and alien spirits that originate from formerly hostile neighboring societies (e.g., emanazwe) are involved in the call to therapeutic cult membership, and that alien sprits, once appeased through the process of cult initiation, become centrally significant in Swazi society.[3]

Yet another interpretive approach is compatible with those discussed thus far. Thoko's decision to become a sangoma may be viewed quite simply as a strategic career choice. Although Swazi and Xhosa belief systems require ritual recruitment to diviner-mediumship, herbalists stated in informal interviews that they pursued healing because they recognized an opportunity to gain wealth, status, and recognition while helping people at the same time; several commented further that formal education was not a prerequisite. Despite the ritual accoutrements of sangoma healing, these specialists may be no less motivated than herbalists by such practical considerations.

Guides may thus diagnose a call to diviner-mediumship when they want another paying apprentice; likewise, individuals wishing to enter a high-status and lucrative occupation may develop or interpret symptoms of illness as ancestral callings to membership in the sangoma cult. The strategic appeal of diviner-mediumship is all the more compelling because there are no other traditional careers open to Swazi or Xhosa women that offer the status, power, autonomy, and income that sangomas enjoy.

Janzen, generalizing about participation in *ngoma* (from a Bantu stem cognate meaning drum, and referring to cults of affliction) therapeutic groups in southern Africa, reaches a similar conclusion. He relates ngoma appeal in part to "chronic anxiety related to jobs" (Janzen n.d.) in the more industrialized and therefore cash-dependent regions of Africa and observes that "chronic inability to retain a job, and the alienation of the urban life for some, are regarded as syndromes appropriate for initiation into an *ngoma* order" (Janzen 1988). He further discusses the ancestral call as an opportunity for resourceful individuals to play a role in ritual leadership:

> It is not appropriate to assume, as some do, that the *twasa* diagnosis or call corresponds to Western psychoanalytic or therapeutic labels. In fact, there may be better reason to suspect that this diagnosis singles out individuals for recruitment to ritual leadership roles on the basis of characteristics of greater sensitivity, ego strength, and cultural receptivity in a time or situation of stress (Janzen n.d.).

No evidence was gleaned from interviews with Thoko that she consciously chose a career path that promised a steady income, status, recognition, emancipation from male dominance, or the realization of latent or frustrated leadership skills. But she did gain enhanced self-esteem and a renewed sense of purpose in life after her initiation and the start of a new career. Nealrly a year after she completed training and returned to Transkei, Thoko's guide told me further details about her former apprentice's progress. Thoko was now known to sangomas by the name of her main empowering spirit, and she had established a successful healing practice that combined elements of biomedicine and traditional Swazi medicine. She had earned enough money to buy a car and to pay the equivalent of U.S.$1,600 in transportation and other costs associated with the litjembe ceremony that ritually symbolized her newly achieved status in her family and home community. She was also able to pay the last of her training fees a month after returning home. Thoko was described by her guide as no longer suffering from the spirit-sent illness that led to her recruitment to the sangoma cult, and her marriage had become harmonious.

The life history method enlarges sociological perspectives of "cults of affliction," the most forceful statement of which is found in Lewis's 1971 study. The personal experiences and conscious motivations of individuals caught up in the historical realities of time and space add real-life context to a view that is otherwise one-dimensional, no matter how compellingly and elegantly it may be presented by its proponent(s). Moreover, life histories allow not only a consideration of multiple and alternative interpretations, as, for example, have been offered here in the telling of Thoko's recruitment to a healing role, but also demand that the cultural insider's interpretation be one of these. Thoko and her guide would never risk affronting the ancestors by explaining their calling in any way other than by spiritual means. Although they may recognize practicality in what they do, the spiritual dimension of diviner-mediumship is what imbues it with special character and meaning.

Notes

1. South African Zionism refers to independent black churches that combine Christian and traditional African beliefs and practices. The name comes from Zion City, Illinois, headquarters of the American missionaries whose teachings led to the establishment of Zionist churches in South Africa at the beginning of this century (Sundkler 1976; West 1975).
2. Traditional Africans have well-defined concepts of the more severe forms of mental disorder, such as the psychoses; these concepts do not differ markedly from each other or from biomedical concepts (Edgerton 1977; Green 1980; Murphy 1976).
3. Despite many close similarities between Zulu and Swazi healing beliefs and practices, there are significant differences between the two groups regarding spirit beliefs. I have become aware of these differences through detailed discussions with Zulu anthropologists Harriet Sibisi and Absolom Vilakazi. The distinctions persist although a significant number of Zulus are inducted into Swazi sangoma cults, then return to South Africa to establish themselves as diviner-mediums.

PART FOUR
Women Healers and Culture Change

Most of the chapters in this book describe healers against a backdrop of culture change, broadly speaking, and medical change, more specifically. For example, the Saraguro Indians Finerman discusses must cope with increasing state interest in their affairs, including government-sponsored health facilities. Nordstrom refers to the growing number of women entering both traditional and modern medical professions in Sri Lanka, a trend that reflects and contributes to changing gender relationships in Sri Lankan society. The women described in the chapters by Singer and Garcia and Green chose ritual healing as a personal solution to women's traditional subordination to men in Puerto Rican and Xhosa society, and to both gender and ethnic struggles as these evolve in the larger social context of the United States and South Africa.

The two chapters in this section, however, bring culture change to the forefront and examine how women's healing, in these two cases, midwifery, has responded to particular sets of sociocultural forces in particular historical contexts. Sargent compares contemporary midwifery and childbirth care practices among rural and urban Bariba in the West African Republic of Benin and shows how traditional patterns yield to forces of development. Reid reconstructs the changes in the ideology and practice of lay midwifery in the United States that resulted in its professionalization during the 1970s.

Sargent's analysis of Bariba women's participation in the medical domain in rural and urban areas illustrates some of the consequences that economic development has had for women in the Third World, particularly in connection with the intensification of capitalist and socialist modes of production in the past several decades. Traditional Bariba women's roles are those associated with domestic production and reproduction, and motherhood is their most valued accomplishment. Although women enter the public arena regularly as traders, and occasionally as midwives and healers, men are the dominant political and religious actors in traditional Bariba society.

Bariba women have not yet made tangible gains in the urban environment, but at the same time they have lost important traditional advantages in both domestic and public domains. Their control over childbirth has been usurped by government maternity services, a change that has removed a traditional source of reward and achievement for mothers. Traditional midwifery is dying out in town, which thus removes one of the few avenues for social prestige open to women. Although women have entered the formal labor market through factory employment, wage labor has not brought them uniform benefits. As in many other areas of the Third World, labor-force participation has resulted in the "double day" for Bariba women. They not only work as wage laborers but also continue to shoulder responsibilities for unpaid domestic labor, including the care of children and other dependent household members (see Hafkin and Bay 1976; Leacock and Safa 1986; and Young, Wolkowitz, and McCullagh 1981, for additional examples). Sargent describes how female Bariba cashew factory employees are considered less reliable than men by supervisors because men take sick leave only for themselves, but women take sick leave for their husbands and children as well. Even in contexts in which women have closed the earning and prestige gaps between themselves and men in the workplace, such as among middle-class whites in the United States, women continue to carry responsibility for routine household chores, a sex-role pattern that frequently intensifies after the birth of the first child. (Hoffman and Manis 1978).

Not all forms of social and cultural change are imposed on women. In some contexts women take social, economic, or political risks to gain strategic benefits both for themselves and for their children. Browner (1986a) provides a particularly vivid example in describing women's political activism in a traditionally conservative Chinantec village in highland Oaxaca. A small number of women tried to persuade the community to accept government-sponsored health and educational programs because they felt the programs would benefit their children and that they in turn would accrue advantages through their children's enhanced opportunities. But the majority of women in the community joined with the men in condemning the activists because of the prevailing sentiment that any changes from outside would threaten village autonomy, as had been true so often in the past. Women's innovations, then, do not always lead to uniform benefits for them or promote feminine solidarity.

The professionalization of midwifery provides an especially clear illustration of the mixed blessings conferred on women by cultural and social change. Traditional midwives in the Third World and lay midwives in the United States have responded to forces of change by making unsatisfactory tradeoffs in which old rewards are relinquished in order to take advantage of new benefits or in response to newly imposed constraints (Newman 1981; Rothman 1982). The dilemma is illustrated vividly by Reid's chapter on U.S. lay midwives. When modern lay midwifery began, in the late 1960s and early 1970s, the prevailing ideology underlying midwives' work was "sisterhood": women helping other women in the universal feminine experience of pregnancy and childbirth. Reid describes the pressures emanating both from outside forces and from within lay midwifery itself that inevitably led toward the professionalization of the occupation. In the process, lay midwives gained certain goals associated with professional status but lost the rewards of sisterhood. Reid contrasts professionalism with sisterhood by locating them in the public and the domestic domains, respectively. The domains are genderized in the sense that as social spaces they are dominated by one sex. But more important, the public and the domestic are social spaces with attributes that persons of either gender assimilate when occupying them. Thus, birth attendants in the public sphere are formally educated, publicly regulated, and organized into professions and semiprofessions, associations based more on legal than moral criteria. Birth attendants in domestic contexts are informally educated and regulated and are bound by moral considerations—those of sisterhood. Signficantly, women's increasing participation in the public/professional mode of childbirth care is not paralleled by growing male interest in domestic/informal birth care. Lay midwifery indeed remains a woman's specialty.

Women's Roles and Women Healers in Contemporary Rural and Urban Benin

Healing roles for Bariba women in contemporary rural and urban settings in the People's Republic of Benin, West Africa, reflect significant structural and ideological modifications occurring throughout the country. Browner, discussing the politics of reproduction in a Mexican village, has argued that "just as it is unproductive to study women's reproductive behavior without analyzing the broader sociopolitical conditions that constrain this behavior, it is equally unproductive to investigate the reproductive goals of a social collectivity without considering the desires and interests of the female members of the group" (Browner 1986b, 710; see also Jordan 1983, 3; MacCormack 1982b, 13). Similarly, an analysis of Bariba women healers requires a consideration of societal norms regarding mothering, appropriate female behavior, and women's expected domains of responsibility. In this chapter I will discuss healing roles for Bariba women in the general context of the changing sociopolitical conditions impinging on women's roles in general and on their reproductive goals and options.

The French anthropologist Lombard, in describing avenues for social mobility available to Bariba women, argued that a primary route to enhanced prestige for a woman was to achieve a position as a midwife (Lombard 1965, 143). A woman's social position, he said, largely reflected that of her father and her husband, with age and rank among wives as contributing factors. A healing role represented the most accessible means to achieving respect and even regional renown. Lombard's statement reflected research conducted primarily in rural Dahomey from 1955 to 1960. In the ensuing twenty-five years, Dahomey has been renamed Benin, and the Bariba—a major ethnic group in the northern provinces who number approximately five hundred thousand in population—have increasingly migrated to urban settings. Both rural and urban Bariba have experienced the impact of national legislation and policies and the increase in the power of institutions like the judiciary, police, and army, and have witnessed the transformation and sometimes the decline of Bariba political and religious institutions. Bariba religion has been perhaps more constrained than Islam, which draws adherents from one-quarter to one-half of the Bariba population. The status of women in society has correspondingly altered economic opportunities available to women. The position of healer and its implications for women require reassessment in light of the fundamental social changes that have occurred in the past two decades.

Gender, Healing, and Status in Theoretical Perspective

In analyzing asymmetries in cultural evaluations of gender, Rosaldo has proposed a "universal, structuralist opposition between domestic and public domains of activity" (M. Z. Rosaldo 1974, 35). She proposes that "women's status will be lowest in those societies where there is a firm differentiation between domestic and public spheres of activity and where women are isolated from one another and placed under a single man's authority, in the home. Their position is raised when they can challenge those claims to authority, either by taking on men's roles or by establishing social ties . . . in a world where women prevail" (M. Z. Rosaldo 1974, 36).

This model appears especially applicable to an understanding of gender in rural Bariba areas of Benin, where a demarcation is evident between the domestic and public domains, with women's responsibilities largely confined to the domestic arena. Politics, warfare, and community concerns of all sorts are primarily the affairs of men, and thus a correct woman does not speak in the presence of men engaged in public pursuits—whether they are elders discussing ritual processes, men of the household preparing for a hunt, or leaders in councils of war. Nor, in principle, do women offer advice behind the scenes. In contrast, child rearing, food processing, and associated tasks requisite to the functioning of a household are the responsibilities of women. However, the association of women with the domestic and men with the public is not absolute. Most rural women engage in petty trade, and a successful few progress to large-scale commercial enterprises; these traders operate in the public domain, although the proceeds of their commerce are often channeled back into the domestic domain, invested in children or the household.

Further, as Lombard argued and as this chapter will demonstrate, women transcend the domestic domain via the route of healing. The role of healer provides an option for women to develop a network of social ties outside the household and to achieve positions of decision-making responsibility. Through personal skill and inclination, women healers tap a source of prestige that enables them to command greater access to material resources as well as enhanced respect (see Ortner and White-head 1981, 15). Ortner and Whitehead argue that modes of prestige allocation are few: "There are ascriptive channels, which assign people to status positions through kin affiliation and natural surface characteristics; there are the achievement channels, which assign prestige according to group or individual success in designated endeavors; and there are sundry hybrids of both modes" (Ortner and Whitehead 1981, 14). For rural Bariba women, gender represents a primary "ascriptive channel" that constrains access to valued sources of power. Midwifery, the central healing role for women, has served as a conduit for women to achieve prestige beyond the limits of the household. For urban women, the emerging proliferation of opportunities in the public domain is further diminishing the boundaries between the domestic and public still evident in rural Bariba society. Following Rosaldo's model, the position of urban Bariba women, as they challenge men's authority in political and economic arenas, appears enhanced relative to their rural counterparts.

Research Site and Methodology

The material presented in this chapter is based on research conducted during 1976–1977 in the rural district of Pehunko and in 1982–1983 in the provincial capital of Parakou. Pehunko, with an estimated population of two thousand, is an agricultural community specializing in the production of cotton and peanuts as well as yams, millet, sorghum, and assorted vegetables and condiments. A thriving market center, Pehunko was historically a renowned chiefdom that until recently resisted the encroachment of both Christianity and Islam. Despite national government constraints on the functioning of indigenous political institutions, the death of the elderly chief of Pehunko in 1981 was followed by intense lobbying among contenders for the position. The chieftaincy thus continues, although officially "feudalism" has been abolished. Pehunko houses a dispensary, an endemic disease center, and a maternity clinic that opened in 1982. Until the arrival of the maternity clinic, almost all births occurred at home, sometimes with the assistance of indigenous midwives, who provided crisis care.

According to the Bariba ideal, women strive to deliver alone, unless an emergency arises during delivery. In this event, a midwife may be called or, if additional assistance is required, a diviner or herbalist, usually male, may be consulted. At the time of the 1982–1983 research, the range of formal therapeutic alternatives in the region included district nurses, the endemic disease nurse, a government nurse-midwife, one obstetrical auxiliary, herbalists, diviners, indigenous midwives, and bone setters. Government nurses were ubiquitously male, and females served as nurse-midwives; among the indigenous practitioners, all midwives were female and the majority of other specialists were male. The hierarchy of indigenous healers will be discussed further below. In addition to these locally available services, Pehunko residents occasionally sought medical assistance at the provincial hospital in Natitingou, located approximately 90 kilometers from the village, or at the hospital in Parakou, 177 kilometers distant. In 1977 motor transport to either of the provincial hospitals was sporadic, but by 1983 public buses traversed these routes several times weekly.

Parakou, the second research site, is an administrative and commercial center, with a population of over sixty thousand, approximately half of whom are Bariba. Bariba from contiguous areas have migrated to Parakou in search of employment as laborers, in the transport sector, in commerce, or increasingly, in one of the five factories that periodically have open hiring. The government civil service also provides a major source of employment, at various ranks, for Parakou residents. Custodial personnel, chauffeurs, and clerks as well as administrators may be categorized as civil servants. Health services in Parakou include the government hospital, two private clinics specializing in gynecology and obstetrics, the endemic disease center for the province, the Social Security Administration Prenatal Clinic, a Family Planning Clinic and Provincial Prenatal Clinic, and an array of indigenous practitioners similar to those described for Pehunko. Although indigenous healers from the several ethnic groups residing in Parakou (Fon, Yoruba, Dassa, Dindi) practice in Parakou, only Bariba healers will be considered here. No census of indigenous healers exists for Parakou, but it is evident from informant commentary that as in rural Bariba communities, indigenous midwives constitute the major category of female healers in the urban setting, and the majority of other specialists are male.

In both Pehunko and Parakou, the research focused on factors implicated in women's decisions to employ obstetrical assistance and the attributes, techniques, and practices of the indigenous midwives who provide the bulk of care for women of reproductive age. Data were collected by means of participant-observation and structured interview schedules. In the region of Pehunko, I interviewed eighteen midwives regarding their practices, observed home deliveries and consultations between midwives and clients, and interviewed 122 women of reproductive age concerning their reproductive histories and preferences for obstetrical care. In Parakou, I interviewed two indigenous midwives, one self-trained midwife running a private clinic, one nurse-midwife clinic proprietor, a male healer running a medicine boutique, two male healers providing general health care, one elderly female practicing primarily child health care, and nurse-midwives staffing the government health facilities. In addition, I interviewed 123 women at home and followed all throughout their pregnancies. These women, in the course of their interviews, discussed their reproductive careers, employment histories, health care preferences and religious beliefs and practices. Finally, a sample of fifty women employed in a cashew factory were interviewed concerning health care, employment aspirations, domestic responsibilities, and reproductive histories.

The Rural Setting

It will be useful to sketch briefly the understanding of the role of women in society that remains prevalent in rural Bariba settlements. A Bariba proverb succinctly describes the condition of women and the implications of gender: Women suffer. The essence of this suffering is unraveled in the thoughts of one Bariba woman, who stated that "to be a mother of children" is to experience suffering, from pregnancy, labor, and delivery through the perils of childhood. The trials of childhood illness, socialization of one's children, and responsibility for their welfare into adulthood make up the expected burdens of a Bariba woman of reproductive age. The proverb proclaiming "women suffer" indicates the fundamental attributes of female gender as understood in Bariba society. Maternity represents the essential goal of the adult woman; without the achievement of motherhood, a woman remains adolescent and unworthy of respect. As one infertile woman remarked, "I would run naked down the street without shame if such an act would give me a child." Even material acquisition, success in commerce, or making the pilgrimage to Mecca does not compensate for the lack of children in assessment of social standing for an adult woman.

Categories of Healing

Healing may be viewed as an extension of the nurturing role considered appropriate for women, given their primary association with the domestic domain. As Rosaldo states, "Women become absorbed primarily in domestic activities because of their role as mothers. Their economic and poltical activities are constrained by the responsibilities of child care, and the focus of their emotions and attentions is particularistic and directed toward children and the home" (M. Z. Rosaldo 1974, 24). Similarly, Ortner observes that children require "supervision and constant care. Mother is the obvious person for this task, as an extension of her natural nursing bond with the children or because she has a new infant and is already involved with child-oriented activities" (Ortner 1974, 77; see also Ortner and Whitehead 1981, 7). Among her duties, the Bariba "mother of children" is expected to assume responsibility for the health and welfare of her children and of others in the household who may seek her advice. This area of responsibility extends to the economic realm, as noted above. Most women, hoping to establish a lucrative commercial enterprise, engage in petty trade. The proceeds from this belong to the trader, but it is expected that her profits will be used for investment in health care as well as in clothing and adornment for her children. Thus extradomestic economic production by women is consumed within the household.

In the domestic domain, age and seniority among wives may be associated with experience in curing. However, even the most junior wife or new mother is expected to care for the mundane ailments of her child—skin disorders, gastrointestinal problems, respiratory infections.

In addition, she is to oversee the proper physical growth and development of her children. Thus mothers collect herbal preparations to ensure that a toddler will grow fat, or to stimulate walking at an early age, soothe teething, or assist articulate speech. If a child falls ill, then choice of an appropriate therapy is the responsibility of its mother, with liberal advice from senior women in the household. Neighborhood specialists may be consulted if encountered casually at an opportune moment or in the event of a worsening condition. When the two-year-old son of Zalia, mother of eight, had bloody diarrhea, for example, she concluded without benefit of counsel from her peers that this was caused by the swollen gums of teething. She treated the child with European antidiarrheal products purchased in the market. Zalia explained that when her first son was an infant, however, she constantly received advice—both solicited and unsolicited—from friends and neighbors. People kept telling her, for example, that the baby's head was overly swollen. An old woman next door told her to make a medicine from a certain type of seed and rub it on his head seven mornings consecutively, before speaking to anyone. She followed this advice. As her own experience as a mother increased, her cousins and nieces began to consult her regarding child care, and now she consults old women healers primarily for unusual or persistent problems.

Similarly, Bekegi, mother of four, observed that her baby had a sore in its anus; because she had never seen such as sore, she consulted her elderly female neighbor. This woman, not known as a formal healer but an experienced parent with many living children, diagnosed a condition caused by ants and prescribed a particular bark infusion as therapy. In addition, Bekegi employed an ointment of black soap that she had learned from her husband's sister in Togo, a neighboring country. In another case, Laratou was concerned because her baby seemed abnormal—the child never ate dirt, although "all children do." She consulted an elderly woman known as a healer to learn if this odd behavior signified that the child would die. The old woman said no, every child has its own "habit"; let the child do what it wants and don't worry.

In addition to providing remedies for common childhood sicknesses, women may also be called upon to recommend and prepare medicines to treat adult household members. Women frequently co-counsel wives concerning routine problems like menstrual complaints as well as for skin problems, respiratory disorders, and gastrointestinal ailments. When I suffered a leg abscess, several neighboring women volunteered therapies for this condition and one prepared a treatment. Women treat themselves for common complaints like malaria or diarrheal diseases and recommend treatments that they have found successful for their own health problems to others suffering similar afflictions. For serious health conditions, however, an adult will usually consult a respected male healer who is known to specialize in the particular disorder afflicting the individual. The hierarchy of healers thus begins with informal healing by household women and progresses to the more formal levels of male and female specialists known as *tingibu* (medicine people, sing. *tingi*). Among tingibu, males are uniformly senior to females. Midwives occupy a curious ranking in this hierarchy, in that some women informally assist at problematic deliveries of kin and neighbors but are not known as specialists. Women who have served an apprenticeship under a midwife—usually an aunt or grandmother—are termed *marusiobu*, one who sits at a delivery. This category overlaps with that of tingibu, with some midwives having attained this specialist status and others considered only technicians rather than true healers.

In analyzing the healing roles available to women, then, three primary categories emerge:

1. Mothering—in contrast to fathering, which involves primarily the roles of economic provider and disciplinarian, the role of the mother intrinsically includes healing. In discussing the nurturing qualities of a mother, Bariba invariably mention the skill of mothers in treating childhood illnesses and in generally protecting the health and emotional well-being of the child. When a mother's knowledge is insufficient to cope with an illness episode, she may then informally consult female kin and respected neighbors. Senior women in the household and older female neighbors are the second line of resort.

2. Informal health care provider—older women with a great deal of experience in treating the health needs of their own children as well as those of other adult household members often volunteer advice to young mothers and are frequently consulted for problematic (but not grave) illnesses. Such women are respected by the community, as is evident in deferential languages and genuflection in greetings, but they do not usually receive gifts or payment in return for their services and they are not titled as marusio or tingi.

3. Specialists—the primary healing specialization available to women is midwifery, which, as noted above, requires an apprenticeship to an established midwife. The practicing midwife is usually a postmenopausal woman with several living children who delivers babies for kin and neighbors on a part-time basis. She uses both ritual measures (incantations, gestures, sympathetic magic) and herbal remedies to ease complicated labors and accelerate delivery (see Sargent 1982). Apprentices are

usually women who have had children themselves. They "carry the medicine gourd" for their mentor until she retires. Midwives commonly offer advice to pregnant women, assist at deliveries, and provide remedies for infant and child illnesses, but they do not routinely offer counsel or remedies for other categories of complaints.

An elderly woman will rarely provide fertility counseling; most fertility specialists are men. One explanation offered by Bariba for this division of labor is that potent ritual means may be necessary to resolve fertility disorders. Therefore a superior and "strong" individual is required for this task. A male healer is more likely to demonstrate the requisite personal and professional characteristics for this undertaking. Because women of reproductive age are considered to pollute medicines, only women past menopause or men may employ truly strong medicines used to combat dangerous or stubborn afflictions. For this reason men make up the majority of senior and respected healers.

However, women are not completely excluded from this category. Among healers known as tingibu are some women, usually members of the possession cult *sambani,* and they are said to have powers of clairvoyance useful in the diagnosis and treatment of illness. Most often their clients are other women. These sambani women assist at complicated deliveries, and some specialize in treatment of disorders such as *tigpiru,* a folk illness that includes swollen ankles and legs, and hemorrhoids, hernia, and a prolapsed uterus or bladder, or *wirugu* (fallen fontanelle). Each healer is known for a particular remedy, and most specialties, with the exception of bone setting, include an occasional female practitioner. There appear to be few "general" practitioners. Specialization, per se, does not augment a healer's prestige. Rather, capacity to enter an altered state is associated with prestige among healers. Women belonging to spirit cults, according to one Pehunko midwife, are those who are truly respected in society. Other women do not offer opinions to men, but a cult member will do so without shame. These sambani cults, whose membership is predominantly female, comprise, in Rosaldo's terms, "a world where women prevail" (M. Z. Rosaldo 1974, 36). Cult members may achieve positions of prominence within the cults but often their influence extends to the community at large, where they are perceived as persons with unusual power.

Thus one young urban man observed that "it is rare for a young woman to have the quality *dam,* or force, but old woman can have this power just as old men do. Some old women even have more dam than men, especially the sambani women." This strength of character and spiritual power, dam, identifies the superior healer, competent to confront mystical forces attacking an afflicted client. Women thus are included among the highest-ranking healers, although it is infrequent that a woman is consulted as a last resort for serious conditions not responsive to treatment. Similarly, in all cases observed in this research, the final resort in cases of obstetrical complications was a male healer, although for reasons of modesty, such an individual might provide advice from outside the delivery area in order to avoid gazing at the woman in labor. In this regard, the Bariba case raises a central problem in gender and healing: why do men predominate as respected healers? Why do more men than women achieve dam? Rosaldo and Lamphere note that "everywhere we find that women are excluded from certain crucial economic or political activities . . . sexual asymmetry is presently a universal fact of human social life" (Rosaldo and Lamphere 1974, 3). Correspondingly, the role of women healers reflects the position of women more broadly construed in Bariba society. Mediated by factors such as age, seniority among wives, and lineage, the position of women in this highly stratified society is subordinate to that of men. Menopause, believed to eliminate the polluting qualities of female gender, is the critical factor allowing women healers—especially possession cult members—to approach the prestige of respected male healers.

Changing Obstetrical Alternatives

In the context of changing therapeutic alternatives in Benin, the Pehunko dispensary has coexisted for forty years with amiable interactions between most resident nurses and local healers. Indigenous midwives occasionally refer complicated cases to the nurse (see Sargent 1982, 115, 118) and sometimes participate in supervising the parturient at the dispensary. In a recalcitrant case, several elderly women might be seen calling consecutively at the clinic at the request of the family. However, in 1982 the government maternity clinic opened in Pehunko to offer specialized obstetrical care, and local authorities attempted to require pregnant women to deliver at the clinic rather than at home.

Currently, local midwives continue to assist at home deliveries but some have expressed concern at the attitude of the new nurse-midwife, who has rejected collaboration with indigenous practitioners. The government nurse-midwife has enlisted the assistance of village officials to fine women suspected of "deliberately" delivering at home. Indigenous midwives commented disparagingly on the attempt to pressure women to deliver at the clinic when customarily, a woman should have no assistance whatsoever at a birth except in the event of an emergency. In one case, a pregnant woman found herself in the predicament of either displeasing her mother-in-law, a respected indigenous midwife, by delivering at the clinic, or risking censure by village authorities. She chose to deliver in the bush, and claimed labor had begun suddenly while she was collecting wood. The nurse-midwife, having noticed that the woman was no longer pregnant, claimed that no labor is that sudden, and fined her. The family refused to pay and eventually the matter was dropped.

The Urban Context

Bariba women in the town of Parakou, regardless of social class or employment affiliatiton, maintain a primary identification as "mothers of children" similar to that expressed by rural women. Educated women employed at high administrative echelons in government civil service express opinions that are not unlike those of petty traders with no formal education regarding the value of children in establishing the identity of respected adult women. The critical contrast between the maternal roles of rural and urban women emerges in the case of cashew factory workers who work fixed hours and are unable to prepare family meals and engage in child care during the day (Sargent 1984, 289). Routine nurturing responsibilities are therefore delegated to relatives, friends, or domestic servants. In addition, all female cashew factory employees interviewed had adopted mixed feeding (breast and bottle) rather than breast feeding alone, due to inflexible work schedules—in contrast to the majority of urban women interviewed who were self-employed or in civil service, with more flexible hours. Women in the factory perceived the shift from breast to bottle feeding as a fundamental modification in the role of the mother. Rural Bariba, for example, consider breast feeding intrinsic to the health and well-being of an infant, as it in fact is, in the absence of alternatives. Thus the primary nurturing function of the mother is to provide breast milk for her child. To date, no rural Bariba in the sample studied has bottle fed; some women did not even know the Bariba word for bottle, "white person's breast." The modified feeding practices of women in the cashew factory as well as in the other urban factories represents a significant, though as yet rare, transformation in mothering responsibilities.

In the more general realm of informal healing, urban women, including those in the factory, continue to retain responsibility for child health, whether in providing home remedies or in making the decision to take a sick child for a clinic consultaiton. Interestingly, factory workers obtain liberal leaves of absence to care for sick children and other relatives. The factory manager complained that although the women are competent cashew sorters, they are not as responsible as men because men take sick leave only for themselves, while women take leave for themselves, their husbands, and their children. In addition, as in the village, factory women offer advice to kin and neighbors regarding routine health problems. Remedies for malaria, for example, were frequently circulated among women as the news of a relevant case arose.

It is in the realm of formal healing that the most obvious contrasts emerge between the rural and urban setting. These distinctions derive largely from structural differences between the two contexts. In Parakou, the existence of the provincial hospital and two private obstetrical clinics has provided a ready alternative to home delivery. Consequently, less than half of urban deliveries are estimated to occur at home (Provincial Director of Public Health, pers. comm.). Moreover, the national government and the provincial administration have strongly discouraged home delivery in town over the past ten years by threatening to fine those "caught" delivering at home. Further, women report that if one experiences complications during home delivery and seeks assistance at the hospital, government health personnel receive the offending patient with criticism and scorn. The woman who delivers at home may also encounter difficulties in obtaining a birth certificate, now recognized as necessary to enable children to attend school.

Thus, although indigenous midwives continue to practice in Parakou, many find that their clientele is dwindling. One urban midwife, Yaayi Bake, a woman in her sixties, observed that she was shifting her practice to infant and child care because mothers continued to consult her for advice on herbs and other preparations for childhood illnesses unresponsive to home treatment and for behavior problems. Similarly, another elderly woman maintains a practice in medicinal scarification for children afflicted by sorcery; it appears that health problems defined as resistant to cosmopolitan medicine such as illness resulting from sorcery or witchcraft remain the province of indigenous practitioners. Adults suffering such afflictions would consult a prominent male healer such as the Land Chief (in Parakou, the authority responsible for ritual well-being of the community). Women healers, however, figure among the respected personnel consulted for mystical illnesses among children.

Correspondingly, the Parakou market includes a section for venders of medicinal plants, and many of these traders are women, often post-menopausal, who collect herbs and roots in the rural environs of the town to sell in the market. Popular among these vendors are those who prescribe for the folk illness tigpiru. This condition is believed to afflict women of reproductive age most often, although men may also become sufferers. Because government health personnel, many of whom are not Bariba, do not respond sympathetically to clients who present themselves with complaints of tigpiru, indigenous healers remain the primary source of relief for this widespread complaint.

In the opinion of the Parakou midwife Bake, indigenous midwifery is declining in town but will persist in the countryside, where government pressures are less strong. In contrast, the urban midwife Sika claimed that she is still called for home deliveries (although she would not name any clients who had delivered at home or invite the researcher to observe her work) and that the sensible urban woman appreciates a healer who collects herbal medications and provides them without cost—as opposed to the maternity clinic, which requires the patient to purchase medication at the pharmacy.

Yet another indigenous midwife resolved the issue of government policy encouraging hospital delivery by transforming her practice. She apprenticed herself to an agreeable physician for a brief period and opened an obstetrical clinic that is supervised by the Department of Public Health. At this clinic, she accepts uncomplicated deliveries, advises her patients to deliver lying down rather than in the customary kneeling position, and refers problematic cases to the hospital. She sometimes employs herbal treatments during labor but does not use analgesics, forceps, or other technological interventions prevalent in cosmopolitan medicine. Her clinic is viewed by the neighborhood women who patronize it as "modern" but more comfortable and personal than the hospital.

Other healers, both male and female, complain of the difficulties of finding an apprentice in town. Young people see little advantage in "carrying the medicine gourd" for an elderly healer when the route to power in the modern sector lies in the formal educational system. In general, fundamental transformations in the bases for social stratification are diverting clientele from indigenous midwives, and the proliferation of alternatives for economic enterprise is directing young women toward avenues other than that of healer to enhance their social position.

Where midwifery formerly served as a unique means for women to transcend the domestic domain, the urban environment offers myriad options, especially for those who are literate. In addition to the route of petty trade, ubiquitous in both rural and urban areas, urban Bariba women may accrue capital to enter profitable long-distance commerce, seek salaried employment in one of several factories, or attempt to enter the civil service. Because the civil service includes levels ranging from custodial staff to clerk and administrative personnel, even women who have not completed secondary school may (with strategic use of their extended family network) obtain government employment. The fifty women employed at the cashew factory, when questioned regarding the ideal job for a woman in Benin today, uniformly mentioned as first choices large-scale trade and employment in the government health bureaucracy. The position of healer or diviner was not mentioned as desirable employment, particularly because most healers operate part-time and are remunerated according to the good will of the patient.

In assessing the future for indigenous midwives—the primary category of female healer in town—the government effort to organize collaboration between indigenous healers and cosmopolitan medical personnel is a relevant consideration. This effort has included the formation of an association for traditional medicine; midwives cannot register with this organization, however, because in its terms they are not defined as legitimate healers. With few exceptions, the government does not recognize women healers as bona-fide practitioners, despite the fact that training programs have been instituted in several areas to upgrade the skills of local midwives. Although the collaborative effort has so far lacked drive (cf. Sargent 1986), the official policy toward midwives does not encourage perpetuation of this specialty. One rural midwife, commenting on the trend away from indigenous midwifery, observed that she would have appreciated learning from clinic staff and had hoped to work together, as in the past, when the indigenous midwife would accompany her client to the dispensary in the event of complications. Now, she said, the "heart" of the nurses is unwelcoming. She has ceased to practice since the opening of the Pehunko maternity clinic in 1982.

In the rural areas, other midwives do continue to assist at home deliveries, but many complain, like their urban couterparts, that apprentices are increasingly difficult to obtain. As government public health policy and health services reach rural communities, indigenous medicine may follow the trend apparent in town. Changes in appropriate gender roles are to date only germinal in villages like Pehunko, where maternity still defines a woman's status and informal healing emerges as an extension of motherhood. Via the formal position of tingi, the medicine person, a woman may achieve the status of true healer, who is "like a man," serving the public domain. These women, often known as clairvoyant, remain respected in both rural and urban sectors; but as possession cults have decreased in public presence due to government interdictions, healers who are cult members are increasingly less visible and less frequently consulted.

Economic and political dynamics appear, then, to be exerting a profound influence on women's roles in the urban area and concomitantly on the ideology of gender. The socialist government, for example, has created official positions for women whose function is to mobilize and "sensitize" the masses of women. This introduces them to concepts of more egalitarian relationships with men and more widespread public political participation, yet ironically closes their old avenues to prestige and influence. Although maternity remains central to the concept of the successful woman, the accretion of other possibilities in the public domain, such as salaried worker, provide alternatives—both symbolic and actual—to traditionally acceptable options, principally that of midwife.

MARGARET REID

Sisterhood and Professionalization: A Case Study of the American Lay Midwife

The key to understanding the dilemma of the American lay midwife is to know that lay midwives started out as friends, as "sisters." Their social organization is based upon the values of sisterhood that themselves derive from the women's movement. But a combination of factors—the desire to progress and improve their working conditions and to allow more women the possibility of a home birth—has led to increasing peer pressure among lay midwives to professionalize and to gain legitimacy through legislation. It is this dilemma, the contrary demands of sisterhood and professionalization, that faces many lay midwives today.

The Status of Lay Midwifery

Midwifery has traditionally been seen as women's work. In some countries today midwives have become organized into a distinct occupational group—that is, the work has become located in the public domain. In other countries midwives remain at the level of traditional birth attendants, and this "traditional" or nonmedical midwifery has tended to remain in the private sphere, located within the family as domestic work (Stacey 1981). The group I focus on here is composed of women drawn mostly from the latter group; they practice home birth in the United States, often without a license. They are called "lay," "empirical," or "non-nurse" midwives. These terms indicate that like many other midwives around the world, the majority hold no formal qualifications or license to practice midwifery. They have learned their skills instead through self-instruction and apprenticeship, and some still practice covertly.

In a few states, lay midwives can practice legally if they have attended an approved course of study and passed a state qualifying examination (as, e.g., in Washington State). In other states, lay midwifery may be legal simply because there are no laws directly outlawing the practice of midwifery or because midwives are merely asked to register themselves as such (as used to be the case in Texas). The remaining states have more specific laws; some prohibit lay midwifery altogether and some also set constraints on the practice of certified nurse-midwifery.

This chapter considers the development of lay midwifery from its beginnings to the later stage of professionalization. Freidson (1970) characterizes a profession as having both a long period of training and an esoteric body of knowledge that creates experts set off from lay persons. Freidson also asserts that a central criterion of a profession is that its members have autonomy over their work: they should not be ruled by other professionals and they should have the ability to carry out decision making on their own behalf. This last characteristic, in Freidson's view, sets apart those few "true" professions such as medicine or law from occupations referred to as "semi-professions," such as nursing, social work, and teaching. Although both professions and semiprofessions ensure standards through the careful selection of students, a series of formal requirements before full membership can be achieved, and possession of a register of members and a code of ethics, a truly autonomous professional body would have few outsiders or lay members on its governing board and minimal accountability to other occupations.

Licensed lay midwives, with their required period of training and specialized knowledge, come under the same banner as other semiprofessionals. They are based in hospitals and with their prescribed education, professional organization, and journals, they possess some of the hallmarks of a profession. Although they work with some independence, they are restricted from attending high-risk labors and deliveries and from using a number of medical technologies. Ultimately, they are accountable to others, most notably physicians.

Unlicensed lay midwives are different. They are domestically based and attend only home births. For this they use some specialized knowledge and undergo a period of training that is of an unspecified time period and empirical rather than abstract. Though they do not meet all of the criteria of a profession, they do work with considerable autonomy, unlike licensed midwives. The work limitations of an unlicensed midwife are not that certain tasks or practices belong to other occupational groups or that they are accountable to other professionals. Rather, the boundaries are set by the empirical limits of the midwife's own skill. The lay midwife working illegally is answerable to no one except her clients and possibly other unlicensed lay midwives. In addition, lay midwives may be subject to prosecution for practicing medicine without a license.

Freidson himself has noted a number of groups who work outside the orthodox framework of society and who do not fit the straightjacket definition of professions (Freidson, quoted in Stacey 1981); it could be argued that lay midwives merely constitute a group of women workers who do not fit the system. But lay midwives work within the female, private sphere and organize their work within that world. What Freidson describes in his analysis of professions is a style of working that is geared toward the public world, the world of business, universities, hospitals, and public institutions. It is a world in which men especially have access to and use of key resources and dominate high-prestige and high-paying occupations. Because lay midwifery is domestically based and informally organized, it is not strictly comparable to professions.

Lay Midwifery: Its Place in American Birth

As in other Western societies, women in the United States are presented with a range of alternatives for the birth attendant and the place of birth. The lay midwife attends home births, but she is only one of several kinds of practitioners that do so. Some are licensed, others are not. Table 12.1 summarizes childbirth care options. Since 98 percent of all births in the United States take place in the hospital, home birth with any type of attendant is an option taken by very few. Of hospital births, most take place in either public or private hospitals under the direct care of an obstetrician, with a certified nurse-midwife (CNM) responsible for a small percentage. The CNM has been trained first as a registered nurse (RN), later becoming a CNM through an extra year's training (in some cases two years). She usually works in close association with an obstetrician, is a member of a professional organization, and her orientation is distinctly medical (Rothman 1982). Whether a CNM can obtain private insurance varies considerably.

TABLE 12.1   Childbirth Care Options

	Hospital	Freestanding Birth Center	Home
Attendant (licensed)	Obstetrician		Obstetrician
	Family Practitioner		Family Practitioner
	CNM[a]	CNM	CNM
Attendant (unlicensed)			Lay Midwife
			Granny Midwife
			Partera

[a]CNM–certified nurse-midwife.

For women not wishing a hospital birth, the free-standing birth center or alternative birth center (ABC) is a possible choice. Staffed by CNMs and often set in a refurbished domestic house, the free-standing ABC offers women a compromise between the institutional atmosphere of hospital and the raw intimacy of a home birth. Free-standing ABCs have become popular and in recent years may well have taken clients from the lay midwife (DeVries 1985). The home is the most radical place of birth in late-twentieth-century America. Most CNMs do not attend (and indeed may not always be legally allowed to attend) home births— DeVries (1985) quotes one study that reported that 4 percent of CNMs would do home deliveries. The number of general practitioners from outlying communities who used to attend a few home births has been reduced to a handful by peer pressure and the threat of having their hospital privileges removed. Home birth, therefore, remains the domain of the traditional lay midwife.

After 1900, when midwives were attending about half of all births, midwives in the United States did not maintain their status as they did in European countries (Donnison 1977; Litoff 1986). Most midwives ceased working in the early decades of this century (for two histories of midwives in the United States, see Donegan 1978 and Litoff 1978). Although illegal in some states, some midwives continued working, mostly in minority communities; examples are the granny midwife, who could be found in black, rural communities (for individual accounts, see Mongeau, Smith, and Maney 1961; Osgood, Hochstrasser, and Deuschle 1966), the *partera*, who worked in Mexican American communities (Buss 1980; E. Kelly 1956), and the midwives who came from separate religious sects such as the Amish in Pennsylvania or the Mormons in Utah.

Anthropologists are sometimes cautious about grouping traditional midwives together because of the internal variations that exist—some are licensed, some are trained in biomedical practices, and others are neither (MacCormack 1982b). However, certain similarities do emerge among "traditional" midwives that link the partera, the granny, and the modern lay midwife with midwives practicing traditionally in many different societies across the world. Few have had formal training, and most acquire their knowledge through apprenticeship with another midwife; they often have a sense of midwifery as a "calling," a vocation. Most adhere to a style of birthing that involves reliance upon herbs and traditional remedies for stimulating the uterus, little use of modern obstetrical instruments, and a lack of orthodox training (MacCormack 1982b; Mongeau, Smith, and Maney 1961; L. Paul 1978b).

Moreover, traditional midwives are culturally compatible with women from their own community. The midwife gains her status not because of her occupational role per se but through her social position as midwife in the community. Since her status depends upon her personal characteristics, the prestige of the midwife can vary considerably (E. Kelly 1956; L. Paul 1978b). Traditional midwives share their clients' assumptions about pregnancy and childbirth which range from beliefs as profound as the meaning of birth to more commonplace notions about the kind of food a pregnant woman should eat and the rituals she should undergo before and after birth. The cultural and epistemological gulf separating patients and biomedical professionals contrasts starkly with the shared values and understandings of traditional midwives and the women who seek their care (Kleinman 1980; MacCormack 1982b; Snow, Johnson, and Mayhew 1978).

Although there are similarities among traditional midwives from different cultures and groups, there are also differences that distinguish, in particular, lay midwives from many other traditional midwives. The granny midwife, on the one hand, started her working life after her children had grown up, and she continued working into old age. The modern lay midwife, on the other hand, began to work when her children were

TABLE 12.2   Number and Percentage Distribution of Live
Births by Place of Delivery, United States, 1950, 1960, 1970, 1975–
1981

Year	Total Live Births	In Hospital No.	%	Out of Hospital No.	%
1950	3,554,149	3,125,975	88.0	428,174	12.0
1960	4,257,850	4,114,368	96.6	143,482	3.4
1970	3,731,386	3,708,142	99.4	23,244	0.6
1975	3,144,198	3,103,323	98.7	40,875	1.3
1976	3,167,788	3,123,439	98.6	44,349	1.4
1977	3,326,632	3,276,732	98.5	49,900	1.5
1978	3,333,279	3,300,659	99.0	31,350	1.0
1979	3,494,398	3,460,484	99.1	33,914	0.9
1980	3,612,258	3,576,370	99.0	35,888	1.0
1981	3,629,238	3,591,582	98.9	37,656	1.1

Source: National Center for Health Statistics, *Vital Statistics of the United States,
1977,* vol. 1: *Natality, 1981,* National Center for Health Statistics, Monthly Vital
Statistics Report 32 (9, suppl.): December 29, 1983. Adapted from DeVries 1985.

young. Other differences also appear. The modern lay midwifery movement has been defined as a woman's cause, influenced by the recent
feminist movement in the United States (Litoff 1986). The granny midwife, though she too was doing woman's work, lacked such consciousness. Although the granny achieved status in her community, the modern
lay midwife has reached beyond her community and is now attempting to
build a profession. Finally, the traditional midwives described in anthropological studies are Third World, usually rural, women, or members of
ethnic and religious minorities in Western countries. The lay midwife
described here is with few exceptions white, middle class, and frequently
has young children. She is a product of the dominant class of her society
and, more often than not, has completed a good number of years of education. Of the forty-nine midwives I studied, only two were nonwhite. The
majority had started a college education; one was over 50, the remainder
were between 25 and 40. All except one had children, although several of
the apprentices had none. Childbirth care by these midwives reflects a

different career choice and a different set of motives from those of more traditional midwives, many of whom can neither read nor write and most of whom follow traditional practices as the only option available.

Nationally, it is impossible to estimate at any one time how many lay midwives are practicing, for figures are unreliable and based at best on guesses. Lay midwives do not file tax returns or appear in official employment figures. What is recorded through statistics is the number of out-of-hospital births that occur annually and whom the attendant was. Lay midwife and other transfers would, of course, count as hospital births; unexpected home births would add to the overall total of out-of-hospital births. Table 12.2 summarizes birth location from 1950 to 1981.

Such data are the only official evidence of the prevalence of the lay midwife, and even this is extrapolated information. Only where lay midwives are licensed does a register of their names exist. Elsewhere, guesses are hopeless. "Estimates vary widely on their numbers," write Sallomi and her colleagues, referring to the number of midwives working in Alabama, "from anywhere betwen ten and fifteen to between 100 and 150" (Sallomi, Pallow, and McMahon 1981). A quick examination of the midwifery guide they construct, however, suggests that in each state there is evidence of some midwifery activity.

Studying Lay Midwifery

The empirical data for this chapter are based on a study of American lay midwives I carried out in 1981–1982 and 1983. I selected a state in which lay midwifery was illegal; I quickly found out, however, that there were "shades of illegality," and in the community I chose to carry out the research lay midwifery was not very underground. Many of the rules I adopted for studying this group are similar to those used in studying other covert groups, well described by Polsky (1969). Trust was built up slowly, and after some months I was able to have access to the midwives across the state and, through their connections, to midwives elsewhere. Five months into the project I was a recognized and tolerated outsider. I attended meetings, visits, and by the end, births with midwives; tape recorded all interviews and meetings when possible; and wrote field-notes at times. Intermittent traveling had allowed me to broaden my sample and my perspective, and the beginnings of a comparative dimension emerged, for I visited midwives who worked with a license and met others who were undergound. Undercover agents have been used to expose midwife activities (as in the famous Santa Cruz bust; see Ruzek 1978), and there were occasional jokes about my presence. In all written accounts I have taken care to disguise the identity of the women, some of whom no longer work as midwives.

The Lay Midwifery Movement: Its Origins

The roots of the present-day U.S. lay midwifery movement can be traced to the late 1960s and the broader "counterculture" that emerged at that time on the West Coast (Hazell 1974). The countercultural movement was primarily composed of middle-class women and men who had rejected mainstream American institutions in favor of a return to a more natural style of living that embraced values and beliefs that were the antithesis of those of an achievement-oriented culture. Their approach to food and clothing, as well as their belief in a more spiritual approach to life, were reflected in their life style, which appeared to have emerged from a combination of political radicalism and an attraction to Eastern religious zeal. Couples wishing to live by their principles had home births. Hazell, in an early study of home birth among this alternative group, describes a typical couple: "One of the main characteristics of this group is a hard-to-define level of self-awareness which manifests itself in an individual concern with proper nutrition and a kitchen stocked with health foods, personal libraries dealing with religious topics, philosophy, positive health, and humanistic psychology" (Hazell 1974, 7).

Until that time, birth had been culturally managed by obstetricians as a strictly medical procedure, with the use of heavy sedation dying out only in the 1960s in some places (Leavitt 1980). In this new countercultural setting, birth took on a different emphasis. It became redefined as a "natural" event that should take place in the home, without technological intervention. It also became a social occasion to which it was appropriate to invite friends. Although unattended home births among alternative life-style couples occurred on the West Coast at the time, this was not always planned. Indeed, it was argued that the major reason they took place was simply because no attendants could be found to help the couple (Brooks 1979); even then doctors refused to attend such a delivery (Hazell 1974). As one midwife confirmed in an interview: "And that's just the way most people were, it was just the husband and the wife, and that was because there wasn't anyone." The only people around to help would be friends who had had babies themselves and other young women who were interested in the idea of home birth, perhaps as a form of self-expression. These were not midwives, then, but "brave ladies who hung out and stayed by your bedside and told you that it was okay and learned a little each time they went to a birth."

In one West Coast community, a few young women started helping each other with their home births and went on to organize a birth collective. They started a birth center that acted both as a support and training center for midwives and also as a place where women could find an attendant for their home birth. The group of "helpers" met regularly and carried out prenatal sessions once a week. Since there was no one who was an "expert," the informal sessions in which the helpers got together and talked about pregnancy and birth served an educational function, each learning from the others.

In keeping with their values, birth helpers rejected technological equipment (except, for some, the stethescope), replacing it with a reliance upon alternative aids like herbal teas and remedies. In the early days the helpers did not obtain antihemorrhage drugs like pitocin but instead "we would carry herbs and we were adamant about it." Some relied upon knowing the mother well and picking up the "vibes" during labor, rather than depending upon what they perceived to be male-created obstetric tools to manage the progress of the labor. Prior to the birth, considerable attention was paid to the diet and life style of the woman, but since she was usually from the same community this was seldom a problem. Later some took to carrying pitocin and attempted to broaden their knowledge of the birth process by consulting biomedical texts.

The West Coast community was not alone in developing a distinct home birth culture, although it was probably the earliest. In the late 1960s a group of women and men emigrated east from California, ending their long trek in Tennessee, where they founded a spiritual community that also became a focus for lay midwifery. It trained midwives and opened its doors to welcome any woman who wished to give birth there (Gaskin 1977). The leader of the spiritual community was male, but his wife (author of the first textbook for lay midwives) took on the role of midwife and encouraged other women in the community to train empirically with her. Much of the West Coast ideology was incorpoated by this group, although being more patriarchal in organization, it did not carry with it the same strong feminist message. Thus their interpretation of birth was as a family event, with less emphasis upon the importance of fulfillment of the woman through the act of birth.

Still other kinds of birth attendants were emerging from a variety of backgrounds. Some were distinctly feminist, reflecting the growing women's health movement (Fremont 1978); others, like a number of lay midwives I interviewed, started out in the early 1970s from a feminist stance that was combined with strong views about the importance of the family. Although their politics may have differed, women from these varied beginnings united in their decision to allow as little technology into the home as possible, and to create alternative birth possibilities for mothers and families.

From its origins in the late 1960s and early 1970s, the lay midwife movement flourished. Official statistics indicate that the number of out-of-hospital births increased, and although the number of women working as home-birth attendants rose (the majority of women I interviewed started working in the 1970s), the number of clients each midwife took on grew at a faster rate. Couples' desire for a home birth put pressure on women wishing to work as lay midwives, which sometimes led them to take on work when they were not sufficiently experienced. One woman recalled: "When I first started attending births, I used to get dizzy at the sight of blood. My head would go real light, and I never wanted to be a midwife, I really didn't. I kept thinking this was the last birth I was ever going to do, because every time I went to a birth, I would get real frightened."

The home-birth clientele broadened to include couples with strong religious or family convictions, and even professional couples. Women began calling midwives from outside their immediate circle—not just friends of friends, but sometimes women with whom they had no previous links: "Every day I get phone calls. Every day someone phones me up and says 'Hi! You don't know me but . . . ' And it's like 'Who are you, and when are you due?' "

This kind of demand had heavy repercussions on the organization of a midwife's work. It changed her relationship with clients, and in many cases her style of work altered to accommodate the larger work load. It also altered her relationship with her sister midwives.

The first transformation to occur was often an internal one, a change in self-perception or self-image. Midwives reported that at some point (different for each midwife), their self-perception shifted from that of a birth helper to that of a midwife. Sometimes this identity change came swiftly, at other times they adjusted more slowly to the way the community now perceived them. It was always a significant change, as one midwife's comments illustrate:

. . . and then the community began to call these helpers "midwives" and they got a title, and with that title there was a whole role they had to perform, and with that role came a lot of work, and within a certain amount of time (it took me a long time) but for most of the women it wasn't all that long before they realized, "I want some money for this. I'm spending maybe sixty hours a week, I'm away from my family, my children and so forth, and I want to be compensated." And with that grew the birth of a professional.

Work Organization and Practice

When midwives first established themselves, they charged little. They felt that they were still in the process of learning and were not hesitant to "put themselves out as a midwife." But with increasing numbers of clients, their costs escalated. More clients from other communities meant greater distances to travel; gas costs and car repair bills also grew. Child care for their own children presented many with continuing worry and expense, as did the necessity to set up and maintain a small library of books for their clients and themselves. Since midwives have to maintain some link with clients day and night (especially near clients' due dates), some form of telephone link was essential. Some midwives bought an answering machine, others used an answering service or added a second phone line to their house. Whatever the solution, it cost money.

Despite the move toward financial recompense, most midwives did not earn enough to make a living but continued to be financially dependent upon their partners. Such dependence created unease in this woman-centered occupation; in all other aspects of their lives, midwives demanded from their partners respect for their work and, in many cases, equality or priority for midwifery over their other roles as wife and mother. Such dependence characterizes other women healers (see, e.g., L. Paul's [1978a] discussion of Mayan midwives) and in large part reflects the status and conditions attached to women's work, rather than the tasks that women carry out per se. Some midwives supported themselves, but their style of practice was very labor intensive, and most felt that they could not take on any more clients than they already had.

Bookkeeping was time consuming. Increased client numbers resulted in midwives spending more time with the "paperwork," working out their finances, keeping records of a client's progress, and attempting to come out with a profit at the end of the month. Being efficient with the paperwork was, many midwives reported, the worst part of the work and the part that, like professionals, they regarded as "dirty work." The process of turning a favor to a friend into a home business was for many midwives slow and difficult, for the business ethic seemed to run against the spirit in which the movement had begun.

The lay midwife, like many other traditional midwives (MacCormack 1982b), carried out a broader range of services with her clients than did the certified nurse-midwife. She supervised her client's diet, tended to her spiritual well-being as well as her physical health during pregnancy, and looked after her family. But the early practitioners reported that midwifery threatened to eat up their personal lives. It left them worn and exhausted, with a family they seldom saw. The increasing number of calls from clients forced many midwives to reorganize their work. Midwives reported that they started restricting the time spent with each client; visits overlapped less with friendship and time spent together was spent more focused upon the pregnancy.

Other time-saving strategies developed. Midwives often recalled that when they started their practice they would go to the birth whenever the woman first called, at the beginning of the labor. Later, however, many realized that it was possible to "spread themselves too thinly," and thus they would tend to keep in touch by telephone until the labor picked up and arrive once labor became established.

Such reductions in time spent with each client introduced additional risks, for the midwife was not always on hand if problems suddenly arose. It was also commonly agreed that clients, not wishing to take on responsibility, took less time to find out about the pregnancy and birth in detail. Instead, the midwife was in charge. As one midwife pointed out, "If you're paying someone a grand for a birth, you're paying someone to take on that responsibility." Thus lay midwives had more clients and more responsibility for their work than ever before.

Despite the fact that midwives attempted to redefine birth as a normal event, the issue of risk was highly problematic. Although it was felt that the notion of safety should not force the midwives into a style of practice that was against their principles, medical standards had to be taken into some sort of consideration. If problems did arise, the midwives knew that they would be judged by medical standards rather than their own. Midwives reacted in various ways to this pressure to become accountable in their work. Some virtually disregarded it. Some bought more equipment, such as a doptone, an ultrasonic device that can monitor more accurately than the fetoscope the fetal heart during the second stage of labor. Others cultivated a local physician whom they could trust and use as a second opinion on issues about which they had doubt (e.g., should a woman with herpes have a home birth?) and approached those with access to legislators in the hope of gaining some support for the licensing of their work. In 1982, an alliance was formed with CNMs, the Midwives' Alliance of North America (MANA); lay midwives hoped that such contact would add respectability and an aura of legitimacy to them.

Thus each midwife went her own way, precariously balancing her family and her work. Most took on more clients, and talked of reducing time and reorganizing work. Some midwives in rural areas introduced a geographical cutoff so that they only accepted as clients women who lived within their area. Others attempted to find ways of obtaining payment from the client with minimum fuss; some managed to rent an office for a day or half a day and rationalize their prenatal care. But in general midwives still made exceptions to the rules, took on clients whom they knew could not pay, had difficulty rejecting clients, and gave generously of their time.

Midwives Together

The lay midwife movement remained fragmented throughout most of the 1970s, with small groups of women working across many states. It has not been politically possible or safe to introduce a midwife register. Too many women drifted in and out of the work, some of the peripheral helpers calling themselves "midwife" to add status to their marginal position. No minimum standards had been established for practice, and there was no way such standards could be maintained. These problems, apparently insurmountable, stood in the path of those who wished to professionalize.

But the situation did change. In 1977 a lay midwife meeting was held in El Paso, Texas. Some two hundred midwives attended and a national register and newsletter had its origins at this meeting (Litoff 1978). Statewide groups with their own newsletters began to be set up.

The link that midwives felt bound them most strongly was still that of their immediate friendship circle, and local groups of midwives were organized around this factor. To these meetings would come midwives from the area, women who had been working on their own or with a few others. The meetings served the same function as earlier ones had: support, education, and as the only form of social control that sisterhood could offer, the internal monitoring of its members.

But these groups, still informal, had problems. The conflicts between the increasing pressure to professionalize and the desire to remain true to the roots of lay midwifery created difficult stresses. Furthermore, the gathering of women from assorted backgrounds and politics and religious beliefs opened up possible divides that sisterhood did not necessarily hold together. Feminist beliefs in sisterhood, egalitarian relations, and shared knowledge and experience were all positive but offered little direction in how to deal with conflict and dissension. The attempts to maintain a nonelitist group, with no leaders or formal hierarchy, led to organizational problems described so acutely by Freeman as "the tyranny of structurelessness" (Freeman 1972–73); masked power and unacknowledged control created stresses that were ideologically difficult to confront. Small wonder that a recurrent sentiment expressed by midwives from a number of states was "I think we have difficulty with group dynamics."

Midwife Meetings

One of the things that strikes me about the association meetings that we have here is that there's always a level of sisterhood that we feel between each other, and we try and incorporate an awareness of that with each group.

In one state, midwife meetings took place once a month and lasted most of the day. Attendance by the whole group was important, and absences were only tolerated if a midwife had to attend a birth or a special family event. The meetings were a mixture of sisterhood and business. When they met, the midwives hugged each other and started each meeting by sitting around in a circle, holding hands, and singing a song or a chant. Throughout the meeting, it was not unusual for the midwives to be physically close to one another, leaning on another's knees if some were sitting on the floor, showing support or sympathy through a hug or touch. The meetings were seen as affirmation of their sisterhood in a symbolic and a physical way. In a world where many were against them, positive support for each other was important, and the hug and the closeness offered tangible evidence of this support.

When I first analyzed these meetings, I assumed that their overall structure was in some way special to the midwives. But studies of women's groups and women's metings from quite diverse sources (e.g., Middleton-Keirn 1978 on spirit-mediums, Carden 1974 on lesbian groups and other feminist meetings) suggest that there were more general aspects of the meetings common to other kinds of women's groups that gather informally and in domestic contexts. Women took their infants to meetings, sewed and embroidered during the business, and discussed cooking and other domestic activities during breaks. Unlike professional men and women who work hard to keep their domestic roles from intruding on business meetings, these women allowed family and work to combine, to flow in and out of the meetings in a way that everyone accepted as normal. Interruptions were accepted, whether it was the telephone or someone handing around tea.

The meetings did follow certain professional conventions; there was an agenda, and someone took minutes, but the midwives incorporated these conventions into their world, and in many other ways did not mimic professional practice. The meetings were held in someone's living room, with the group ranged over easy chairs, sitting casually. There was none of the enforced formality of a professional meeting, with special rituals, formalized language, and carefully controlled emotions. Instead, the discussion was conducted in feminist rhetoric with emphasis on listening to each other, consideration for one another's point of view, fairness, and being open. Emotions ran strong at times. Because of their unlicensed status, these lay midwives were adamant about their work and their relationships with sister midwives. As one midwife burst out at a meeting: "Whether it's legal or not, that's beside the whole point. What I need to do inside me is to be out and out straight with everything and everybody. And I don't give a shit about the law." The agendas for the meetings ranged over talk of forthcoming events, women wishing to join the group, possible ways of developing legislation, discussion of a particular incident of general importance (e.g., a letter or a visit from an official inquiring about a midwife's work, or how a midwife handled a particular event). The group struggled with unresolved tensions that emerged, particularly over the issue of backup, which in turn reflected the larger problem of maintaining standards.

The system of backup relied upon the support of another midwife, who would come to the scene of the birth if there were problems—a difficult presentation, a tear that required stitching that the first midwife could not do, and so on. By calling upon another midwife, the initial midwife avoided the contact with the medical authorities that would occur if the woman had to be transported to a hospital. But by its very nature, the backup system involved bringing another midwife into a potentially hazardous situation. Midwife backup demanded loyalty and support from sister midwives, but though one might back up another midwife out of sisterhood, disagreements still occurred. Midwives sometimes discovered that they were friends with someone whom they thought did not practice very well. The discovery was painful to a group who had thought that friendship was everything. As one said: "I think that it's been hard for us to come from the friendship level and try to create a professional attitude about each other. I think that's been tough."

One group had drawn up criteria for selecting and rejecting clients, but although it defined regulatory procedures that would include client selection, the rules were still written flexibly and considerable variation occurred in practice. This group had two forms of dealing with disagreements among sister midwives, types of social control very similar to those used by professionals themselves (see Bosk 1979, Freidson 1970, and Millman 1976 for discussions of peer review within medicine). The first was to sanction another midwife informally, at a meeting. Millman, discussing peer review in surgery, argues that doctors have developed what amounts to a code, a special rhetoric for telling another surgeon that his or her work is shoddy (Millman 1976). But although the lay midwife reviews at meetings were similar in function to those of physicians, they were less skilled at the procedure. The reviews were tense, defensive, and emotional. One midwife told me of a somewhat acrimonious meeting where another had said to her afterward: " 'I don't like the way you attacked me at this last meeting.' I wasn't attacking her. I said, 'Marianne, we were talking about professionalism and how to handle something. It had nothing to do with you personally. I love you.' "

The second form of sanction was to expel the individual from the group. In the group I became most familiar with, several midwives had been rejected. Lacking the institutionalized devices that professionalism creates for removing unqualified practitioners from the ranks, the midwives did what they could, recognizing their limitations: "We can't really tell another person what to do. In the end, the final line is that we really can't, even if they get ostracized. They can still get out and keep doing it somewhere else."

Midwife groups changed from the early days. They conformed less to the ideal type of radical feminist health care deliverers, though this had occurred through gradual modifications to the original practice rather than through any sudden or considered shift. The desire to take on more clients, to appeal to a broader range of women, and to look beyond the immediate confines of their own community and its needs were all influencing factors. Unlike the grannies and other traditional midwives before them, lay midwives had adopted a cosmopolitan approach and saw themselves as pioneers of a new, national movement. Contrasting the success of orthodox midwifery in the United Kingdom with its lack of success in the United States, Anisef and Basson (1979) argue that occupational visibility is one of the critical factors leading to professionalization. U.S. lay midwives, even those who worked without a license, were becoming more visible, whether through their informal contacts with local physicians and with those involved in legislation, through renting an office for their work, or through the media attention that was paid them.

An analysis of the development of lay midwifery must at this point underline the paradox of their situation. By the end of the 1970s and the beginning of the 1980s, lay midwives were poised between two worlds. Most lay midwives remained working within the domestic sphere, but they were no longer just a group of friends helping each other out. They were beginning to move into the public world and make contact with professionals. Although many seemed determined to gain legalization, they were aware of the problems it brought as well as those it solved. If lay midwives became licensed, they would most likely have to become accountable to the very group that had prompted the movement in the first instance, members of the medical profession. What does such a move mean to lay midwifery?

Professionalization

In recent years, several states have changed their legislation to recognize the practice of lay midwifery. Women who previously worked underground in these states can now practice in the open, advertise their services, and seek collaboration and professional opinion from other health workers. Legislation is thoroughly dealt with by DeVries in his book, *Regulating Birth* (1985). The process will not be dealt with further here, but the consequences of working legally will be described to illustrate the continuum that exists from birth helper to professional lay midwife.

The changes that took place when midwifery became legal were in many ways simply an extension of the process that has been charted in this chapter. Relationships with clients and sister midwives became more formal, work more businesslike. The radical nature of original lay midwifery had already been modified; now legislation spelled out the parameters even more clearly. These may not be what the lay midwives wanted, but compromises were the price they paid for wider credibility and acceptability and for freedom to work without worrying about being prosecuted. Although midwives working illegally continued to choose their apprentices on the basis of personal attributes, one of the conditions of working with a license was that women wishing to train as lay midwives had to apply to an approved school and pass the appropriate examinations. (The exact conditions varied from state to state, but the end result was the same). In Washington State in 1984, students were required to pay $3,750 for each twelve-month session, a stipulation that ruled out those who could not move to the state or did not have the money. In the first year students attended a course of lectures and seminars, and years two and three were taken up with fulfilling other requirements by attending a set number of births and passing a final examination.

One important issue of concern for those involved in running the school was the selection criteria for students seeking admission. With the law as it stood, the academic requirements had been fixed, and all students were required to take a minimum of credits in certain basic sciences before acceptance was possible. The school's administrator voiced her fears: "I'm almost afraid that it's going to get so hard, that we will require so much before people even come into the school, that it's going to rule out a lot of people who would really be good midwives, but maybe can't take Chemistry 200 or something. That could happen."

The school certainly offered students the opportunity to participate in far more births within three years than would a midwife working without a license. But the school, with its input from the university medical facility and other health workers, the requirement of examinations, and the emphasis on formal, organized knowledge, represented a very different kind of education from that gained by the original birth helper, with all her enthusiasm and native intelligence. As a pioneer midwife said of the early lay midwife, "She is self-trained, which makes her who she is. You can't buy that training, that training comes real hard, real personally."

From the limited literature and my own interviews with licensed midwives from two states, it seemed that the essence of the original movement could still be found in the more open relationships such midwives maintained with their clients. One licensed lay midwife who had practiced for a number of years described what she felt was still special about lay midwifery: "I think they're more accessible, there's less professional distance. I think they feel more comfortable being related to as a co-person, or something like that. I think it's more open as far as sharing information. Maybe they're just closer to that themselves, having evolved as parents or something that's not potentially got the elitism or professionalism."

But "doing births" becomes a business, and this midwife reported that she was highly organized, was required to keep records, and found client relations more formal. "It's slightly less of a social thing because it's more of a job where we try and support ourselves."

The licensed lay midwife, then, created a working situation that resembled that of other semiprofessionals. She earned enough to support herself, worked in an office, had contacts with others in the health field, including physicians, and indeed was answerable to both them and to the state. As a matter of course, licensed lay midwives collected statistics on their births, including the percentage of women transported to the hospital.

Others have drawn attention to the tendency of midwives, once licensed, to interpret events through the medical model (Weitz and Sullivan 1985). This is not unexpected, given the educational requirements of the student midwife. The licensed lay midwives I interviewed stressed that they felt they had to be above criticism, and that to do this they had to follow the law to the last word. In each state, the law specified the kinds of births that they could undertake at home, what type of drugs and herbs they could (and could not) use, under what conditions they would have to transport a woman in labor, and so on. Some accepted these stipulations more than others, but on the whole the pressure was toward an increasingly conservative practice. Where ambiguity existed, the midwives were able to exercise judgment. But the freewheeling "gut" reactions of midwives working autonomously were inappropriate within the new working conditions of those licensed, and there was less talk of intuition and vibes.

What about sisterhood? Licensed lay midwifery is still a relatively recent phenomenon and one can only speak of tendencies, but it appears that the closeness of the informal network diminishes with the coming of legislation. Writing about "Jane," the illegal abortion service in Chicago, Bart quotes one of the leaders as saying "the illegal is the crux of it . . . [it] swept us all together" (Bart 1981). One example of the lack of solidarity among licensed lay midwives involves the issue of accountability. DeVries noted that in a state where lay midwifery was legal, a licensed midwife was taken to task for administering herbs, an illegal act in that state. There was none of the kind of midwife support shown her, when her case was heard in court, that had been given to a lay midwife who was being tried for working illegally in a state where she could not be licensed (DeVries 1985).

In the interviews, several licensed midwives spoke of the lack of a need to come together as a group (although this is not necessarily others' experience). Their interdependence had disappeared, and instead they had become solo practitioners. "There are too many factions," I was told about legal lay midwifery in one major city, where certified nurse-midwives, English- and Dutch-trained midwives, and licensed non-nurse midwives all attended home births. "Everyone feels like their training is better than other people's training, so there's not anything in it for them to come together in a group."

The essence of lay midwifery always lay in its irreverence for the biomedical approach to childbirth. The radical challenge was both to the way birth was carried out and to the model of professionalism that dominated hospital birth. At the time of this writing, licensed lay midwifery appears to be maintaining some of this irreverence. But the development of modern lay midwifery suggests that lay midwives cannot continue to work in the domestic sphere and gain respectability in the public sphere. Sisterhood and professionalism are very different doctrines, stemming from different worlds and relating symbolically to different genders. The challenge that faces lay midwives is one familiar to those working within the radical feminist movement. Can midwives set up and achieve an alternative woman-centered occupation that lies outside the traditional sphere of professional groups but is accepted by them and has access to professional resources and rewards? Or, in order to achieve those rewards, do midwives have to conform to the demands of (and be dominated by) professional authorities? The future of lay midwifery is not yet clear, although the continued pressure for licensure in major states like California suggests that they may well have accepted integration and domination as the viable option.

Notes

The research documented in this chapter was in part funded by the Nuffield Foundation. My thanks to them, and to the editor of this collection, Carol McClain, for her helpful suggestions on an earlier draft of the manuscript.

REFERENCES CITED

Aamodt, A.
  1977   "Socio-Cultural Dimensions of Caring in the World of the Papago
          Child and Adolescent." In *Transcultural Nursing Care of Infants and
          Children*, ed. M. Leininger. Salt Lake City: University of Utah School
          of Nursing.
  1978   "The Care Component in a Health and Healing System." In *The
          Anthropology of Health*, ed. E. Bauwens. St. Louis: C. V. Mosby.
Ainsworth, M.D.S.
  1977   "Attachment Theory and Its Utility in Cross-Cultural Research." In
          Culture and Infancy, ed. P. H. Leiderman, S. R. Tulkin, and A.
          Rosenfeld. New York: Academic Press.
Amarasingham, L. R.
  1980   "Movement among Healers in Sri Lanka: A Case Study of a Sinha-
          lese Patient." *Culture, Medicine and Psychiatry* 4:71–92.
Anderson, W., and D. Helm
  1979   "The Physician-Patient Encounter: A Process of Reality Negotiation."
          In *Patients, Physicians, and Illness*, ed. E. Jaco. New York: Free Press.
Anisef, P., and P. Masson
  1979   "The Institutionalization of a Profession." *Sociology of Work and
          Occupations* 6 (3): 353–372.
Ardener, E.
  1972   "Belief and the Problem of Women." In *The Interpretation of Ritual*,
          ed. J. S. La Fontaine. London: Tavistock.
Ardener, S., ed.
  1975   *Perceiving Women*. London: Malaby Press.
  1978a   *Defining Females: The Nature of Women in Society*. New York: John
          Wiley & Sons.
  1978b   "Introduction: The Nature of Women in Society." In *Defining Fe-
          males. See* S. Ardener 1978a.
Arms, S.
  1975   *Immaculate Deception*. Boston: Houghton Mifflin.
Backstrand, J., and S. Schensul
  1982   "Co-Evolution in Outlying Ethnic Communities: The Puerto Ricans
          of Hartford, Ct." *Urban Anthropology* 11 (1): 9–37.
Baer, H.
  1979   "A Psychocultural View of a Modern Day Prophet among the Mor-
          mons." *Journal of Psychological Anthropology* 2 (2): 177–195.
  1981   "Prophets and Advisors in Black Spiritual Churches." *Culture, Medi-
          cine and Psychiatry* 5:145–170.

1984   *The Black Spiritual Movement.* Knoxville: University of Tennessee Press.

Bakhtin, M.
1968   *Rabelais and His World.* Trans. Helen Iswolsky. Cambridge: Harvard University Press.

Baquero, H., R. Sosa, R. Baquero, and E. Pinto
1981   "Ecuador: TBA Training Programme, Supervision, Evaluation, and Follow-Up Services." In *The Traditional Birth Attendant in Seven Countries,* ed. A. Mangay-Maglacas and H. Pizurki. World Health Organization Public Health Papers no. 75. Geneva: WHO.

Barrett, L. E.
1973   "The Portrait of a Jamaican Healer: African Medical Lore in the Caribbean." *Caribbean Quarterly* 19:6–19.

1976   "Healing in a Balmyard: The Practice of Folk Healing in Jamaica, W.I." In *American Folk Healing,* ed. W. D. Hand. Berkeley: University of California Press.

Barry, H., M. K. Bacon, and I. L. Child
1957   "A Cross-Cultural Survey of Some Sex Differences in Socialization." *Journal of Abnormal and Social Psychology* 55:327–332.

Bart, P.
1981   "Seizing the Means of Reproduction: An Illegal Feminist Abortion Collective—How and Why It Worked." In *Women, Health and Reproduction,* ed. H. Roberts. London: Routledge & Kegan Paul.

Bastien, J.
1980   "Herbal Curing of the Qollahuaya Andenas." Paper presented at the annual meeting of the American Anthropological Association, Washington, D.C.

1981   "Metaphorical Relations between Sickness, Society, and Land in a Qollahuaya Ritual." In *Health in the Andes,* ed. J. Bastien and J. Donahue. Washington, D.C.: American Anthropological Association.

Bates, E. B., and J. W. Dittemore
1932   *Mary Baker Eddy: The Truth and the Tradition.* London: George Routledge & Sons.

Bell, D.
1983   *Daughters of the Dreaming.* Melbourne: McPhee Gribble.

Belote, J.
1984   "Changing Adaptive Strategies among the Saraguros of Southern Ecuador." Ph.D. dissertation, Department of Anthropology, University of Illinois, Urbana-Champaign.

Berger, I.
1976   "Rebels or Status Seekers? Women as Spirit Mediums in East Africa." In *Women in Africa. See* Hafkin and Bay 1976.

Berger, J.
1981   Foreword to *Sicilian Lives,* by D. Dolchi. New York: Pantheon.

Berger, P. L., and T. Luckmann
   1966   *The Social Construction of Reality: A Treatise on the Sociology of Knowledge.* New York: Doubleday.
Blum, R., and E. Blum
   1970   *The Dangerous Hour: The Lore of Crisis and Mystery in Rural Greece.* New York: Charles Scribner's Sons.
Boaz, F.
   1943   "Recent Anthropology." *Science* 98:334–337.
Borker, R.
   1985   "Domestic/Public: Concepts and Confusions." Paper presented at the annual meeting of the American Anthropological Association, Chicago.
Bosk, C.
   1979   *Forgive and Remember: Managing Medical Failure.* Chicago: University of Chicago Press.
Bossen, L.
   1983   "Sexual Stratification in Mesoamerica." In *Heritage of Conquest Thirty Years Later,* ed. C. Kendall, J. Hawkins, and L. Bossen, pp. 35–71. Albuquerque: University of New Mexico Press.
Bourguignon, E.
   1976   *Possession.* San Francisco: Chandler & Sharp.
Bowlby, J.
   1971   *Attachment and Loss.* Vol. 1, *Attachment.* Harmondsworth: Penguin.
Braden, C. B.
   1955   *Christian Science Today: Power, Policy, Practice.* Dallas: Southern Methodist University Press.
Brooks, T.
   1979   "Medically Unattended Home Birth." In *Compulsory Hospitalization or Freedom of Choice in Childbirth?* Vol. 2, ed. D. Stewart and L. Stewart. Chapel Hill: NAPSAC.
Brown, J. K.
   1985   Introduction to *In Her Prime. See* Brown and Kerns 1985.
Brown, J. K., and V. Kerns, eds.
   1985   *In Her Prime: A New View of Middle-Aged Women.* Boston: Bergin & Garvey.
Browner, C. H.
   1985a   "Criteria for Selecting Herbal Remedies." *Ethnology* 24:13–32.
   1985b   "Plants Used for Reproductive Health in Oaxaca, Mexico." *Economic Botany* 39:482–504.
   1986a   "Gender Roles and Social Change: A Mexican Case Study." *Ethnology* 25:89–106.
   1986b   "The Politics of Reproduction in a Mexican Village." *Signs* 12:710–724.
   1987   "Producción, Reproducción, y la Salud de la Mujer: Un Estudio

de Caso de Oaxaca, México." Paper presented at the annual meeting of the Society for Applied Anthropology, Oaxaca, Mexico.

Browner, C. H., and E. Lewin
1982   "Female Altruism Reconsiderd: The Virgin Mary as Economic Woman." *American Ethnologist* 9:61–75.

Buss, F. L.
1980   *La Partera: Story of a Midwife*. Ann Arbor: University of Michigan Press.

Carden, M. L.
1975   *The New Feminist Movement*. New York: Russell Sage.

Cheney, C., and G. Adams
1978   "Lay Healing and Mental Health in the Mexican-American Barrio." In *Modern Medicine and Medical Anthropology in the United States–Mexico Border Population*, ed. B. Velimirovic. Pan-American Health Organization Scientific Publication no. 359.

Chiñas, B. L.
1973   *The Isthmus Zapotecs: Women's Roles in Cultural Context*. New York: Holt, Rinehart and Winston.

Clark, M.
1970   *Health in the Mexican-American Culture*. Berkeley: University of California Press.

Collier, J. F.
1974   "Women in Politics." In *Women, Culture, and Society*. *See* Rosaldo and Lamphere 1974.

Collier, J. F., and S. J. Yanagisako, eds.
1987   *Gender and Kinship*. Stanford: Stanford University Press.

Colson, A.
1976   "Binary Oppositions and Treatment of Sickness among the Arawaio." In *Social Anthropology and Medicine*, ed. J. Loudon. London: Academic Press.

Comaroff, J.
1981   "Healing and Cultural Transformation: The Tswana of Southern Africa." *Social Science and Medicine* 15B:367–378.

1982   "Medicine: Symbol and Ideology." In *The Problem of Medical Knowledge: Examining the Social Construction of Medicine*, ed. P. Wright and A. Teacher. Edinburgh: Edinburgh University Press.

Comas Diaz, L.
1981   "Puerto Rican Espiritismo and Psycho-Therapy." *American Journal of Orthopsychiatry* 51:636–645.

Cosminsky, S.
1976   "Cross-Cultural Perspectives on Midwifery." In *Medical Anthropology*, ed. X. Francis, S. J. Grollig, and H. B. Haley, pp. 229–248. The Hague: Mouton.

1978   "Midwifery and Medical Anthropology." In *Modern Medicine and Medical Anthropology in the United States–Mexico Border Population*, ed. B. Velimirovic. PAHO Scientific Publication no. 359.

1982   "Knowledge and Body Concepts of Guatemalan Midwives." In *Anthropology of Human Birth. See* Kay 1982.

1983   "Traditional Midwifery and Contraception." In *Traditional Medicine and Health Care Coverage*, ed. R. Bannerman et al., pp. 142–162. Geneva: World Health Organization.

Crabtree, D. F.
1970   "Women's Liberation and the Church." In *Women's Liberation and the Church*, ed. S. B. Doely. New York: Association Press.

Crapanzano, V.
1973   *The Hamadsha.* Berkeley: University of California Press.

1977   Introduction to *Case Studies in Spirit Possession*, ed. V. Crapanzano and V. Garrison, pp. 1–40. New York: John Wiley & Sons.

1980   *Tuhami: Portrait of a Moroccan.* Chicago: University of Chicago Press.

1984   "Life Histories" (review article). *American Anthropologist* 86 (4): 953–960.

Currier, R.
1966   "The Hot-Cold Syndrome and Symbolic Balance in Mexican and Spanish-American Folk Medicine." *Ethnology* 5:251–263.

Dakin, E. F.
1929.   *Mrs. Eddy: The Biography of a Virginal Mind.* New York: Charles Scribner's Sons.

Davis, E.
1981   *Heart and Hands: A Guide to Midwifery.* Santa Fe: John Muir.

Davis, C., K. Black, and K. MacLean
1977   *Oral History: From Tape to Tape.* Chicago: American Library Association.

de la Fuente, J.
1949   *Yalalag: Una Villa Zapoteca Serrana.* Mexico City; Museo Nacional de Antropología.

Delgado, M.
1977   "Puerto Rican Spiritualism and the Social Work Profession." *Social Casework* 10:451–458.

Dennis, P. A.
1979   "Inter-Village Conflict and the Origin of the State." In *Social, Political and Economic Life in Contemporary Oaxaca*, ed. A. Williams, pp. 43–66. Publications in Anthropology no. 24. Nashville: Vanderbilt University.

DeVries, R.
1985   *Regulating Birth: Midwifery, Medicine and the Law.* Philadelphia: Temple University Press.

Dibble, C. E., and A.J.O. Anderson, eds.
1969   *The Florentine Codex,* by Fray Brernardino de Sahagun. Book 6, *Rhetoric and Moral Philosophy,* no. 14, pt. 7, p. 167. Santa Fe: School of American Research and the University of Utah.

Dinerman, I. R.
1982   *Migrants and Stay-at-Homes: A Comparative Study of Rural Migration from Michoacán, Mexico.* Center for U.S.–Mexican Studies. Monograph Series no. 5. San Diego: University of California, San Diego.

Dobbie, E.
1942   *The Anglo-Saxon Poetic Records, A Collected Edition.* Vol. 6, *The Anglo-Saxon Minor Poems.* New York: Columbia University Press.

Donegan, J. B.
1978   *Women and Men Midwives: Medicine, Morality and Misogyny in Early America, 1860 to the Present.* Westport, Conn.: Greenwood Press.

Donnison, J.
1977   *Midwives and Medical Men.* London: Heinemann Educational.

Douglas, M.
1966   *Purity and Danger: An Analysis of Concepts of Pollution and Taboo.* London: Routledge & Kegan Paul.
1970   *Natural Symbols: Explorations in Cosmology.* New York: Vintage Books.

Dow, J.
1986   "Universal Aspects of Symbolic Healing: A Theoretical Synthesis." *American Anthropologist* 88 (1): 56–69.

Dwyer, K.
1982   *Moroccan Dialogues: Anthropology in Question.* Baltimore: Johns Hopkins University Press.

Eddy, M. B.
1910   *Science and Health with Key to the Scriptures.* Boston: Trustees under the Will of Mary Baker G. Eddy.

Edgerton, R.
1977   "Conceptions of Psychosis in Four East African Societies." In *Culture, Disease, and Healing,* pp. 358–366. *See* Landy 1977.

Edwards, M., and M. Waldorf
1984   *Reclaiming Birth: History and Heroines of American Childbirth Reform.* Trumansburg, N.Y.: Crossing Press.

Eliade, M.
1946   *Shamanism: Archaic Techniques of Ecstasy.* New York: Pantheon Books.

England, R. W.
1954   "Some Aspects of Christian Science as Reflected in Letters of Testimony." *American Journal of Sociology* 59:448–453.

Epstein, S.
    1967   "A Sociological Analysis of Witch Belief in a Mysore Village." In
            Magic, Witchcraft and Curing, ed. J. Middleton. Austin: University
            of Texas Press.
Erasmus, C. J.
    1952   "Changing Folk Beliefs and the Relativity of Empirical Knowledge."
            Southwestern Journal of Anthropology 8:411–428.
    1955   "Work Patterns in a Mayo Village." *American Anthropologist* 57 (2):
            322–333.
Evans-Pritchard, E. E.
    1937   *Witchcraft, Oracles, and Magic among the Azande.* London: Oxford
            University Press.
Faithorn, E.
    1975   "The Concept of Pollution among the Kafe of the Papua New Guinea
            Highlands." In *Toward an Anthropology of Women. See* Reiter 1975.
Falk, N. and R. Gross
    1980   *Unspoken Worlds: Women's Religious Lives in Non-Western Cul-
            tures.* San Francisco: Harper & Row.
Federal Writers Project of the Works Progress Administration in North Caro-
lina, Tennessee, and Georgia (FWPWPA)
    1975   *These Are Our Lives.* New York: W. W. Norton. First published
            1939.
Finerman, R. D.
    1982   "Pregnancy and Childbirth in Saraguro: Implications for Health Care
            Delivery in Southern Ecuador." *Medical Anthropology* 6:269–277.
    1983   "Experience and Expectation: Conflict and Change in Traditional
            Family Health Care among the Quichua of Saraguro." *Social Science
            and Medicine* 17:1291–1298.
    1984   "A Matter of Life and Death: Health Care Change in an Andean
            Indian Community." *Social Science and Medicine* 18:329–334.
    1985   "Health Care Decisions in an Andean Indian Community: Getting
            the Best of Both Worlds." Ph.D. dissertation, Department of Anthro-
            pology, University of California, Los Angeles.
    1987   "Inside Out: Women's World View and Family Health in an Ecuador-
            ian Indian Community." *Social Science and Medicine* 25:1157–1162.
Finke, R. A.
    1986   "Mental Imagery and the Visual System." *Scientific American* 254
            (3): 88–95.
Finkler, K.
    1981   "Dissident Religious Movements in the Service of Women's Power."
            Sex Roles 7 (5): 481–495.
    1983   "Studying Outcomes of Mexican Spiritualist Therapy." In *The An-
            thropology of Medicine,* ed. L. Romanucci-Ross, D. E. Moerman,
            and L. R. Tancredi. New York: Praeger.

246   References Cited

1985   *Spiritualist Healers in Mexico: Successes and Failures of Alternative Therapeutics.* New York: Praeger.
Flores-Ochoa, J.
1966   *Pastoralists of the Andes.* Philadelphia: Institute for the Study of Human Issues Press.
Ford, C. S.
1945   *A Comparative Study of Human Reproduction.* Yale University Publications in Anthropology no. 32. New Haven: Human Relations Area Files Press.
Foster, G. M.
1953   "Relationships between Spanish and Spanish-American Folk Medicine." *Journal of American Folklore* 66:201–217.
1967   *Tzintzuntzán: Mexican Peasants in a Changing World.* Boston: Little, Brown.
1973   *Traditional Societies and Technological Change.* New York: Harper & Row.
1976   "Disease Etiologies in Non-Western Medical Systems." *American Anthropologist* 78:773–782.
Foster, G. M., and B. Anderson
1978   *Medical Anthropology.* New York: John Wiley & Sons.
Fox, M.
1973   "Power and Piety: Women in Christian Science." Ph.D. dissertation, New York University.
1978   "Power in Piety: Christian Science Revisited." *International Journal of Women's Studies* 1 (4): 401–416.
Fox, M., M. Gibbs, and D. Auerbach
1985   "Age and Gender Dimensions of Friendship." *Psychology of Women Quarterly* 9:489–502.
Frank, G.
1979   "Finding the Common Denominator: A Phenomenological Critique of Life History Method." *Ethos* 7:68–94.
Frank, J. D.
1961   *Persuasion and Healing: A Comparative Study of Psychotherapy.* Baltimore: Johns Hopkins University Press.
1974   *Persuasion and Healing: A Comparative Study of Psychotherapy.* Revised edition. New York: Schocken.
Freed, S. A., and R. S. Freed
1967   "Spirit Possession as Illness in a North Indian Village." In *Magic, Witchcraft, and Curing,* ed. J. Middleton. Garden City, N.Y.: Natural History Press.
Freeman, J.
1972–73 "The Tyranny of Structurelessness: A Critical Review." *Berkeley Journal of Sociology* 17:151–164.

Freidson, E.
1970   *Profession of Medicine*. New York: Dodd Mead.
1977   "The Future of Professionalization." In *Health and the Division of Labour,* ed. M. Stacey, M. Reid, C. Heath, and R. Dingwall. London: Croom Helm.

Freemont
1978.   *See* Fremont Women's Clinic/Birth Collective

Fremont Women's Clinic/Birth Collective
1978   "A Working Lay Midwife Home Birth Program, Seattle, Washington: A Collective Approach." In *21st Century Obstetrics Now!* Vol. 2, ed. D. Stewart and L. Stewart. Chapel Hill: NAPSAC.

Furst, P. ed.
1972   *Flesh of the Gods*. New York: Praeger.

FWPWPA. *See* Federal Writers Project.

Galdston, I., ed.
1959   *Man's Image in Medicine and Anthropology*. Monograph 4, Institute of Social and Historical Medicine, New York Academy of Medicine. New York: International Universities Press.

Garcia, R., M. de Jesus, and M. Singer
1987   "Indigenous Treatment for Alcoholism in the Hispanic Community." In *Alcohol Use and Abuse among Hispanic Adolescents,* ed. M. Singer, L. Davison, and F. Yalin. Hartford, Conn.: Hispanic Health Council.

Garrison, V.
1977   "Doctor, Espiritista or Psychiatric? Health Seeking Behavior in a Puerto Rican Neighborhood." *Medical Anthropology* 1:65–91.

Gaskin, I. M.
1977   *Spiritual Midwifery*. Summertown, Tenn.: The Book Publishing Co.

Gaviria, M., and R. Winthrop
1976   "Supernatural Influences on Psychopathology: Puerto Rican Folk Beliefs about Mental Illness." *Canadian Psychiatry Association Journal* 21:361–369.
1979   "Spirit or Psychiatrist: Treatment of Mental Illness among Puerto Ricans in Two Connecticut Towns." *Journal of Operational Psychiatry* 10:40–46.

Geiger, S.N.G.
1986   "Women's Life Histories: Method and Content." *Signs* 11:334–351.

Ginzberg, C.
1982   *The Cheese and the Worms*. Trans. J. Tedeschi and A. Tedeschi. New York: Penguin.

Glick, L. B.
1967   "Medicine as an Ethnographic Category: The Gimi of the New Guinea Highlands." *Ethnology* 6:31–56.

Gombrich, R.
1971   *Precept and Practice: Traditional Buddhism in the Rural Highlands of Ceylon.* Oxford: Clarendon Press.
Gonzales-Wippler, M.
1982   *The Santería Experience.* Englewood Cliffs, N.J.: Prentice-Hall.
Good, B. J., and M. D. Good
1981   "The Meaning of Symptoms: A Cultural Hermeneutic Model for Clinical Practice." In *The Relevance of Social Science for Medicine,* ed. L. Eisenberg and A. Kleinman. Boston: D. Reidel.
Goodale, J. C.
1980   "Gender, Sexuality, and Marriage: A Kaulong Model of Nature and Culture." In *Nature, Culture, and Gender. See* MacCormack and Strathern 1980.
Goodenough, W.
1966   *Cooperation in Change.* New York: John Wiley.
Goody, J., and S. J. Tambiah
1973   *Bridewealth and Dowry.* Cambridge: Cambridge University Press.
Gordon, D.
1978   *Therapeutic Metaphors.* Cupertino, Calif.: Meta Publications.
Gould, H. A.
1965   "Modern Medicine and Folk Cognition in Rural India." *Human Organization* 24:201–208.
Graham, H.
1985   "Providers, Negotiators, and Mediators: Women as the Hidden Carers." In *Women, Health, and Healing: Toward a New Perspective,* ed. E. Lewin and V. Oleson. New York: Tavistock.
Green, E. C.
1980   "Roles for African Traditional Healers in Mental Health Care." *Medical Anthropology* 4:489–522.
1985   "Traditional Healers, Mothers and Childhood Diarrheal Disease in Swaziland: The Interface of Anthropology and Health Education." *Social Science and Medicine* 20 (3): 277–285.
Green, E. C., and L. Makhubu
1984   "Traditional Healers in Swaziland: Toward Improved Cooperation between the Traditional and Modern Health Sectors." *Social Science and Medicine* 18 (12): 1071–1079.
Hafkin, N. J., and E. G. Bay, eds.
1976   *Women in Africa: Studies in Social and Economic Change.* Stanford: Stanford University Press.
Halifax, J.
1979   *Shamanic Voices.* New York: E. P. Dutton.
Halpern, J., and B. Kerewsky-Halpern
1972   *A Serbian Village in Historical Perspective.* New York: Holt, Rinehart and Winston.

Hamer, J., and I. Hamer
1966   "Spirit Possession and Its Socio-Psychological Implications among the Sidamo of Southwest Ethiopia." *Ethnology* 5:392–408.
Hammond, D., and A. Jablow
1976   *Women in Cultures of the World.* Menlo Park, Calif.: Cummings Publishing Co.
Hammond-Tooke, W. D.
1962   *Bhaca Society.* Cape Town: Oxford University Press.
Harris, O.
1978   "Complementarity and Conflict: An Andean View of Women and Men." In *Sex and Age as Principals of Social Differentiation,* ed. J. La Fontaine, pp. 21–40. London: Academic Press.
1981   "Households as Natural Units." In *Of Marriage and the Market: Women's Subordination Internationally and Its Lessons.* See Young, Wolkowitz, and McCullagh 1981.
Harvey, Y. K.
1979   *Six Korean Women: The Socialization of Shamans.* New York: West Publishing Co.
1980   "Possession Sickness and Women Shamans in Korea." In *Unspoken Worlds,* pp. 31–52. *See* Falk and Gross 1980.
Harwood, A.
1977   *Rx: Espiritist as Needed.* New York: John Wiley & Sons.
Hazell, L.
1974   *Birth Goes Home.* Seattle: Catalyst.
Helman, C.
1984   *Culture, Health, and Illness.* Bristol, England: John Wright.
Henderson, S.
1974   "Care-Eliciting Behavior in Man." *Journal of Nervous and Mental Disease* 159 (3): 172–181.
Herrick, J.
1983   "The Symbolic Roots of Three Potent Iroquois Medicinal Plants." In *The Anthropology of Medicine,* ed. L. Romanucci-Ross, D. E. Moerman, and L. R. Tancredi. New York: Praeger.
Herzfeld, M.
1986   "Closure as Cure; Tropes in the Exploration of Bodily and Social Disorder." *Current Anthropology* 27 (2): 107–120.
Hidalgo, H., and E. Hidalgo Christensen
1979   "Two Women: A Story of Success." In *The Puerto Rican Woman,* ed. E. Acosta-Belen, pp. 142–159. New York: Praeger.
Hoch-Smith, J., and A. Spring
1978   Introduction to *Women in Ritual and Symbolic Roles,* ed. J. Hoch-Smith and A. Spring. New York: Plenum Press.
Hoffman, L. W., and J. D. Manis
1978   "Influences of Children on Marital Interaction and Parental Satisfac-

250   References Cited

tion and Dissatisfaction." In *Child Influences on Marital and Family Interaction,* ed. R. M. Lerner and G. B. Spanier. New York: Academic Press.

Holland, W. R.
1963   *Medicina Maya en los Altos de Chiapas.* Mexico City: Instituto Nacional Indigenista y Secretaría de Educación Pública.

Holmberg, D.
1983   "Shamanic Soundings: Femaleness in the Tamang Ritual Structure." *Signs* 9: 40–58.

Huston, P.
1979   *Third World Women Speak Out.* New York: Praeger.

Janzen, J. M.
1978   The Quest for Therapy in Lower Zaire. Berkeley: University of California Press.
1986   "Hippocrate de le Desserto, Galen de la Savanna." *Kos: Rivista di Cultura e Storia della Scienze Medichi* 20, III (Feb./Mar.): 39–61. Quoted here is the English version, entitled "The Meeting of Allopathic and Indigenous Medicine in the African Context."
1988   "Health, Religion and Medicine in Central and Southern Africa." In *Caring and Curing: Health and Medicine in the World Religious Traditions,* ed. L. Sullivan. New York: Macmillan.
n.d.   "On the Comparative Study of Medical Systems: Ngoma, A Collective Therapy Mode in Central and Southern Africa." Manuscript.

Johnson, A.
1975   "Time Allocation in a Machiguenga Community." *Ethnology* 14:310–321.

Jones, D.
1966   *Sanapia: Comanche Medicine Woman.* New York: Holt, Rinehart and Winston.

Jones, E., and C. L. Zoppel
1979   "Personality Differences among Blacks in Jamaica and the United States." *Journal of Cross-Cultural Psychology* 10:435–456.

Jordan, B.
1983   *Birth in Four Cultures.* Montreal: Eden Press.

Kakar, S.
1982   *Shamans, Mystics, and Doctors: A Psychological Inquiry into India and Its Healing Traditions.* Boston: Beacon Press.

Kapferer, B.
1983   *A Celebration of Demons.* Bloomington: Indiana University Press.

Karadžić, V. S.
1896   *Srpske Narodne Pjesme.* Vol. 4. Belgrade: Stamparija Kraljevine Srbije.

Kay, M., ed.
1982   *Anthropology of Human Birth.* Philadelphia: F. A. Davis.

Kearney, M.
1978   "Spiritual Healing in Mexico." In *Culture and Curing: Anthropological Perspectives on Traditional Beliefs and Practices*, ed. P. Morley and R. Wallis, pp. 19–39. Pittsburgh: University of Pittsburgh Press.

Keesing, R. M.
1985   "Kwaio Women Speak: The Micropolitics of Autobiography in a Samoan Island Society." *American Anthropologist* 87:27–39.

Kelly, E.
1956   "An Anthropological Approach to Midwifery Training in Mexico." *Journal of Tropical Pediatrics* 1:200–205.

Kelly, J.
1967   "The Influence of Native Customs on Obstetrics in Nigeria." *Obstetrics and Gynecology* 30:608–612.

Kelly, R. C.
1976   "Witchcraft and Sexual Relations." In *Man and Woman in the New Guinea Highlands*, ed. P. Brown and G. Buchbinder. Washington, D.C.: American Anthropological Association.

Kemper, S.
1980   "Time, Person and Gender in Sinhalese Astrology." *American Ethnologist* 7:744–757.

Kendall, L.
1984   "Wives, Lesser Wives, and Ghosts: Supernatural Conflict in a Korean Village." *Asian Folklore Studies (Nagoya)* 43 (2): 214–225.

1985   *Shamans, Housewives, and Other Restless Spirits: Women in Korean Ritual Life.* Honolulu: University of Hawaii Press.

1988   *The Life and Hard Times of a Korean Shaman: Of Tales and the Telling of Tales.* Honolulu: University of Hawaii Press.

n.d.   "Healing Thyself: A Korean Shaman's Afflictions." *Social Science and Medicine*, forthcoming.

Kerewsky-Halpern, B.
1981   "Text and Context in Serbian Ritual Lament." *Canadian-American Slavic Studies* 15:51–60.

1983   "Watch Out for Snakes! Ethnosemantic Misinterpretations and Interpretation of a Serbian Healing Charm." *Anthropological Linguistics* (Fall): 309–325.

1985   "Trust, Talk, and Touch in Balkan Folk Healing." *Social Science and Medicine* 21 (3): 319–325.

Kerewsky-Halpern, B., and J. M. Foley
1978a   "The Power of the Word, Healing Charms as an Oral Genre." *Journal of American Folklore* 91 (362): 903–924.

1978b   "*Bajanje*: Healing Charms in Rural Serbia." In *Culture and Curing: Anthropological Perspectives on Traditional Beliefs and Practices*, ed. P. Morley and R. Wallis, pp. 40–56. Pittsburgh: University of Pittsburgh Press.

Kiev, A.
  1968   *Curanderismo: Mexican-American Folk Psychiatry.* New York: Free
          Press.
Kleinman, A.
  1980   *Patients and Healers in the Context of Culture.* Berkeley: University
          of California Press.
Kluckhohn, C.
  1945   "The Personal Document in Anthropological Science." In *The Use of
          Personal Documents in History, Anthropology, and Sociology,* ed. C.
          Kluckhohn and R. Angell, pp. 78–173. New York: Social Science
          Research Council.
  1970   *Navaho Witchcraft.* Boston: Beacon Press. First published in 1944.
Koss, J.
  1975   "Therapeutic Aspects of Puerto Rican Cult Practices." *Psychiatry*
          38:160–171.
  1976   "Religion and Science Related; A Case History of Spiritualism in
          Puerto Rico." *Caribbean Studies* 16:22–43.
  1980   "The Therapist-Specialist Training Project in Puerto Rico: An Experi-
          ment to Relate the Traditional Healing System to the Public Health
          System." *Social Science and Medicine* 14B:255–266.
  1987   "Expectations and Outcomes for Patients Given Mental Health Care
          or Spiritist Healing in Puerto Rico." *American Journal of Psychiatry*
          144:56–61.
Kuper, H.
  1947   *An African Aristocracy: Rank among the Swazi.* Oxford: Oxford Uni-
          versity Press.
Laderman, C.
  1983   *Wives and Midwives: Childbirth and Nutrition in Rural Malaysia.*
          Berkeley: University of California Press.
  1987   "The Ambiguity of Symbols in the Structure of Healing." *Social Sci-
          ence and Medicine* 24 (4): 293–302.
La Fontaine, J. S.
  1972   Introduction to *The Interpretation of Ritual,* ed. J. S. La Fontaine.
          London: Tavistock.
Lambert, M. J., D. A. Shapiro, and A. E. Bergin
  1986   "The Effectiveness of Psychotherapy." In *Handbook of Psychother-
          apy and Behavior Change,* 3d ed., ed. S. L. Garfield and A. E.
          Bergin. New York: John Wiley & Sons.
Lamphere, L.
  1974   "Strategies, Cooperation, and Conflict among Women in Domestic
          Groups." In *Women, Culture, and Society. See* Rosaldo and Lam-
          phere 1974.
Landers, R.
  1971   *The Ojibwa Woman.* New York: W. W. Norton. First published
          1938.

Landy, D., ed.
1977   *Culture, Disease, and Healing.* New York: Macmillan.
Lang, R.
1972   *Birth Book.* Felton, Calif.: Genesis Press.
Langer, S. K.
1942   *Philosophy in a New Key.* Cambridge: Harvard University Press.
Langness, L. L.
1965   *The Life History in Anthropological Science.* New York: Holt, Rinehart and Winston.
Langness, L. L., and G. Frank
1981   *Lives: An Anthropological Approach to Biography.* Novato, Calif.: Chandler & Sharp.
Last, M.
1986   "The Professionalization of African Medicine: Ambiguities and Definitions." In *The Professionalization of African Medicine. See* Last and Chavunduka 1986.
Last, M., and G. Chavunduka
1986   *The Professionalization of African Medicine.* Manchester: Manchester University Press.
Lawless, E. J.
1983   "Shouting for the Lord: The Power of Women's Speech in the Pentecostal Religious Service." *Journal of American Folklore* 96 (382): 434–459.
Leach, E.
1966   "Ritualization in Man in Relation to Conceptual and Social Development." *Philosophical Transactions* (London) Royal Society B, 251:247–526.
Leacock, S., and R. Leacock
1975   *Spirits of the Deep.* Garden City, N.Y.: Anchor Books.
Leacock, E., and H. I. Safa, eds.
1986   *Women's Work: Development and the Division of Labor by Gender.* Boston: Bergin & Garvey.
Leavitt, J. W.
1980   "Birthing and Anesthesia: The Debate over Twilight Sleep." *Signs* 6:147–165.
Lebra, W. P.
1966   *Okinawan Religion: Belief, Ritual, and Social Structure.* Honolulu: University of Hawaii Press.
Lee, R.
1976   "Interaction between Chinese and Western Medicine in Hong Kong: Modernization and Professional Inequality." In *Medicine in Chinese Cultures,* ed. A. Kleinman et al. Washington, D.C.: U.S. Government/Fogarty International Center.
Leslie, C. M.
1960   *Now We Are Civilized: A Study of the World View of the Zá-*

potec Indians of Mitla, Oaxaca. Detroit: Wayne State University Press.

1977   "Pluralism and Integration in the Indian and Chinese Medical Systems." In *Culture, Disease, and Healing. See* Landy 1977.

Levin, L., A. Katz, and E. Holst

1979   *Self Care: Lay Initiatives in Health.* New York: Prodist.

Lévi-Strauss, C.

1967   *Structural Anthropology.* New York: Basic Books.

1969   *The Elementary Structures of Kinship.* Boston: Beacon Press.

Lewin, E.

1979   "The Nobility of Suffering: Illness and Misfortune among Latin American Immigrant Women." *Anthropological Quarterly* 52 (3): 152–158.

Lewis, I. M.

1966   "Spirit Possession and Deprivation Cults." *Man,* n.s. 1 (3): 307–309.

1969   "Spirit Possession in Northern Somaliland." In *Spirit Mediumship in Africa,* ed. J. Beattie and J. Middleton, pp. 188–219. New York: Africana Publications.

1971   *Ecstatic Religion: An Anthropological Study of Spirit Possession and Shamanism.* Baltimore: Penguin Books.

1986   *Religion in Context: Cults and Charisma.* Cambridge: Cambridge University Press.

Lieban, R. W.

1981   "Urban Philippine Healers and Their Contrasting Clientele." *Culture, Medicine and Psychiatry* 5:217–231.

Litman, T. J.

1971   "Health Care and the Family: A Three Generation Analysis." *Medical Care* 9:67–81.

1974   "The Family as a Basic Unit in Health and Medical Care: A Socio-Behavioral Overview." *Social Science and Medicine* 8: 495–519.

1979   "The Family in Health and Health Care: A Social-Behavioral Overview." In *Patients, Physicians, and Illness,* 3rd ed., ed. E. G. Jaco, pp. 69–101. New York: Free Press.

Litoff, J. B.

1978   *American Midwives: 1860 to the Present.* London: Greenwood Press.

1986   *The American Midwife Debate: Sourcebook on Its Modern Origins.* London: Greenwood Press.

Little, R.

1980   "Explorations and Individual Lives: A Reconsideration of Life Writing in Anthropology." *Dialectical Anthropology* 5:210–226.

Logan, M.

1973   "Humoral Medicine in Guatemala and Peasant Acceptance of Modern Medicine." *Human Organization* 32:385–395.

1977   "Anthropological Research on the Hot-Cold Theory of Disease:

Some Methodological Suggestions." *Medical Anthropology* 1 (4): 87–112.

Lombard, J.
1965   *Structures de Type Féodal en Afrigue Noire.* The Hague and Paris: Mouton.

Long, J. K.
1973   "Jamaican Medicine: Choices between Folk Healing and Modern Medicine." Ph.D. dissertation, Department of Anthropology, University of North Carolina.

Lord, A. B.
1968   *The Singer of Tales.* New York: Atheneum.

McClain, C.
1975   "Ethno-obstetrics in Ajijic." *Anthropological Quarterly* 48 (1): 38–56.

MacCormack, C. P.
1980   "Nature, Culture and Gender: A Critique." In *Nature, Culture, and Gender. See* MacCormack and Strathern 1980.
1982a   "Health, Fertility and Birth in Moyamba District, Sierra Leone." In *Ethnography of Fertility and Birth,* ed. C. P. MacCormack, pp. 115–139. London: Academic Press.
1982b   "Biological, Cultural and Social Adaptation." In *Ethnography of Fertility and Birth,* ed. C. P. MacCormack, pp. 1–24. London: Academic Press.

MacCormack, C., and M. Strathern, eds.
1980   *Nature, Culture, and Gender.* Cambridge: Cambridge University Press.

Macklin, J.
1974   "Belief, Ritual and Healing: New England Spiritualism and Mexican Spiritualism Compared." In *Religious Movements in Contemporary America,* ed. I. Zaretsky and M. P. Leone, pp. 383–417. Princeton: Princeton University Press.

Madsen, W.
1964   "The Mexican Americans of South Texas." In *Case Studies in Cultural Anthropology,* ed. G. Spindler. New York: Holt, Rinehart and Winston.

Makhubu, L. P.
1978   *The Traditional Healer.* Mbabane: University of Botswana and Swaziland.

Maltz, D.
1985   "Analytical Concepts and Their Semantic Ambiguity: Public and Domestic with Some Insights from Scotland." Paper presented at the annual meeting of the American Anthropological Association, Chicago.

Manzanedo, H. G., E. G. Walters, and K. R. Lorig
1980   "Health and Illness Perceptions of the Chicano." In *Twice a Minority:*

Mexican-American Women, ed. M. B. Melville. St. Louis: C. V. Mosby.

March, K. S., and R. L. Taqqu
  1986   *Women's Informal Associations in Developing Countries; Catalysts for Change?* Boulder: Westview Press.

Martin, K., and B. Voorhies
  1975   *Female of the Species.* New York: Columbia University Press.

Martinez, R., ed.
  1978   *Hispanic Culture and Health Care.* St. Louis: C. V. Mosby.

Martinez, C., and H. Martin
  1979   "Folk Diseases among Urban Mexican-Americans: Etiology, Symptoms, and Treatment." In *Culture, Curers, and Contagion,* ed. N. Klein. Novato, Calif.: Chandler & Sharp.

Marwick, B. A.
  1966.   *The Swazi.* London: Frank Cass.

Mathews, H. F.
  1985   " 'We are Mayordomo': A Reinterpretation of Women's Roles in the Mexican Cargo System." *American Ethnologist* 12:285–301.

Maynard, E.
  1974   "Guatemalan Women: Life under Two Types of Patriarchy." In *Many Sisters; Women in Cross-Cultural Perspective,* ed. C. J. Matthiasson, pp. 77–98. New York: Free Press.

Mead, M.
  1978   "The Originality of Milton Erickson." *American Journal of Clinical Hypnotherapy* 20 (3): 4–5.

Meisch, L. A.
  1980–81 "Costume and Weaving in Saraguro, Ecuador." *Textile Museum Journal* 19–20:55–64.

Mella, P.
  1987   "Effects of Educated Professionals on the Health and Care of Women in Tanzania." *Health Care for Women International* 8:239–248.

Messing, S. D.
  1958   "Group Therapy and Social Status in the Zar Cult of Ethiopia." In *Culture and Mental Health,* ed. M. K. Opler. New York: Macmillan.
  1967   "Group Therapy and Social Status in the Zar Cult of Ethiopia." In *Magic, Witchcraft, and Curing,* ed. J. Middleton, pp. 285–294. Garden City, N.Y.: Natural History Press.

Meswick, S.
  1982   "Migration, Health and Schooling: A Case Study of Puerto Rican Adolescents in Urban Connecticut." Ph.D. dissertation, Department of Anthropology, University of Connecticut.

Metraux, A.
  1959   *Voodoo in Haiti.* London: Oxford University Press.

Metzger, D., and G. Williams
  1963   "Tenejapa Medicine I: The Curer." *Southwestern Journal of Anthropology* 19:216–234.
Middleton-Keirn, S.
  1978   "Convivial Sisterhood—Spirit Mediumship and Client-Core Network among Black South African Women." In *Women in Ritual and Symbolic Roles,* ed. J. Hoch-Smith and A. Spring. New York: Plenum Press.
Millman, M.
  1976   *The Unkindest Cut.* New York: Morrow.
Miranda King, L.
  1979   "Puertorriqueñas in the United States: The Impact of Double Discrimination." In *The Puerto Rican Woman,* ed. E. Acosta-Belen, pp. 124–133. New York: Praeger.
Mitchell, G.
  1981   *Human Sex Differences: A Primatologist's Perspective.* New York: Van Nostrand Reinhold.
Mitchell, M. F.
  1980   "Class, Therapeutic Roles, and Self-Medication in Jamaica." Ph.D. dissertation, Medical Anthropology, University of California at Berkeley and San Francisco.
Mogul, K. M.
  1982   "Overview: The Sex of the Therapist." *American Journal of Psychiatry* 139:1–11.
Mongeau, B, H. L. Smith, and A. C. Maney
  1961   "The 'Granny' Midwife: Changing Roles and Functions of a Folk Practitioner." *American Journal of Sociology* 66:497–505.
Morsy, S.
  1978   "Sex Roles, Power, and Illness." *American Ethnologist* 5: 137–150.
Murko, M.
  1929   *La Poésie Populaire Epique en Yougoslavie au Début du XXe Siècle.* Paris: Librairie Ancienne Honoré Champion.
Murphy, J.
  1976   "Psychiatric Labelling in Cross-Cultural Perspective." *Science* 191:1019–1027.
Murphy, Y., and R. F. Murphy
  1974   *Women of the Forest.* New York: Columbia University Press.
Nadelson, L.
  1981   "Pigs, Women, and the Men's House in Amazonia: An Analysis of Six Mundurucú Myths." In *Sexual Meanings. See* Ortner and Whitehead 1981.
Nag, M., B. White, and R. Peet
  1978   "An Anthropological Approach to the Study of the Economic Value of Children in Java and Nepal." *Current Anthropology* 19 (2): 293–306.

Nash, J.
  1967   "Death as a Way of Life: The Increasing Resort to Homicide in a
          Maya Indian Community." *American Anthropologist* 69:455–470.
Neumann, E.
  1972   *The Great Mother: An Analysis of the Archetype.* Bollingen Series.
          Princeton: Princeton University Press.
Newman, L. F., ed.
  1981   "Midwives and Modernization." Special issue of *Medical Anthropol-
          ogy* 5 (1).
  1985   *Women's Medicine: A Cross-Cultural Study of Indigenous Fertility
          Regulation.* New Brunswick and London: Rutgers University Press.
Ngubane, H.
  1975   *See* Sibisi
  1977   *Body and Mind in Zulu Medicine: An Ethnography of Health and
          Disease in Nyuswa-Zulu Thought and Practice.* New York: Academic
          Press.
  1981   "Aspects of Clinical Practice and Traditional Organization of Indige-
          nous Healers in South Africa." *Social Science and Medicine* 15B:361–
          366.
Nichter, M.
  1981   "Negotiation of the Illness Experience: The Influence of Ayurvedic
          Therapy on the Psychosocial Dimensions of Illness." *Culture, Medi-
          cine and Psychiatry* 5:5–24.
Nordstrom, C.
  1984   "The Illness Episode and the Reconstruction of Meaning." Paper
          presented at the annual meeting of the Anthropological Association.
  1986   "Meaning and Knowledge in Medical Pluralism: Sri Lanka." Ph.D.
          dissertation. University of California, Berkeley.
Obeyesekere, G.
  1963a   The Great Tradition and the Little in the Perspective of Sinhalese
          Buddhism." *Journal of Asian Studies* 22:139–153.
  1963b   "Pregnancy Cravings (Dola-Duka) in Relation to Social Structure
          and Personality in a Sinhalese Village." *American Anthropologist*
          65:323–342.
  1966   "The Buddhist Pantheon in Ceylon and Its Extensions." In *Anthropo-
          logical Studies in Theravada Buddhism,* ed. M. Nash, pp. 1–86. New
          Haven: Yale University Press.
  1969   "The Cultural Background of Sinhalese Medicine." *Journal of the
          Indian Anthropological Society* 4:117.
  1975   "Some Comments on the Nature of Traditional Medical Systems." In
          Medicine in Chinese Cultures, ed. A. Kleinman et al. Washington,
          D.C.: U.S. Government/Fogerty International Center.
  1976   "The Impact of Ayurvedic Ideas on the Culture and the Individual in

Sri Lanka." In *Asian Medical Systems*, ed. C. Leslie. Berkeley: University of California Press.

1977   "Psychocultural Exegesis of a Case of Spirit Possession in Sri Lanka." In *Case Studies in Spirit Possession*, ed. V. Crapanzano and V. Garrison. New York: John Wiley & Sons.

1981   *Medusa's Hair: An Essay on Personal Symbols and Religious Experiences*. Chicago and London: University of Chicago Press.

O'Connell, M. C.
1982   "Spirit Possession and Role Stress among the Xesibe of Eastern Transkei." *Ethnology* 21:21–38.

Okley, J.
1975   "Gypsy Women: Models in Conflict." In *Perceiving Women. See* S. Ardener 1975.

O'Nell, C. W., and H. A. Selby
1968   "Sex Differences in the Incidence of Susto in Two Zapotec Pueblos: An Analysis of the Relationships between Sex Role Expectations and a Folk Illness." *Ethnology* 7:95–105.

Ortiz de Montellano, B. R., and C. H. Browner
1985   "Chemical Bases for Medicinal Plant Use in Oaxaca, Mexico." *Journal of Ethnopharmacology* 13:57–88.

Ortner, S. B.
1974   "Is Female to Male as Nature Is to Culture?" In *Woman, Culture, and Society. See* Rosaldo and Lamphere 1974.

Ortner, S. B., and H. Whitehead, eds.
1981   *Sexual Meanings: The Cultural Construction of Gender and Sexuality*. Cambridge: Cambridge University Press.

Osgood, K., D. L. Hochstrasser, and K. W. Deuschle
1966   "Lay Midwifery in Southern Appalachia." *Archives of Environmental Health* 12:750–770.

Paige, K. E., and J. M. Paige
1981   *The Politics of Reproductive Ritual*. Berkeley: University of California Press.

Parker, R. L., S. M. Shah, C. A. Alexander, and A. K. Neumann
1979   "Self-care in Rural Areas of India and Nepal." *Culture, Medicine and Psychiatry* 3:3–28.

Parry, M. (coll.), and A. B. Lord (ed. and trans.)
1954   *Serbo-Croatian Heroic Songs*. Cambridge and Belgrade: Harvard University Press and Srpska Akademija Nauka.

Parvati, J.
1978   *Hygieia, a Woman's Herbal*. Berkeley: Freestone.

Paul, B. D.
1955   *Health, Culture and Community: Case Studies of Public Reactions to Health Programs*. New York: Russell Sage Foundation.

260 References Cited

Paul, L.
1978a "Careers of Midwives in a Mayan Community." In *Women in Ritual and Symbolic Roles*, ed. J. Hoch-Smith and A. Spring, pp. 129–149. New York: Plenum Press.
1978b "Recruitment to a Ritual Role: The Midwife in a Maya Community." *Ethos* 6:449–467.

Paul, L., and B. Paul
1975 "The Maya Midwife as a Sacred Specialist." *American Ethnologist* 2:707–726.

Pelto, P., and G. Pelto
1978 *Anthropological Research*. Cambridge: Cambridge University Press.

Petrović, A.
1939 *Rakovica: Socijalno-zdravstvene i Higijenske Prilike*. Belgrade: Biblioteka Centralnog Higijenskog Zavoda.

Petrović, P. Ž.
1970 "Bajanje"; "Metla." In *Srpski Mitološki Recnik*, pp. 16–18; 202. Belgrade: Nolit.

Phillips, A. S.
1973 *Adolescence in Jamaica*. Kingston: Jamaica Publishing House.

Pokorny, J.
1953 *Indogermanisches Etymologisches Wörterbuch*. Berne: A. Franke.

Pollack, M.
1983 *Health Problems in Sri Lanka: An Analysis of Morbidity and Mortality Data*. Washington, D.C.: American Public Health Association.

Polsky, N.
1969 *Hustlers, Beats and Others*. Harmondsworth: Pelican Books.

Poole, F.J.P.
1981 "Transforming 'Natural' Women: Female Ritual Leaders and Gender Ideology among Bimin-Kuskusmin." In *Sexual Meanings*. *See* Ortner and Whitehead 1981.

Press, I.
1971 "The Urban Curandero." *American Anthropologist* 75:741–756.

Prince, R.
1982 "Shamans and Endorphins, Hypothesis for a Synthesis." *Ethos* 10:409–423.

Quinn, N.
1977 "Anthropological Studies on Women's Status." *Annual Review of Anthropology* 6:181–225. Palo Alto, Calif.: Annual Reviews.

Radenković, L.
1986 *Mesto Isterivanja nečiste sile u narodnim bajanjima slovensko-balkanskog areala*. Belgrade: Glasnik Etnografskog Muzeja, L.

Radin, P.
1957 *Primitive Religion*. New York: Viking Press. First published 1937.

Redfield, R.
1970   *A Village That Chose Progress.* Chicago: University of Chicago Press.
Reichel-Dolmatoff, G.
1976   "Training for the Priesthood among the Kogi of Columbia." In *Enculturation in Latin America,* ed. J. Wilbert. Los Angeles: UCLA Latin America Center Publications.
Reiter, R., ed.
1975   *Toward an Anthropology of Women.* New York: Monthly Review Press.
Rivers, W.H.R.
1927   *Medicine, Magic, and Religion.* London: Kegan Paul, Trench, Trubner and Co.
Rogers, C. R.
1957   "The Necessary and Sufficient Conditions of Therapeutic Personality Change." *Journal of Consulting Psychology* 21 (2): 95–102.
Rogler, L., and A. Hollingshead
1961   "The Puerto Rican Spiritualist as Psychiatrist." *American Journal of Sociology* 67:269–275.
Romalis, S.
1981   *Childbirth: Alternatives to Medical Control.* Austin: University of Texas Press.
1985   "Struggle between Providers and Recipients: The Case of Birth Practices." In *Women, Health, and Healing: Toward a New Perspective,* ed. E. Lewin and V. Oleson. New York: Tavistock.
Rosaldo, M. Z.
1974   "Woman, Culture, and Society: A Theoretical Overview." In *Woman, Culture, and Society. See* Rosaldo and Lamphere 1974.
1980   "The Use and Abuse of Anthropology: Reflections on Feminism and Cross-Cultural Understanding." *Signs* 5:389–417.
Rosaldo, M. Z., and L. Lamphere, eds.
1974   *Woman, Culture, and Society.* Stanford: Stanford University Press.
Rosaldo, R.
1976   "The Story of Tukbaw: 'They Listen as He Orates.' " In *The Biographical Process: Studies in the History of Psychology of Religion,* ed. F. E. Reynolds and D. Capps, pp. 121–151. The Hague and Paris: Mouton.
Rosen, S., ed.
1982   *My Voice Will Go with You—The Teaching Tales of Milton H. Erickson.* New York: W. W. Norton.
Rossi, A. S.
1977   "A Biosocial Perspective on Parenting." *Daedalus* 106 (2): 1–32.
Rothman, B. K.
1982   *In Labor: Women and Power in the Birthplace.* London: Norton.

Rubel, A. J., and J. Gettelfinger-Krejci
1976   "The Use of Hallucinogenic Mushrooms for Diagnostic Purposes among Some Highland Chínantecs." *Economic Botany* 30:235–248.

Ruiz, P., and J. Langrod
1976   "The Role of Folk Healers in Community Mental Health Services." *Community Mental Health Journal* 12 (4): 392–398.

Russell, S. D.
1984   "Curing and Commerce: Changes in an Indigenous Medical Practice in a Highland Philippine Town." *Social Science and Medicine* 18 (2): 129–137.

Ruzek, S.
1978   *The Women's Health Movement.* New York: Praeger.

Salgado, R. M.
1974   "The Role of the Puerto Rican Spiritist in Helping Puerto Ricans with Problems of Family Relations." Ph.D. dissertation, Columbia University Teachers College.

Sallomi, P., A. Pallow, and M.P.O. McMahon
1981   "Midwifery and the Law." *Mothering* 21 (Fall): 63–83.

Sandoval, M.
1979   "Santería as a Mental Health Care System." *Social Science and Medicine* 13B:137–151.

Sargent, C. F.
1982   *The Cultural Context of Therapeutic Choice: Obstetrical Decisions among the Bariba of Benin.* Dordrecht: D. Reidel.
1984   "Obstetrical Choice among Urban Women in Benin." *Social Science and Medicine* 20 (3): 287–292.
1986   "Prospects for the Professionalization of Indigenous Midwifery." In *The Professionalization of African Medicine. See* Last and Chavunduka 1986.

Šaulić, N.
1929   *Srpske Narodne Tužbalice.* Belgrade: Srpska Kraljevska Akademija.

Scheff, T. J.
1975   "Labelling, Emotion, and Individual Change." In *Labelling Madness,* ed. T. J. Scheff, pp. 75–89. Englewood Cliffs, N.J.: Prentice-Hall.
1979   *Catharsis in Healing, Ritual, and Drama.* Berkeley: University of California Press.

Schensul, S., and J. J. Schensul
1982   "Helping Resource Use in a Puerto Rican Community." *Urban Anthropology* 11 (1): 59–79.

Schlegel, A.
1975   "Three Styles of Domestic Authority: A Cross-Cultural Study." In *Being Female: Reproduction, Power, and Change,* ed. D. Raphael. The Hague: Mouton.

Schreiber, J., and L. Philipott
1978   "Who Is a Legitimate Health Care Professional? Changes in the Practice of Midwifery in the Lower Rio Grande Valley." In *Modern Medicine and Medical Anthropology in the United States–Mexico Border Population,* ed. B. Velimirovic. Pan-American Health Organization Scientific Publication no. 359.

Schutz, A.
1962   *Collected Papers.* Vol. 1. Ed. M. Natanson. The Hague: Martinus Nijhoff.

Seaga, E.
1968   "Healing in Jamaica." In *True Experiences in Exotic ESP,* ed. M. Ebon. New York: Signet.

Sharon, D.
1978   *Wizard of the Four Winds.* New York: Free Press.

Shepperson, G.
1970   "The Comparative Study of Millenarian Movements." In *Millennial Dreams in Action,* ed. S. L. Thrupp. New York: Shocken Books.

Sibisi (Ngubane), H.
1975   "The Place of Spirit Possession in Zulu Cosmology." In *Religion and Social Change in Southern Africa,* ed. M. G. Whissen and M. West. Cape Town: David Philip.

Silva, T. K.
1983   "Community, Disease and Participatory Approaches." *Economic Review* (June): 26–28.

Simeonov, L. A.
1975   *Better Health for Sri Lanka.* World Health Organization.

Simmel, G.
1950   *The Sociology of Georg Simmel.* Trans. K. Wolff. Glencoe: Free Press.

Singer, M.
1984   "Spiritual Healing and Family Therapy: Common Approaches to the Treatment of Alcoholism." *Family Therapy* 11 (2): 155–162.

n.d.   "Choosing Folk Treatment: A Profile of Clients in Espiritismo." Hispanic Health Council, Hartford, Conn. Manuscript.

Singer, M., and M. Borrero
1984   "Indigenous Treatment for Alcoholism: The Case of Puerto Rican Spiritism." *Medical Anthropology* 8:246–273.

Singer, M., and R. Garcia
1984   "La Guérison Spirite dans une Communauté Portoricaine." *Mouvements Religieux* 45:1–3.

Slade, D. L.
1975   "Marital Status and Sexual Identity: The Position of Women in a Mexican Peasant Society." In *Women Cross-Culturally: Change and Challenge,* ed. R. Rohrlich-Leavitt, pp. 129–148. The Hague: Mouton.

Snow, L. F.
    1973   " 'I Was Born Just Exactly with the Gift': An Interview with a Voo-
            doo Practitioner." *Journal of American Folklore* 86:272–281.
    1977   "Popular Medicine in a Black Neighborhood." In *Ethnic Medicine in
            the Southwest,* ed. E. Spicer, pp. 19–95. Tucson: University of Ari-
            zona Press.
Snow, L. F., S. J. Johnson, and H. E. Mayhew
    1978   "The Behavioural Implications of Some Old Wives' Tales." *Obstet-
            rics and Gynecology* 51:727–732.
Spector, R.
    1979   *Cultural Diversity in Health and Illness.* New York: Appleton-Century
            Crofts.
Spiro, M. E.
    1952   "Ghosts, Ifaluk and Teleological Functionalism." *American Anthro-
            pologist* 54 (40): 497–503.
    1978   *Burmese Supernaturalism,* expanded ed. Philadelphia: Institute for
            the Study of Human Issues Press.
    1979   *Gender and Culture: Kibbutz Women Revisited.* New York: Schocken.
Spring, A.
    1978   "Epidemiology of Spirit Possession among the Luvale of Zambia." In
            Women in Ritual and Symbolic Roles, ed. J. Hoch-Smith and A.
            Spring. New York: Plenum Press.
Sri Lanka Department of Information
    1981   *Facts about Sri Lanka.* Colombo: Department of Information
Sri Lanka Ministry of Health
    1982   *Annual Health Bulletin.* Colombo: Ministry of Health.
    1983   *Annual Health Bulletin.* Colombo: Ministry of Health.
Stacey, M.
    1981   "The Division of Labour Revisited, or Overcoming the Two Adams"
            in *Practice and Progress: British Sociology 1950–1980,* ed. P. Ab-
            rams, R. Deem, J. Finch, and P. Rock. London: Allen & Unwin.
Stebbens, K. R.
    1984   "Second-Class Mexicans; State Penetration and Its Impact on Health
            Status and Health Services in a Highland Chinantec Municipio in
            Oaxaca." Ph.D. dissertation, Michigan State University.
Stern, P., ed.
    1986   *Women, Health, and Culture.* Washington: Hemisphere/Harper &
            Row.
Stewart, N., J. Belote, and L. Belote
    1976   "Transhumance in the Central Andes." *Annals of the Association of
            American Geographers* 66:337–397.
Strathern, M.
    1972   *Women In Between.* New York: Seminar.

1980   "No Nature, No Culture: The Hagen Case." In *Nature, Culture and Gender. See* MacCormack and Strathern 1980.

1981   "Self-Interest and the Social Good: Some Implications of Hagen Gender Imagery." In *Sexual Meanings. See* Ortner and Whitehead 1981.

Sundkler, B.

1976   *Zulu Zion.* London: Oxford University Press.

Swain, M. B.

1982   "Being Cuna and Female: Ethnicity Mediating Change in Sex Roles." In *Sex Roles and Social Change in Native Lower Central American Societies,* ed. C. A. Loveland and F. O. Loveland. Urbana: University of Illinois Press.

Tambiah, S. J.

1968   "The Magical Power of Words." *Man,* n.s. 17:175–208. Malinowski Memorial Lecture 1968.

Taussig, M. T.

1980   "Reification and the Consciousness of the Patient." *Social Science and Medicine* 14B:3–13.

Torrey, E. F.

1972   *The Mind Game.* New York: Bantam.

Trevathan, W.

1980   "The Independent Midwives of the 1970s." Paper presented at the annual meeting of the American Sociological Association.

Turner, R. P.

1970   "Witchcraft as Negative Charisma." *Ethnology* 9:366–372.

Turner, V.

1967   *The Forest of Symbols.* Ithaca: Cornell University Press.

1969   *The Ritual Process: Structure and Anti-Structure.* Chicago: Aldine.

Ugalde, A.

1973   "Contemporary Mexico: From Hacienda to PRI, Political Leadership in a Zapotec Village." In *The Caciques,* ed. R. Kern, pp. 119–135. Albuquerque: University of New Mexico Press.

UNICEF-WHO Committee on Health Policy

1977   *Community Involvement in Primary Health Care: A Study of the Process of Community Motivation and Continued Participation.* Geneva: World Health Organization.

Vasquez Calzada, J. L.

1976   "Demographic Aspects of Migration." In *Labor Migration under Capitalism: The Puerto Rican Experience.* History Task Force, Centro de Estudios Puertoriqueños, pp. 223–236. New York: Monthly Review Press.

Vogt, E. Z.

1969   *Zinacantán: A Maya Community in the Highlands of Chiapas.* Cambridge: Belknap Press of the Harvard University Press.

Wardwell, W. I.
   1963   "Limited, Marginal and Quasi-Practitioners." In *Handbook of Medical Sociology,* ed. H. E. Freeman, S. Levine, and L. S. Reeder. Englewood Cliffs, N.J.: Prentice-Hall.
Waxler, N. E.
   1976   "Social Change and Psychiatric Illness in Ceylon: Traditional and Modern Conceptions of Disease and Treatment." In *Culture Bound Syndromes: Ethnopsychiatry and Alternative Therapies,* ed. W. P. Lebra, pp. 22–40. Honolulu: University of Hawaii Press.
   1979   "Is Outcome for Schizophrenia Better in Nonindustrial Societies?" *Journal of Nervous and Mental Disease* 167:144–158.
Weber, M.
   1947   *The Theory of Social and Economic Organization.* Trans. A. M. Henderson and T. Parsons. New York: Oxford University Press.
Wedenoja, W.
   1978   "Religion and Adaptation in Rural Jamaica." Ph.D. dissertation, Department of Anthropology, University of California, San Diego.
   1980   "Modernization and the Pentecostal Movement in Jamaica." In *Perspectives on Pentecostalism: Case Studies from the Caribbean and Latin America,* ed. S. D. Glazier, pp. 27–48. Washington, D.C.: University Press of America.
   1988   "The Origins of Revival, a Creole Religion in Jamaica." In *Culture and Christianity: The Dialectics of Transformation,* ed. G. Saunders. Westport, Conn.: Greenwood.
Weitz, R., and D. Sullivan
   1985   "Licensed Lay Midwifery and the Medical Model of Childbirth." *Sociology of Health and Illness* 7:36–54.
West, M.
   1975   *Bishops and Prophets in a Black City.* Cape Town: David Philip.
Whitecotton, J. W.
   1977   *The Zapotecs: Princes, Priests, and Peasants.* Norman: University of Oklahoma Press.
Whiting, B. B., and J. M. Whiting
   1975   *Children of Six Cultures: A Psycho-Cultural Analysis.* Cambridge: Harvard University Press.
Whyte, M. K.
   1978   *The Status of Women in Preindustrial Societies.* Princeton: Princeton University Press.
Wijeratne, G.
   1979   "Development of Health Manpower with a View to the Possibilities of Integrating Western and Traditional Systems of Medicine." Manuscript.
Wilson, B.
   1970   *Religious Sects.* New York: McGraw-Hill.

Wirz, P.
1954   *Exorcism and the Art of Healing in Ceylon.* Leiden: E. J. Brill.
Wolf, E. R.
1955   "Types of Latin American Peasantry: A Preliminary Discussion."
        American Anthropologist 57:452–471.
1957   "Closed Corporate Peasant Communities in Mesoamerica and Cen-
        tral Java." *Southwestern Journal of Anthropology* 13:1–18.
Wolf, M.
1972   *Women and the Family in Rural Taiwan.* Stanford: Stanford Univer-
        sity Press.
Woods, C., and T. Graves
1976   "The Process of Medical Change in a Highland Guatemalan Town."
        In *Medical Anthropology,* ed. F. Grollig and H. Haley. The Hague:
        Mouton.
Worsley, P.
1982   "Non-Western Medical Systems." In *Annual Review of Anthropol-
        ogy,* vol. 11, ed. B. J. Siegel, A. R. Beals, and S. A. Tyler, pp. 315–
        348. Palo Alto, Ca.: Annual Reviews, Inc.
Yalman, N.
1971   *Under the Bo Tree.* Berkeley: University of California Press.
Young, A.
1976   "Some Implications of Medical Beliefs and Practices for Social An-
        thropology." *American Anthropologist* 78 (1): 5–24.
1983   "The Relevance of Traditional Medical Cultures to Modern Primary
        Health Care." *Social Science and Medicine* 17:1205–1211.
Young, J. C.
1981   *Medical Choice in a Mexican Village.* New Brunswick: Rutgers Uni-
        versity Press.
Young, K.
1976   "The Social Setting of Migration: Factors Affecting Migration from a
        Sierra Zapotec Village in Oaxaca, Mexico." Ph.D. dissertation, Uni-
        versity of London.
1978   "Modes of Appropriation and the Sexual Division of Labour: A Case
        Study from Oaxaca, Mexico." In *Feminism and Materialism: Women
        and Modes of Production,* ed. A. Kuhn and A. M. Wolpe, pp. 124–
        154. London: Routledge & Kegan Paul.
Young, K., C. Wolkowitz, and R. McCullagh, ed.
1981   *Of Marriage and the Market: Women's Subordination Internationally
        and Its Lessons.* Boston: Routledge & Kegan Paul.
Zempleni, A.
1977   "From Symptom to Sacrifice: The Story of Khady Fall." In *Case
        Studies in Spirit Possession,* ed. V. Crapanzano and V. Garrison, pp.
        87–139. New York: John Wiley & Sons.

Index